Jet Reports with Microsoft Dynamics GP

Ian Grieve

Copyright © 2020 Ian Grieve

Published by azurecurve Publishing

Notice of Rights

All rights reserved. No part of this book may be reproduced, stored in a retrieval system, or transmitted in any form or by any means, without the prior written permission of the publisher, except in the case of brief quotations embedded in critical articles or reviews.

Notice of Liability

Every effort has been made in the preparation of this book to ensure the accuracy of the information herein. However, the information contained in this book is sold without warranty, either express or implied. Neither the author, publisher, nor its dealers and distributors will be held liable for any damages caused or alleged to be caused directly or indirectly by the instructions contained in this book, or by the software or hardware products described within.

Trademark Notice

Rather than indicating every occurrence of a trademarked name as such, this book uses the names only in an editorial fashion and to the benefit of the trademark owner with no intention of infringement of the trademark.

First published: June 2020

ISBN 979-8-6576981-6-9

https://publishing.azurecurve.co.uk

About the Author

Ian Grieve is the Lead ERP Consultant at ISC Software Solutions Ltd., a Microsoft Partner, VAR and ISV headquartered in the United Kingdom of Great Britain & Northern Ireland and with an office in the Republic of Ireland. He is an Advanced Credentialed Professional in Microsoft Dynamics GP by the Association of Dynamics Professionals and was a Microsoft® Most Valuable Professional for Microsoft Dynamics GP between 2013 and 2018.

Ian has worked with Microsoft Dynamics GP since 2003 and, over the years since then, has dealt with all aspects of the product life-cycle from presales, to implementation, to technical and functional training, to post go-live support and subsequent upgrades and process reviews.

Ian is the author of several books for Microsoft Dynamics GP:

- *Microsoft Dynamics GP 2013 Financial Management*.
- *Implementing the Microsoft Dynamics GP Web Client* (first and second editions).
- *Microsoft Dynamics GP Workflow* (first, second and third editions).

And is the co-author, with Mark Polino, of two further books for Microsoft Dynamics GP:

- *Microsoft Dynamics GP 2013 Cookbook*.
- *Microsoft Dynamics GP 2016 Cookbook*.

In his spare time, Ian runs the *azurecurve|Ramblings of a Dynamics GP Consultant* (https://www.azurecurve.co.uk/) blog dedicated to Microsoft Dynamics GP and related products; in 2017 he launched the *azurecurve|Microsoft Dynamics GP Table Reference* website (https://gptables.azurecurve.co.uk/k); to add required functionality to his blog, he became a plugin developer (https://development.azurecurve.co.uk/) for WordPress and, more recently, ClassicPress.

Acknowledgement

Thanks to my parents for their support through the years and my employer, ISC Software, for giving me the opportunity to work with clients in many different fields and, not least, for being open to me taking on outside projects such as this book and its predecessors.

I also owe thanks to all of the clients I have worked with over the years, whose needs and questions have prompted me to learn ever more about Microsoft Dynamics GP, thereby putting me in a position to write this book.

Thanks to the Technical Reviewers, Hemant Parmar and Laura Bowie for their valuable feedback which helped to make the book better.

About the Reviewers

Hemant Parmar

Hem has worked in and headed up Finance departments in a variety of for profit and not for profit organizations. Across the years, he has worked with numerous financial systems and been the lead on the implementation several of them following detailed end user reviews.

Hem's initial exposure to Microsoft Dynamics GP was in 2015. Following a merger, he worked alongside Ian Grieve on implementing Microsoft Dynamics GP as a unified financial system for the new group. Hem was involved in selecting and implementing Jet Reports in December 2019 as a group-wide reporting tool and has been involved in building reports since.

Laura Bowie

Laura is a Senior ERP Consultant with a Microsoft Gold Partner and VAR in the UK. Starting her career as an Application Support Engineer she has progressed to her current role due to her hard work and willingness to learn under the guidance of Ian Grieve for several years.

Laura has worked with Microsoft Dynamics GP since April 2010 and, over the years since then, has dealt with all aspects of the product life-cycle from presales, to implementation, to technical and functional training, to post go-live support and subsequent upgrades and process reviews. Laura is now embarking on the new challenge of learning Microsoft Dynamics 365 Business Central to diversify her skill set and to gain knowledge in the newest Microsoft ERP offering.

Table of Contents

Preface   1

Chapter 1: Introduction to Jet Reports   5

   Versions of "Jet Reports"   5

   How Jet Reports works   7

   Types of reporting   7

   Replacement for Management Reporter   7

   Summary   7

Chapter 2: Implementing Jet Reports   9

   Components   9

      Jet Excel Add-in   9

      Jet Service Tier   9

      Jet Hub   9

   Prerequisites   10

      Jet Reports 2019 or higher   10

      Excel Add-In   10

      Jet Service Tier   11

      Jet Hub   11

   Download Jet Reports   12

   Install the Jet Server Components   13

   Install the Jet Client Components   17

   Deploying the Jet SQL objects   19

   Summary   21

Chapter 3: Configuring Jet Reports   23

   Configuration using the Jet Administration Console   23

      Activating Jet Reports   23

      Creating a data source   24

      Creating users   26

   Running Jet Excel Add-in for the first time   28

Summary	28
Chapter 4: Introducing the Excel Add-in	**29**
Jet Action Add-in	29
Mode	29
Report	30
Tools	30
Jet Hub	31
Distribution	31
Settings	31
Information	32
Summary	32
Chapter 5: Report Structure	**33**
Worksheets	33
Special rows and columns	33
Report page layout	34
Options page	34
Formatting	35
Summary	36
Chapter 6: Using the functions in the Excel Add-in	**37**
Available functions	37
NL function	37
Return a single record	38
Return all records	38
Return range of records	38
Return field for a date range of records	39
Handling a blank filter	39
NF function	40
Use NL function to return a record key	40
Use NF function to return a field using a record key	41
NP function	41

Evaluate a formula	41
Date filter	42
GL function	42
Return list of accounts	42
Return Account Name	43
Return the YTD balance for a period	43
Return the opening balance for period	43
Return the period balance for period	44
Return the balance for period last year	44
Return a budget period balance	45
Summary	45
Chapter 7: Creating and using an Options page	**47**
Create a new Options page	47
Lookup on Fiscal Year	48
Lookup on Fiscal Period	48
Lookup on Company	49
The Options page	50
Using an Options page	51
Summary	51
Chapter 8: Create a Summary Trial Balance	**53**
Design the report	53
Create the Report page	54
Create the Options page	54
Set Options on Report page	57
Add Record Key for Account Master	58
Add Account Index and Account	59
Add Account Description	59
Add Opening Balance	60
Add Debit and Credit	61
Add Net Change	62

Add Closing Balance	62
Hide zero value rows	62
Report ready for testing	63
Run report	63
Summary	64
Chapter 9: Create a Detailed Trial Balance	**65**
Design the report	65
Add transaction detail column headers	66
Update Record Key for Account Master	66
Add Record Key for Year-to-Date Transaction Open	66
Add Journal Entry	67
Add Reference	68
Add Transaction Date	68
Add Currency	68
Add Source Document	69
Add Debit	69
Add Credit	69
Add Description	69
Run report	69
Summary	70
Chapter 10: Create a Balance Sheet	**71**
Design the report	71
Create the Report page	73
Create the Options page	74
Set Options on Report page	77
Output options	78
Add categories	78
Add current year	79
Add previous year	80
Add variance	81

Add section totals	81
Add Total Assets	81
Add Total Liabilities and Shareholders's Equity	81
Run report	82
Summary	83
Chapter 11: Create an Income Statement	**85**
Design the report	85
Create the Report page	86
Create the Options page	87
Set Options on Report page	90
Output options	91
Add categories	91
Add current period	92
Add current year	93
Add current period for previous year	94
Add previous year	95
Add period variance	95
Add period variance for previous year	95
Add section totals	96
Add Net Operating Income	96
Add Net Income	96
Run report	96
Adding extra companies	97
Making a consolidation page	97
Run report	98
Summary	98
Chapter 12: Create a Summary Payables Aged Trial Balance	**99**
Design the report	99
Create the Report page	100
Create the Options page	101

Set Options on Report page	104
Add settings from Payables Management setup	104
Add parameters to report	108
Add Record Key for PM Vendor Master File	109
Add Vendor Master fields	109
Add count of vouchers	110
Add Due balance for a vendor	111
Add sum of credit transactions	111
Add sum of debit transactions	112
Add Due amount	113
Add Current Balance for a vendor	113
Add sum of credit transactions	113
Add sum of debit transactions	114
Add Due amount	115
Add aging period 2 balance	115
Add aging period 3 balance	116
Add aging period 4 balance	117
Hide vendors with no due balance	118
Add field for counting creditors	118
Add total count of vendors	118
Add total count of vouchers	118
Add Due total	118
Add Aging Period totals	119
Report ready for testing	119
Run report	119
Summary	120
Chapter 13: Create a Purchase Order by Vendor report	**121**
Design the report	121
Create the Report page	122
Create the Options page	123

Set Options on Report page	126
Add parameters to report	126
Add Record Key for PM Vendor Master File	127
Add Vendor Master fields	127
Add Record Key for Purchase Order Work	128
Add Purchase Order Work fields	129
Add Record Key for Purchase Order Line	129
Add Purchase Order Line fields	130
Add Account Number to Purchase Order Lines	131
Add subtotals for Purchase Order Lines	132
Add Record Key for Purchase Order History	132
Add Purchase Order History fields	133
Add Record Key for Purchase Order Line History	134
Add Purchase Order Line History fields	135
Add Account Number to Purchase Order Line History	135
Add subtotals for Purchase Order Line History	136
Add vendor total for purchase orders	136
Hide rows when no data to display	136
Calculation for Vendor Master rows	137
Calculation for Purchase Order Work rows	137
Calculation for Purchase Order Line rows	137
Calculation for Purchase Order Work subtotal row	137
Calculation for Purchase Order History rows	137
Calculation for Purchase Order Line rows	137
Calculation for Purchase Order Work subtotal row	137
Calculation for purchase order total row	138
Report ready for testing	138
Run report	138
Summary	139
Chapter 14: Report creation tools	**141**

Report Wizard	141
Table Builder	147
Create Table Builder report	147
Amend Table Builder template	150
Browser	150
Snippets	151
Add snippet	151
Edit snippet	152
Replace snippet	152
Rename snippet	153
Delete snippet	153
Organize snippets	153
Share snippet	154
Sample snippets	154
Summary	155
Chapter 15: Using Jet Hub	**157**
Introducing Jet Hub	157
Accessing Jet Hub	157
Uploading reports	158
Upload through Jet Hub	158
Upload through the Excel add-in	160
Running a report	161
Opening a report	163
Run History	164
Versions	165
Scheduling a report	165
Summary	166
Index	**169**

Preface

Microsoft Dynamics GP is a popular enterprise resource planning (ERP) application used by tens of thousands of sites around the world to keep the accounting, financial, distribution and manufacturing functions running day in and day out.

While Microsoft Dynamics GP includes a number of different reporting tools "out of the box" which cover a number of different reporting needs, they are usually not intended for end-users to modify and provide different reporting meaning users need to learn several reporting tools and run reports from different areas of the system.

One of these reporting tools is Management Reporter which was intended for financial reporting and was very popular with accountants for self-serving their financial reports. In 2016 Microsoft made two announcements; development on Management Reporter would cease, with the product being retired in a few years, and that they had gone into partnership with the company producing Jet Reports.

Partners and clients have started making moves to transition from Management Reporter to Jet Reports; unfortunately, there is no migration tool so reports need to be recreated in Jet Reports.

As well as a replacement for Management Reporter, Jet Reports allows a much wider range of reports to be produced; it allows not only financial reporting, but also operational reporting.

Who This Book Is For

This book is aimed at Dynamics GP users, partners and consultants who need to migrate from Management Reporter, improve or standardize reporting from Microsoft Dynamics GP.

This book assumes you have a reasonable understanding of Microsoft Dynamics GP and Microsoft Excel, including worksheet formula and building workbooks.

What This Book Covers

This book introduces the reporting tool Jet Reports for Microsoft Dynamics GP, including the installation and configuration of the Excel Add-in, Jet Service Tier and Jet Hub.

The book then moves onto showing the functionality available through the Excel-Addin and how the four available Jet Functions can be used to create reports.

The creation of seven example reports are covered with step-by-step instructions before the report creation tools, which can be used to quickly and easily create reports, are

Jet Reports with Microsoft Dynamics GP

covered.

The final chapter centers on the use of Jet Hub, which provides a web portal for users to run and view reports.

How This Book Is Structured

Chapter 1, Introduction to Jet Reports, *introduces Jet Reports and explains what type of reporting for which it can be used.*

Chapter 2, Implementing Jet Reports, *covers the installation of Jet Reports including the Jet Service Tier and Jet Hub.*

Chapter 3, Configuring Jet Reports, *shows how to configure Jet Reports once it has been installed.*

Chapter 4, Introducing the Excel Add-in, *introduces the Excel Add-in and the features available.*

Chapter 5, Report Structure, *shows how reports can be structured to make maintaining them easier.*

Chapter 6, Using the functions in the Excel Add-in, *shows how each of the four Jet Functions can be used.*

Chapter 7, Creating and using an Options page, *covers the creation and use of an options page in reports.*

Chapter 8, Create a Summary Trial Balance, *steps through the creation of a Summary Trial Balance report.*

Chapter 9, Create a Detailed Trial Balance, *shows how to make the Summary TB from the previous chapter into a Detailed report.*

Chapter 10, Create a Balance Sheet, *covers the creation of a formatted Balance Sheet.*

Chapter 11, Create an Income Statement, *covers the creation of an Income Statement and how to make it an intercompany/consolidated version.*

Chapter 12, Create a Summary Payables Aged Trial Balance, *shows how to create a Summary Payables Trial Balance report.*

Chapter 13, Create a Purchase Order by Vendor Report, *covers the creation of an operational report on purchase orders.*

Chapter 14, Report Creation Tools, *introduces the tools which can be used to make creating reports easier.*

Chapter 15, Using Jet Hub, *shows how users can access Jet Reports via web access and*

Preface

without a local install of Jet Reports.

Download example reports

All the reports covered in this book can be downloaded from:

> https://pub.azrcrv.co.uk/jetgpsamplereports

What You Need For This Book

You will require the following for this book:

- One Windows Server 2019 with a domain controller.
- One Windows Server 2019 with Microsoft SQL Server 2019 installed.
- One Windows Server 2019 to install the Jet Service Tier.
- One PC, or server, with Windows 10, or Windows Server 2019, with Microsoft Dynamics GP and Microsoft Excel installed.
- The Fabrikam, Inc. sample company deployed.

Windows Server 2016 and SQL Server 2016 or 2017 are acceptable replacements for the Windows Server 2019 and SQL Server 2019 listed above as both are fully compatible with Microsoft Dynamics GP and Jet Reports.

A test company database is a suitable alternative to Fabrikam, but the examples in this book use the sample data in Fabrikam.

For a new standalone test system, all of the above could be located on a single server although I typically keep the domain controller separate.

Conventions

To help you get the most from this book and keep track of what is happening, a number of stylistic conventions have been used throughout this book.

The key styles of text used in this book to distinguish between different types of information are:

- New terms and important words are **bolded**.
- Words you would type are shown as MSDYNGP\srvc.jet.
- Key combinations are shown as *Win+R*.

Errata

Every care has been taken to ensure the accuracy of the books content, but mistakes do happen. If you find a mistake in this book we would be grateful if you could report this to us; reporting an error means we can fix the error and improve future editions of the book.

Please report errors by visiting https://pub.azrcrv.co.uk/submit-errata, select the book in question from the drop down list and enter the details of the errata in the textbox.

Reader Feedback

Feedback from readers is always welcomed as it will enable us to improve future titles. Please let us know what you think about this book, in particular what you liked and disliked.

If you are having problems with any aspect of the book, or have questions about the content you can contact us at https://pub.azrcrv.co.uk/questions.

Piracy

The Internet is a marvelous invention, but it does represent an ongoing problem for the protection of published works. If you happen across any unlicensed copies of our works, in any form, please provide us with the website name or link, so that we can pursue a remedy, by email at copyright@azurecurve.co.uk.

Introduction to Jet Reports

Microsoft Dynamics GP includes several different reporting tools, but they are all limited in the data they can report on and many of them are not easily modified by end-users. As such many users will adopt third party reporting solutions.

Jet Reports is one of the most popular third-party reporting tools for Microsoft Dynamics GP. It allows for the production of financial and operational reporting from Microsoft Dynamics GP using data from any module, including third party ones.

Versions of "Jet Reports"

Technically there is only one version of the reporting tool called Jet Reports, but the name "Jet Reports" has been around for a long time.

Initially the company itself was called Jet Reports and they had two products: Jet Essentials and Jet Enterprise which were the standard reporting product and the data warehouse version of Jet.

The company introduced Jet Express when they went into partnership with Microsoft and the existing Jet Essentials product was renamed Jet Professional.

The company then rebranded from Jet Reports to Jet Global Data Technologies and the products were renamed:

- Jet Express became Jet Basics.
- Jet Professional became Jet Reports (the only version ever called this, but the mid-tier product has generally been called Jet Reports by users, regardless of the official name).
- Jet Enterprise became Jet Analytics.

Jet Reports with Microsoft Dynamics GP

Since then Jet Global Data Technologies has been acquired by insight Software.

The table, below, shows the differences between the three products.

Version comparison	Jet Basics	Jet Reports	Jet Analytics
Real-Time reporting direct from Microsoft Dynamics GP	✓	✓	✓
Financial Reporting from any GL account or Account Category	✓	✓	✓
Prebuilt templates for reports and dashboards	20+ pre-built reports	45+ pre-built reports	60+ pre-built reports and dashboards
Multi-company consolidation of separate companies into a single report	✓	✓	✓
Access, run and collaborate with reports (and budgets) on mobile and web via Jet Hub using any form-factor device		✓	✓
Integration with Jet Budgets for controlled fiscal planning with governed spreadsheets for budget input, automated workflows, and seamless actual-to-plan reporting and analysis		✓	✓
Operational and business reporting with complete access to all tables, views, fields, modules, third-party add-ons and customizations in Microsoft Dynamics GP		✓	✓
Multi-company reporting with consolidation of data from multiple databases		✓	✓
Schedule and automate report distribution		✓	✓
Manage sharing, version control, report permissions and search capabilities		✓	✓
Any report format and design with Excel formulas		✓	✓
Snippets allow users to save Excel and report logic for repeat use		✓	✓
Business dashboards allow users to quickly see trends,			✓

discover relations and identify issues	
Data warehouse automation for consistent analysis and governance on all sources of data for one version of the truth	✓
Pre-defined OLAP cubes for Sales, Finance, Inventory, Purchasing, AP and AR for KPIs and business intelligence	✓
Support for quick and easy drag-and-drop customization of the data warehouse and cubes	✓
Additional layer of security to provide control over who sees the data	✓

This book will be covering only the middle-tier product, Jet Reports.

How Jet Reports works

The core element of Jet Reports is the Excel Add-in which adds a new tab to the action pane as well as four new Jet functions which can be used to extract data from Microsoft Dynamics GP. A Jet Function is essentially an excel formula which makes special calls via the Excel Add-in to retrieve information from the Microsoft Dynamics GP company databases.

Types of reporting

The core strength of Jet Reports is that while the **GL** function allows for easy financial reporting from the General Ledger, the **NL** function allows data from any table or SQL view to be used in reports.

Replacement for Management Reporter

The **Jet Basics** version is intended as the direct replacement for Management Reporter and was announced as part of the partnership with Microsoft. The **GL** function is the method in which Management Reporter reports can be reproduced; this book will look at the **GL** function in **Chapter 6, Using the functions in the Excel Add-in**, and again in later chapters such as **Chapter 8, Create a Summary Trial Balance report**.

Summary

In this chapter we have introduced Jet Reports and covered the type of reporting it allows. In the next chapter, we'll take a look at implementing Jet Reports.

2

Implementing Jet Reports

In this chapter we're going to take a look at the implementation of Jet Reports from the components which can be installed, to the prerequisites and then stepping through the installation of them.

Components

There are three components to Jet Reports with two of them optional and only one of them, the Jet Excel Add-in, required.

Jet Excel Add-in

Jet Reports is a Microsoft Excel Add-in that integrates Excel with Microsoft GP or any database which has an OLE or ODBC driver available, allowing you to create reports with simple worksheet functions.

The Jet Excel Add-in allows you to enter formula which read directly from a database directly into a worksheet; standard Excel charts, sparklines and slicers can be used in conjunction with the returned data.

Jet Service Tier

The Jet Service Tier is a Windows service which enables communications between the Jet Excel Add-in and the Jet Services Database (on a SQL Server).

Jet Hub

Jet Hub is a web portal which allows users access to their reports through a simple web interface using virtually any form-factor device.

Users accessing Jet Hub do not need to have any software installed to view or generate reports. Within Jet Hub they can quickly find a specific report, set report parameters and run the report to get real-time data and view it in Excel Online.

Prerequisites

The prerequisites for Jet Reports will vary depending on which components are going to be installed.

Jet Reports 2019 or higher

Regardless of the components being installed, the database connection is always the same.

System Requirements	
Database Connection	• Microsoft Dynamics GP version 9 or later • Microsoft SQL Server 2005 or later[1] • OLE or ODBC compliant database

[1] The version of SQL Server must be supported by the operating system being used.

Excel Add-In

The Jet Excel Add-in is the component used by designers to create reports and by viewers to refresh and schedule reports.

System Requirements	
Operating System[1]	• Microsoft Windows 10 • Microsoft Windows Server 2008 SP2 - 2016 • Microsoft Windows 8.0 and 8.1 • Microsoft Windows 7 SP1
Microsoft Office[2]	• Microsoft Office 2007 - 2019[1] • Microsoft Office 365 (2013-2016 Desktop Edition Only) (delivered through Microsoft's *Semi-annual Channel*)
Prerequisites	• Microsoft .Net Framework 2.0, 3.5. and 4.5 or higher (including 'ADOMD.NET for SQL Server 2005')
Hardware (minimum)	• Processor: 1.4GH • RAM: 2GB • Disk space: 2GB

Languages Supported	Czech, Danish, Dutch, English, Finnish, French, German, Greek, Hungarian, Icelandic, Italian, Japanese, Norwegian, Polish, Portuguese, Russian, Spanish, Swedish

[1] Both 32-bit and 64-bit versions, if applicable.
[2] Jet Global recommends that only one installation of MS Office be present. Jet Global cannot support installations where multiple copies of MS Office are installed on a single system.

Jet Service Tier

The Jet Service Tier allows centralized storage of data source settings and use of Jet Hub.

System Requirements	
Server OS	• Microsoft Windows Server 2008SP2 - Server 2016 (64-bit if using with Jet Hub)
Client OS	• Microsoft Windows 10, Windows 8.1, Windows 8, Windows 7 SP1, Windows Vista SP2
Prerequisites	• Microsoft .Net Framework 4.5[1] • TLS Certificate • Active Directory or Office 365 authentication[2] • Microsoft IIS v7.0 or higher • SQL Server 2008 or higher
Hardware (minimum)	• Processor: 1.4GH • RAM: 8GB • Available Disk Space: 10GB

[1] including ADOMD.NET for SQL Server 2005
[2] AD or O365 is required for credential authentication when logging in to Jet Hub.

Jet Hub

The Jet Hub allows users to access Jet Reports through the browser without any desktop software, such as the Jet Excel Add-in, installed.

User Requirements	

Internet Browser[1]	• Windows
	    o Internet Explorer 11 or higher
	    o Google Chrome[2]
	    o Firefox[2]
	    o Edge[2]

| Prerequisites | - OneDrive[3] or
- OneDrive for Business[3] |

[1] Jet Hub requires that cookies be enabled in the browser.
[2] Most recent release.
[3] Only required for opening reports in Excel Online. Most free OneDrive accounts are supported - please test.

Server Requirements	
Operating System (64-bit)	- Microsoft Windows Server 2008R2 - Server 2016 (recommended)
- Supported: Microsoft Windows 10, Windows 8.1, Windows 8.0, Windows 7 SP1
Prerequisites	- Microsoft .Net Framework 4.5[1]
- Security Certificate (e.g., SSL/TLS)
- Active Directory or Office 365 authentication
- Microsoft IIS v7.0 or higher
- SQL Server 2008 or higher
Hardware (minimum)	- Processor: 1.4GH
- RAM: 8GB
- Available Disk Space: 10GB
Security	- Organizations wishing to provide data to remote devices outside of their network should purchase a domain-validated Security Certificate (SSL/TLS) from an outside vendor in order to do so.
Languages Supported	Czech, Danish, Dutch, English, Finnish, French, German, Greek, Hungarian, Icelandic, Italian, Japanese, Norwegian, Polish, Portuguese, Russian, Spanish, Swedish

[1] including ADOMD.NET for SQL Server 2005.

Download Jet Reports

The Jet Reports software is available for download from the **insight software** website (https://insightsoftware.com/downloads/). The download is of a zip file containing all of the necessary software:

Chapter 2: Implementing Jet Reports

Download Software

Jet Analytics
(formerly Jet Enterprise)

Download Jet Analytics
Getting Started
Download Sample Reports
Prior Build Downloads
Training
Support

Jet Reports
(formerly Jet Professional, Jet Essentials)

Download Jet Reports
Getting Started
Download Sample Reports
Prior Build Downloads
Training
Support

Install the Jet Server Components

The official instructions for installing Jet Reports suggests that installing the Jet Server Components (the Jet Service Tier and Jet Hub) can be done on the SQL Server, but I would very strongly advise against this, most especially if the Jet Hub is going to be externally accessible.

The Jet Service Tier and Jet Hub can be installed on the same or different servers, but if making the Jet Hub externally accessible, I'd recommend that they be on different servers to allow for maximum security.

For this book, I am only installing it for local access, so will have a separate SQL Server, with the Jet Service Tier and Jet Hub sharing a server.

To install the Jet Service Tier and Jet Hub, perform the following steps:

1. Extract the files from the downloaded zip file and run the **Jet Reports.exe**.

Jet Reports with Microsoft Dynamics GP

2. Accept the default of **Active Directory** and click **Next**.

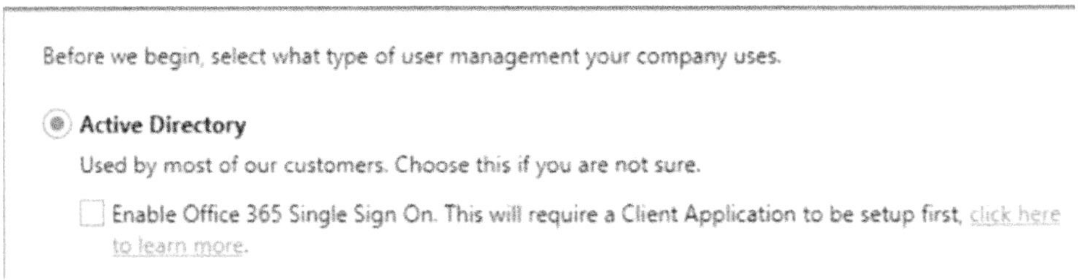

> Before we begin, select what type of user management your company uses.
>
> ⦿ **Active Directory**
> Used by most of our customers. Choose this if you are not sure.
>
> ☐ Enable Office 365 Single Sign On. This will require a Client Application to be setup first, click here to learn more.

3. Jet Service Tier and Jet Hub are the **Server Components,** so select this and click **Next**.

> Choose an installation option:
>
> Client Components
>
> Server Components

4. As we are installing both Jet Service Tier and Jet Hub, leave both checkboxes marked and click **Next**.

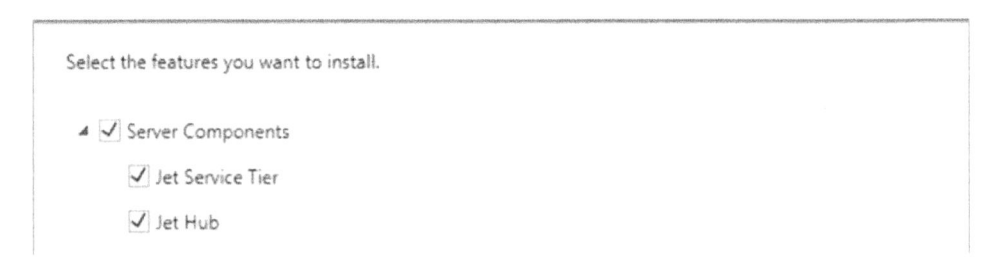

> Select the features you want to install.
>
> ▲ ☑ Server Components
>   ☑ Jet Service Tier
>   ☑ Jet Hub

5. Enter your **Activation Code** and click **Next** (you can leave the Activation Code blank and enter it later).

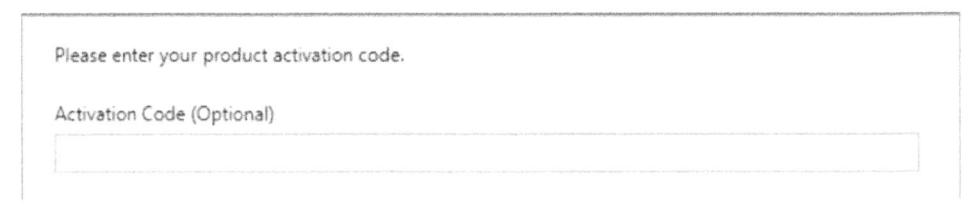

> Please enter your product activation code.
>
> Activation Code (Optional)

6. Jet recommend using **NETWORK SERVICE** as the service for the **Jet Service Tier**. If you are going to manually sort out your firewall rules, unmark the **Add rules to Windows Firewall**.

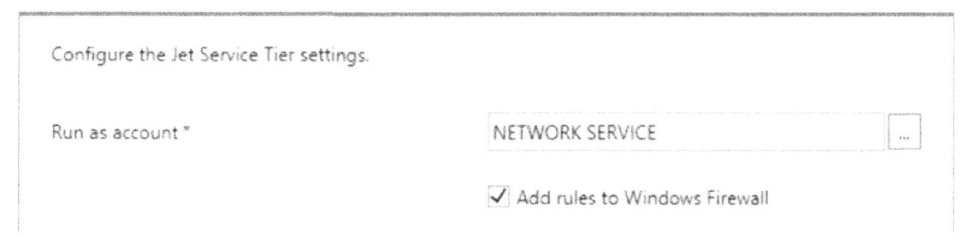

> Configure the Jet Service Tier settings.
>
> Run as account *   NETWORK SERVICE
>
> ✓ Add rules to Windows Firewall

7. Click **Next** to continue.

8. The Network Connection settings all need to be set:

    a. The **Jet Service Tier host** is the fully-qualified domain name (FQDN) of the server you're installing it on.

    b. The **Port** will default to **7090**, but can be changed.

    c. **Jet Hub URL** is the URL users will use to access the Jet Hub.

> Configure the Network Connection settings.
>
> Jet Service Tier host *   GP2019JET.azurecurve.local
>
> Jet Service Tier port *   7090
>
> Jet Hub URL *   https://GP2019JET.azurecurve.local

9. Once entered, click **Next**.

10. You can click the **Enabling IIS features** checkbox to manually install the required functions, but I am opting to mark the **Automatically enable all required IIS features**.

> Configure the Jet Hub settings.
>
> Enabling IIS features
>
> ⦿ Automatically enable all required IIS features (recommended)
>
> ◯ I will manually enable the IIS features required by the Jet Hub.

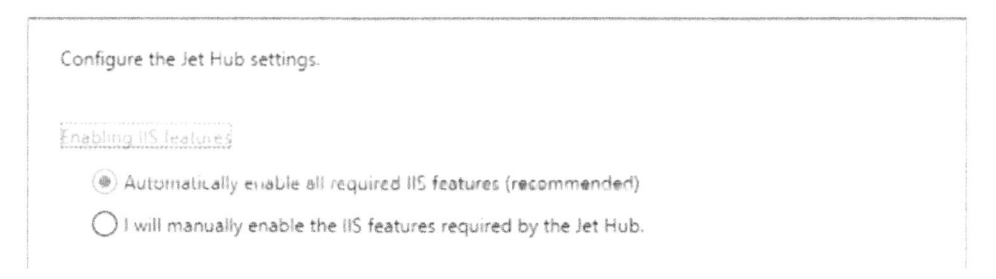

11. Click **Next** to continue.

12. A **SQL Server Instance** need to be supplied to hold the **JetServices** database; the database name can be changed if required.

13. Select the authentication method for connecting to the SQL Server Instance; this user needs to have permissions to create a database.

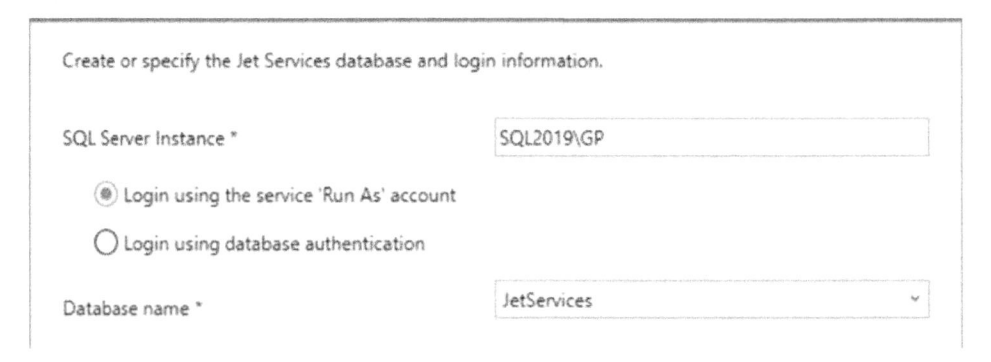

Jet Reports with Microsoft Dynamics GP

> Create or specify the Jet Services database and login information.
>
> SQL Server Instance *: SQL2019\GP
>
> ◉ Login using the service 'Run As' account
> ○ Login using database authentication
>
> Database name *: JetServices

14. Click **Next** to continue.

> **Jet Setup**
>
> **JET GLOBAL**
> DATA TECHNOLOGIES
>
> The setup is ready to make changes to your system. Please click the Install button to perform the requested operations.

15. To begin the installation, click **Install**.

16. Once the installation is complete, click **Finish**.

That completes the installation of the **Jet Service Tier** and **Jet Hub**, but there is a final configuration step required, which is to bind the SSL certificate to the **Jet Hub** website:

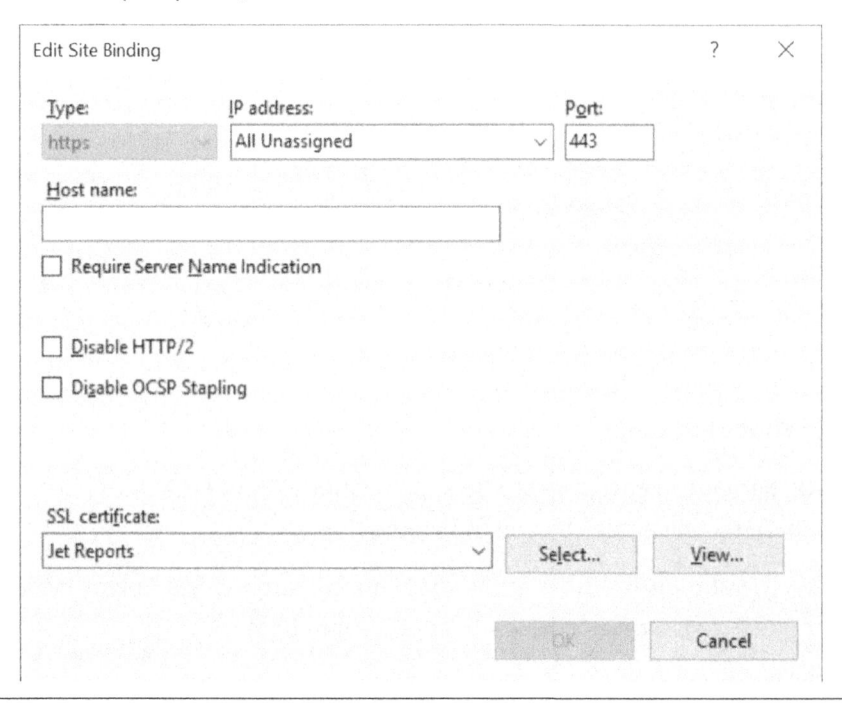

> Edit Site Binding
>
> Type: https IP address: All Unassigned Port: 443
>
> Host name:
>
> ☐ Require Server Name Indication
>
> ☐ Disable HTTP/2
> ☐ Disable OCSP Stapling
>
> SSL certificate: Jet Reports   Select... View...
>
> OK Cancel

1. Open **Internet Information Services (IIS) Manager**, select the **Jet Hub** website and, under **Actions >> Edit Site** click **Bindings**.

2. Select the **https** binding and click **Edit**.

3. Select the **SSL Certificate** and click **OK** to save the change.

Jet Service Tier and **Jet Hub** are now fully installed; **Jet Hub** requires a data source to be created before it can be used. We will do this once we have installed the **Client Components**.

Install the Jet Client Components

There are two elements to the **Jet Client Components**; the Jet Excel Add-in which needs to be installed on every client on which users will develop or generate reports created with Jet Reports; and the **Jet Administration Console** which only needs to be installed once, although it can be installed multiple times.

The **Jet Excel Add-in** provides the additional functionality to Excel which allows reports to be designed and generated.

The **Jet Administration Console** provides access to configuring the settings deployed via the **Jet Service Tier** (which includes the shared data sources).

To install the **Client Components**, perform these steps

1. Launch the downloaded setup utility.

2. Select the same **user management** selected when installing the **Server Components** and click **Next**.

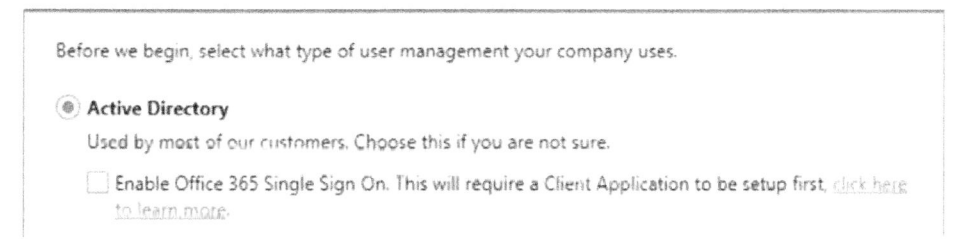

> Before we begin, select what type of user management your company uses.
>
> ⦿ **Active Directory**
> Used by most of our customers. Choose this if you are not sure.
>
> ☐ Enable Office 365 Single Sign On. This will require a Client Application to be setup first, click here to learn more.

3. Select **Client Components** and click **Next**.

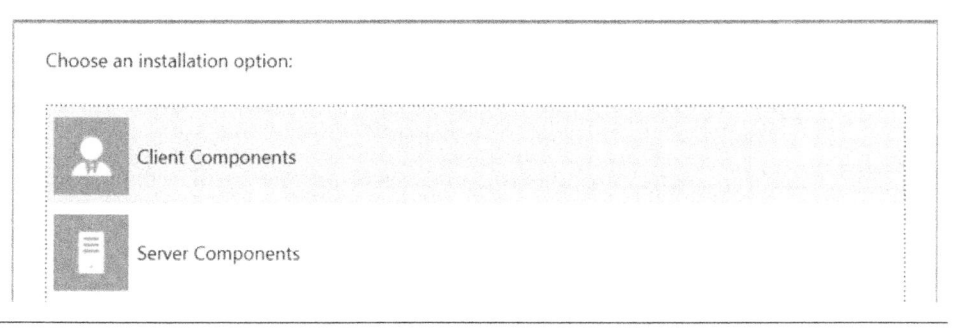

> Choose an installation option:
>
> Client Components
>
> Server Components

4. Select the **Client Components** (**Jet Excel Add-in** and **Jet Administration Console**), make sure none of the **Server Components** are selected and click **Next**.

5. Enter your **Activation Code** and click **Next**.

6. Enter the same **Network Connection settings** as entered on the **Server Component** install and click **Next**.

7. Click **Install** to begin the installation.

8. Once the installation is complete, click **Finish**.

The Jet Excel Add-in and Jet Administration Console are now both installed and ready for use.

Deploying the Jet SQL objects

With the **Server** and **Client Components** installed, there is one final installation step to complete before we can configure the data source and start using **Jet Reports**. To do this final installation step, perform the following:

1. Launch **Microsoft Dynamics GP** and log into a company (the **Jet GP Updater** connects with the client to access field names so needs it running).

2. Navigate to the **Jet Reports** install folder (C:\Program Files (x86)\JetReports) and launch the **Jet GP Updater.exe**..

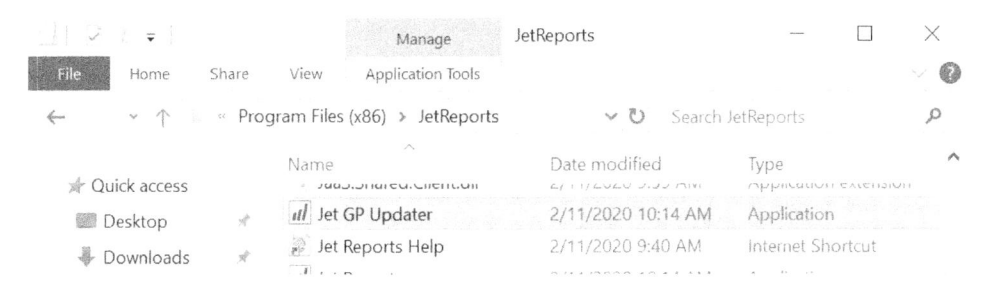

3. Enter the **SQL Server Instance name** and enter the **Dynamics Database** (which in this example is a named system database called **DJET** instead of the more common default one of **DYNAMICS**).

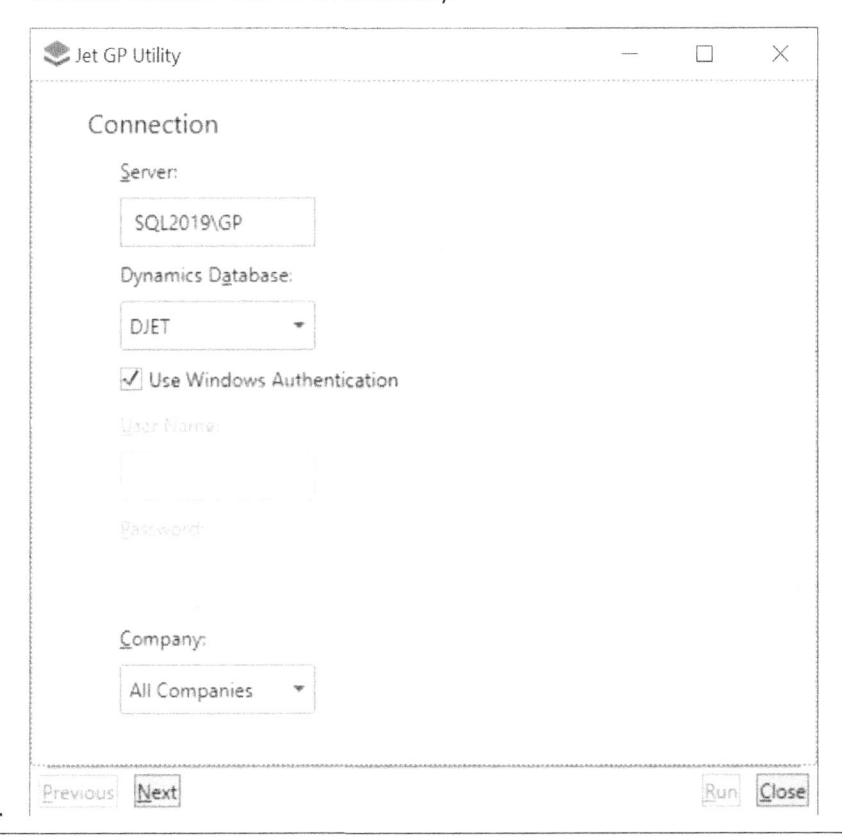

4.

Jet Reports with Microsoft Dynamics GP

Decide if you're using **Windows Authentication** and, if not, enter a SQL logon username and password. Whichever you use, needs to have permissions to deploy and configure SQL objects.

Decide which company to update; I have opted for **All Companies** and click **Next**.

5. Make sure all checkboxes are marked and click **Run**.

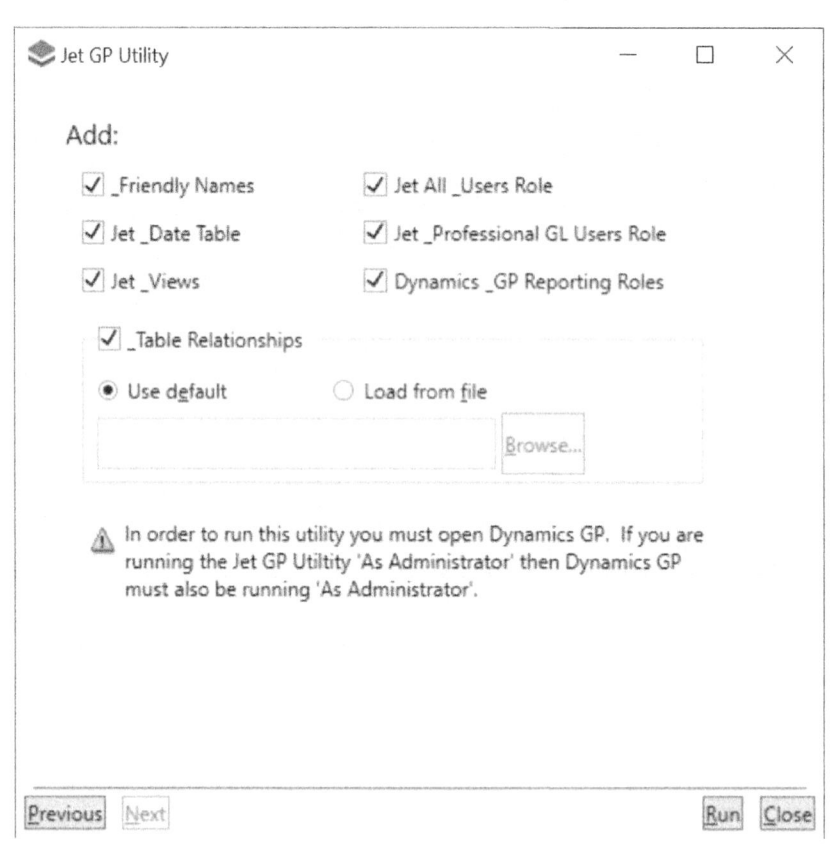

6. When prompted, click **Yes** to confirm the databases are to be updated.

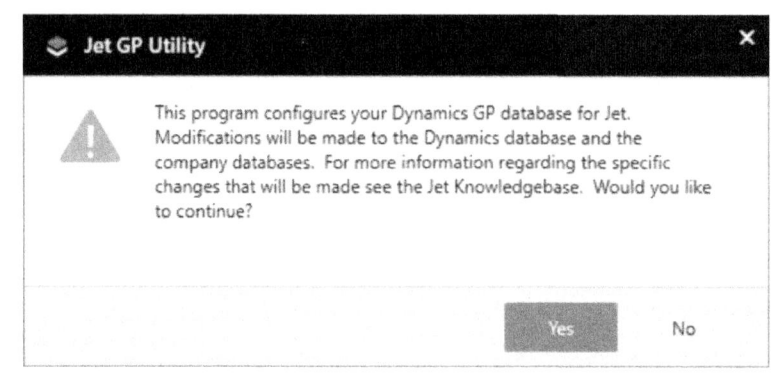

7. The update may take a while to run through, but will return and show the update status.

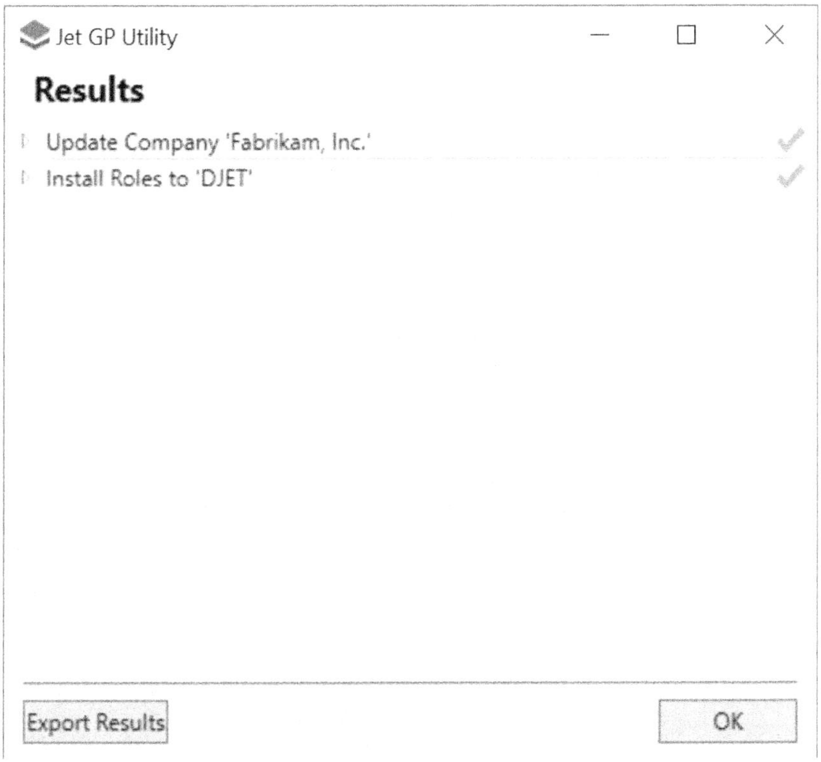
Jet GP Utility
Results
Update Company 'Fabrikam, Inc.'
Install Roles to 'DJET'
Export Results
OK

8. Click **OK** to close the **Results** window and then close the **Jet GP Utility** by clicking **Close**.

Summary

In this chapter, we've taken a look at the components and perquisites of Jet Reports and then stepped through the installation of the Jet Client and Server Components. In the next chapter, we'll take a look at configuring Jet Reports.

3

Configuring Jet Reports

In this chapter we're going to take a look at the steps required to configure Jet Reports so that we can start to create reports.

Configuration using the Jet Administration Console

The recommended approach is to use the **Jet Administration Console** to configure Jet Reports; doing it this way means you do the configuration once and it is automatically rolled out to all users. If you configure Jet Reports manually, then you need to do the configuration individually for each user on each computer.

Activating Jet Reports

If you did not enter the activation code during the installation, then you need to activate it now. Activate Jet Reports by performing these steps:

1. Launch the **Jet Administration Console**.

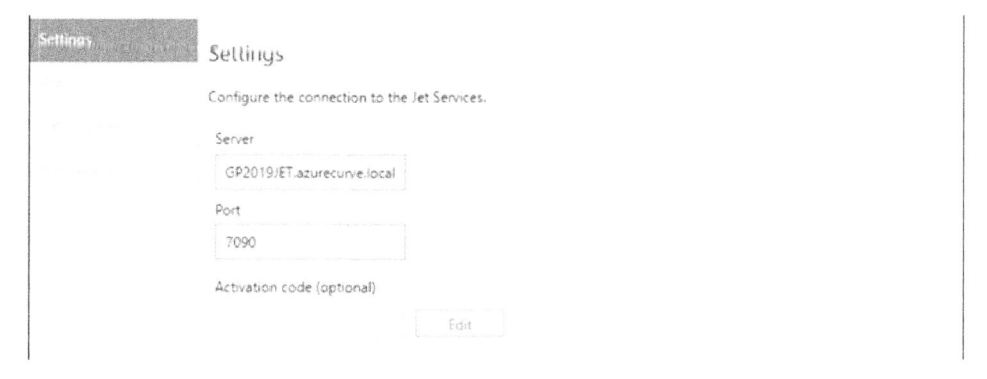

   ![Settings screen showing Server field with "GP2019JET.azurecurve.local", Port field with "7090", and an Activation code (optional) field with an Edit button]

2. Make sure the **Server** and **Port** fields are correctly set for the **Jet Service Tier** using

the details used during installation.

3. Click the **Connect** button on the action pane.

4. Click **OK** on the "successfully connected..." message when it is displayed.

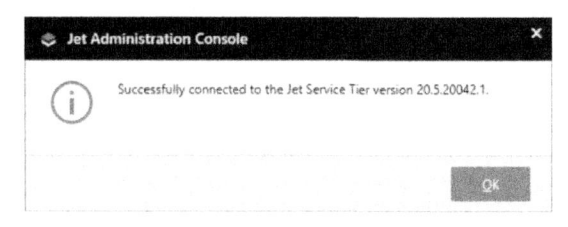

5. Click the **Edit** button next to the **Activation Code** field.

6. Enter your activation code (which will be supplied by the jet partner you ordered Jet Reports through) and hit **Save**.

Jet Reports will now be activated and ready for use.

Creating a data source

Data sources are best created through the **Jet Administration Console** as they can then be rolled out to users automatically; when we create a user, we'll show you how to assign data sources to them.

To use the **Jet Administration Console** to create a data source follow these steps:

1. Select **Data Sources** on the navigation pane.

2. Click **Add** on the action pane.

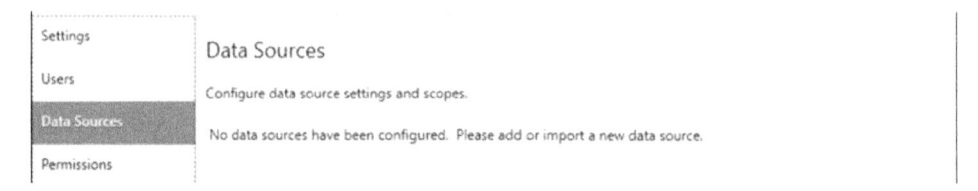

3. Enter the **Name** to be used for the data source; this should be unique and identifiable.

4. Select a **Database Type** of **Dynamics GP**.

5. Set the **Connection Method** to **On Premises**.

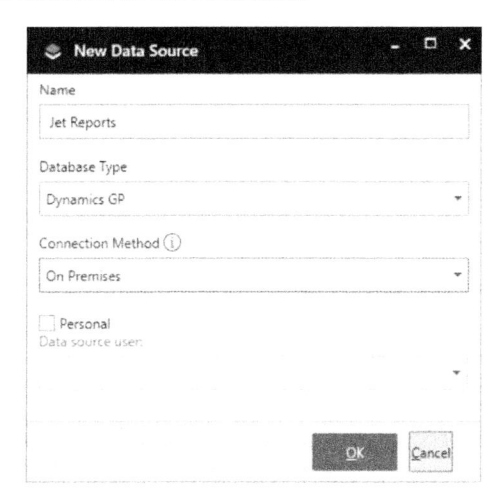

6. Click **OK**.

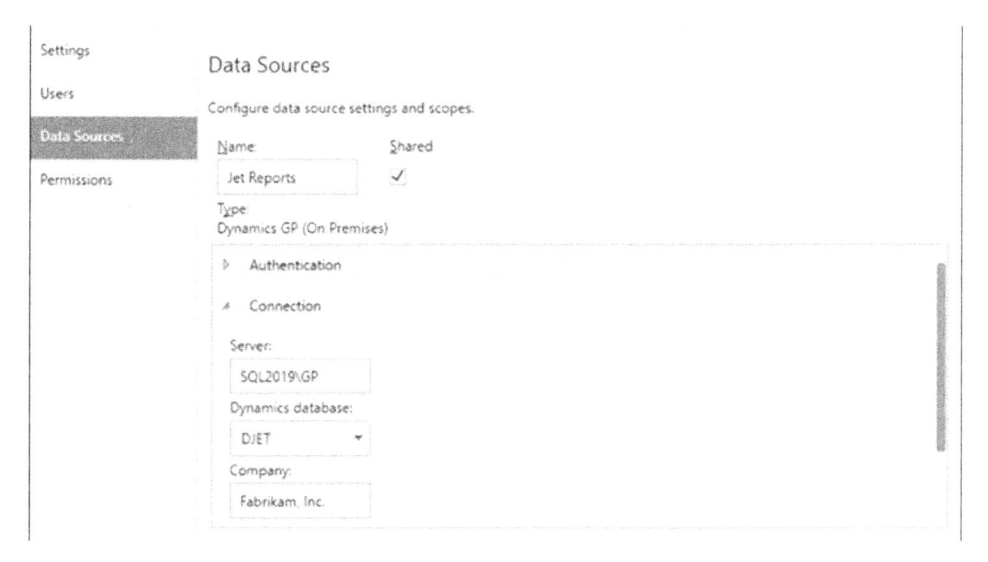

7. In the **Data Sources** pane expand **Connection**.

8. Enter the full **Instance** name of the **SQL Server** hosting the **Microsoft Dynamics GP** databases in the **Server** field.

9. Select the **Dynamics Database** from the dropdown list (typically this would be called **DYNAMICS**, but my environment has a named system database.

10. Enter the name of the default **Company**; this is free-form entry and has to be exactly the same as the company name in the **Company** Setup window in Microsoft Dynamics GP on the **Administration area page** » **Setup** » **Company**.

11. Click and expand the **Display** heading.

12. Mark **Enable Friendly Names for this data source**; this is not required, but users generally handle the friendly names better than the physical names (**PM Creditor Master** compared to **PM00200**).

13. Enter Great Plains in the **Friendly Names Group** field (this is free form text entry so must be exactly entered for the friendly names to work).

14. The **Display format** will default to **Captions**, but can be changed to one of four options:

    a. **Captions** which is the friendly name; e.g. **PM Creditor Master**.

    b. **Names** which is the physical name; e.g. **PM00200**.

    c. **Caption (Name)**; e.g. **PM Creditor Master (PM00200)**.

    d. **Name (Caption)**; e.g. **PM00200 (PM Creditor Master)**.

15. The recommended setting is **Caption (Name)** as this works best for normal users while allowing technical users to still easily use the physical names.

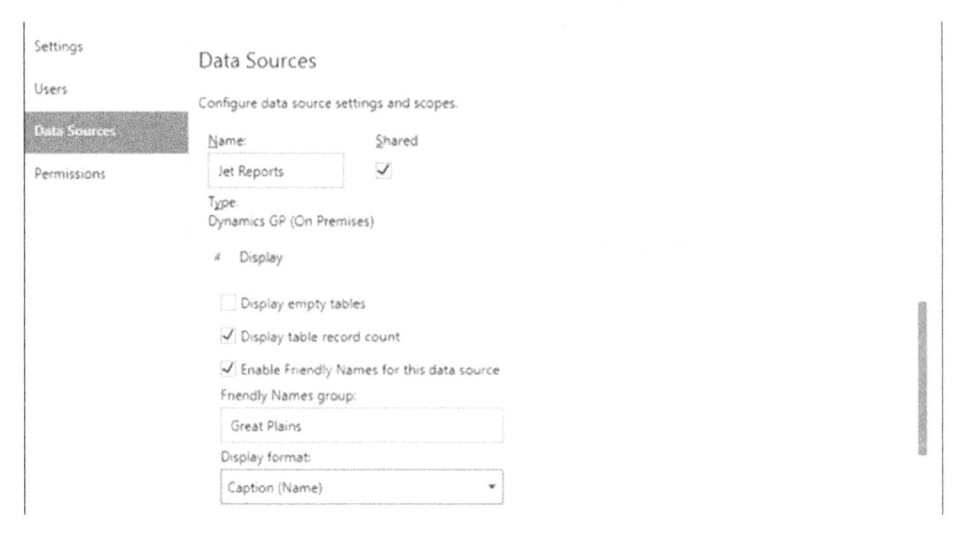

16. Click **Save** to save the data source.

Creating users

With a data source created, we can create additional users and give them access to a data source. Do this by following these steps in the **Jet Administration Console**:

1. Select **Users** in the navigation pane.

2. Click the **Add** button on the action pane.

3. Enter the name of the user(s) you want to add and select them from the list as they appear.

Settings
Users
Data Sources
Permissions
Users
Add, remove, and edit Jet Reports users.
Type
Full Name
Name
Domain
Security Level
Allow Personal Data Sources
AZURECURVE

4. When all required users have been selected, click **Add**.

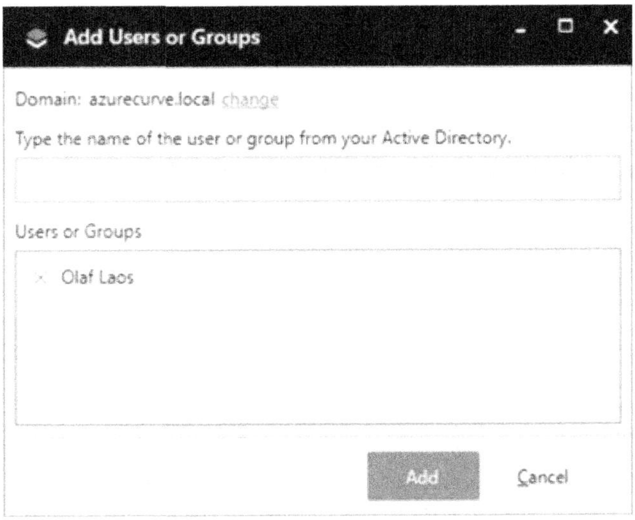
Add Users or Groups
Domain: azurecurve.local change
Type the name of the user or group from your Active Directory.
Users or Groups
Olaf Laos
Add
Cancel

5. Use the **Security Level** box to set the user as a **User** or **Administrator** (the former can only view and generate reports others have designed, whereas the latter can also design reports).

Settings
Users
Data Sources
Permissions
Users
Add, remove, and edit Jet Reports users.
Type
Full Name
Name
Domain
Security Level
Allow Personal Data Sources
AZURECURVE
User
Olaf Laos
olafl
AZURECURVE
User
Administrator

6. Click **Save**.
7. Select **Permissions** on the navigation pane.
8. The available data sources will be listed alongside the users, with a checkbox to grant access.

9. When all users have been assigned the required data sources, click **Save**.

Users are now created and configured with access to the data source to the Microsoft Dynamics GP data source. They can now run the **Jet Excel Add-in** and use Jet Reports to design reports.

Running Jet Excel Add-in for the first time

The first time a user runs **Jet Reports** they will be prompted to participate, or not, in the **Customer Experience Improvement Program**.

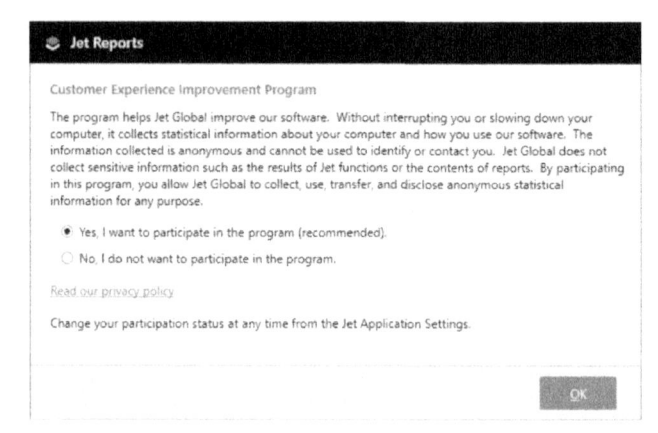

After they have made their choice and clicked **OK**, Excel will finish loading the **Jet** tab into the action pane.

Summary

In this chapter we have covered the configuration of **Jet Reports** by activating it, creating a data source to Microsoft Dynamics GP and adding users with the required permissions. In the next chapter, we'll take a look at the functions available on the **Jet** tab of the action pane made available by the **Jet Excel Add-in**.

4

Introducing the Excel Add-in

The **Jet Excel Add-in** adds a tab to the action pane in Excel which provides access to all of the functionality for the design and running of reports. In this chapter we're going to take a look at the functionality it adds.

Jet Action Add-in

The **Jet Excel Add-in** allows Excel to integrate with Microsoft Dynamics GP or any other database which has an **OLE** or **ODBC** driver available so that reports can be created with simple worksheet functions.

The add-in provides a number of functions which allows data to be read direct from the database and refreshed within Excel.

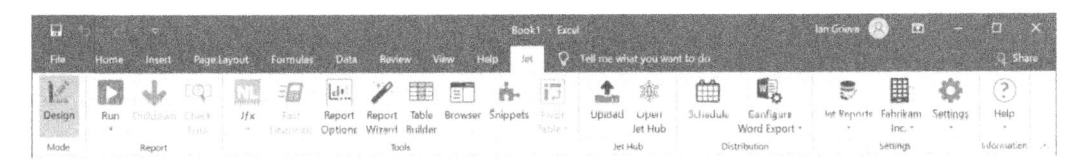

Mode

The first section of the Jet tab is the **Mode**. To create or modify a report you need to click this button to take Jet into design mode. We'll cover report design in a later chapter.

Jet Reports with Microsoft Dynamics GP

Report

The second section of the Jet tab is the **Report** tab.

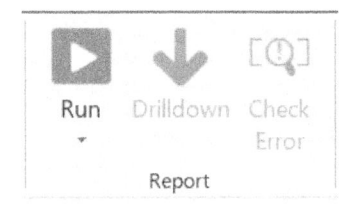

1. The **Run** button will generate the report using the current design and refresh the data from the data source. If in **Design** mode, clicking run will take you from design mode into run mode.

2. The **Drilldown** button will drill down into the selected cell.

3. The **Check Error** button can be used to diagnose a value of **"#VALUE"** in a cell containing a Jet function.

Tools

The **Tools** tab contains the functionality for designing reports.

1. The **Jfx** button gives access to the Jet functions which are used to design reports.

2. The **Report Options** button allows you to easily create an options page; this will be covered in depth in **Chapter 5, Report Structure**.

3. The **Report Wizard** button launches the **Report Wizard tool** which allows reports to be created through a wizard driven process.

4. The **Table Builder** button launches the **Table Builder tool** which allows table reports to be created through a drag and drop process.

5. The **Browser** button launches the **Browser** which allows NL and associated NF functions to be placed onto a worksheet using drag and drop from the **Browser** window.

6. The **Snippets** button opens the **Snippets** window which allows reusable snippets to be created and used repeatedly. This tool is useful for storing sections which

will be used on multiple different reports.

All of the above are covered in detail in later chapters of this book.

Jet Hub

The **Jet Hub** gives users the ability to view reports via the web browser.

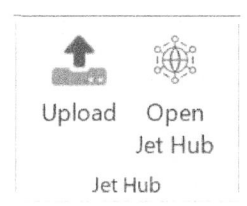

1. When users design reports they are stored on the user's computer or a shared network drive; to make them available to users of the **Jet Hub**, the **Upload** button will upload the report to the **Jet Hub**.
2. The **Open Jet Hub** button will launch the **Jet Hub** in your default browser.

Distribution

The **Distribution** tab provides access to the distribution methods for a Jet Report.

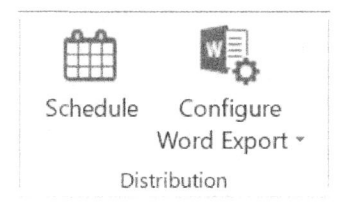

1. **Schedule** allows a report to be scheduled to run at a specific date and time; recurrence is supported so a report could be scheduled to run daily, weekly or any other desired basis.
2. **Configure Word Export** allows a report to be configured for export to Microsoft Word in order that it can be distributed in a readable format. Reports generated to Word are often then converted to PDF before distribution.

Settings

The **Settings** tab on the **Jet** tab contain the default data source and app settings.

1. The first button is the default data source with the name on the button being the name of the selected data source.

2. The second button is the default company and will show the name of the selected Microsoft Dynamics GP company.

3. The third button, **Settings**, gives access to the **App Settings** and **Data Source Settings**.

Information

The **Information** section of the **Jet** tab gives access to the **Help Centre**, **Feedback** and **About** window.

Summary

In this chapter we have introduced the functionality of the **Jet Reports Excel Add-in**; we'll take a more detailed look into some specific functions over the next chapters. In the next chapter, we'll be taking a look at how a report would be structured.

5

Report Structure

In this chapter we're going to take a look at how a report can best be structured in design mode to allow easy understanding of the design.

Worksheets

Technically, a report only requires a single worksheet which is the one which contains the report design; however, almost every report will also include options which the user needs to specify when they run the report. These options should be created on a dedicated page.

It's also quite common for reports to be created in a style similar to Management Reporter where there are separate sheets for the Financial, Account and Transaction levels of detail.

Special rows and columns

The first row of a report is a special row which should not contain any output elements of the report. The first row can be used to define whether a report should be shown or hidden and can be used to control the width of a column.

	A	B	C	D
1	Auto+Hide+Values+Lock	Hide+?	Hide	Fit

Cell **A1** will always contain **Auto+Hide+Values** and should not be changed, unless it is to add **+Lock** which will stop users unhiding hidden columns or pages.

Cells **B1** contains **Hide+?** which will hide this column and allow an Excel formula to be used to show/hide a row based on an **IF** command.

Cell **C1** contains the word **Hide** which will automatically cause this column to be hidden when the report is run.

Cell **D1** contains **Fit** which will automatically resize the column to the width of the data it contains when the report is run.

A report will typically have options which the user is prompted to enter or select when running the report. It is more efficient if these options are on a separate worksheet and brought through to the report sheet using the **NP** function; this is typically done in column **A**.

Column **B** is used to show/hide a row based on a formula such as:

| B9 | ▼ | : | × | ✓ | *fx* | =IF($G9 > 0,"Show","Hide") |

Column **C** is used for a row key, such as an **Account Category Number** or **NL** replicator.

Report page layout

The report page should contain the special rows and columns outlined above, but after this the report can be laid out in any way required.

Typically when I create a report, the report title would go in cell **E5**, the column headings starting in **E7** and the report output starting in **E8**. If there is a record key column not being output this would go in column **D** with the heading in **D7** and the data starting in row **D8**.

Options page

Most reports will need options for the user to set at runtime; the most common options are year and period. All report options should be contained within a dedicated **Options** worksheet.

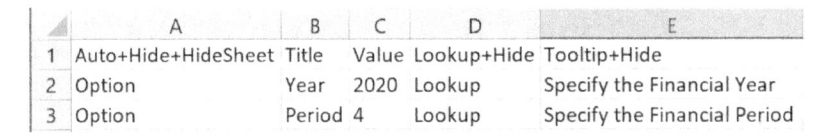

	A	B	C	D	E
1	Auto+Hide+HideSheet	Title	Value	Lookup+Hide	Tooltip+Hide
2	Option	Year	2020	Lookup	Specify the Financial Year
3	Option	Period	4	Lookup	Specify the Financial Period

The first row of an **Options** page is a special row where the cells specify the content of the columns:

- Cell **A1** contains **Auto+Hide+HideSheet** which will hide both that column and the entire worksheet when the report is run; column **A** should contain the keyword **Option** which tells **Jet** this is a row containing an option for the user to set.

- Cell **B1** contains the word **Title** and will be used as the title column in the **Report Options** window when the report is generated; column **B** contains the titles for the option.

- Cell **C2** contains **Value** and will be the value entered by the user in the **Report Options** window; column **C** contains the default values which the user can override.

- Cell **D1** contains **Lookup+Hide** and column **D** contains an **NL** function with a type of **LOOKUP**. Creating this function will be covered in **Chapter 6, Using the functions in the Excel Add-in**.

- Cell **E1** contains **Tooltip+Hide** and column **E** contains the tooltips which should be shown to users when they hover their mouse over a field in the **Report Options** window.

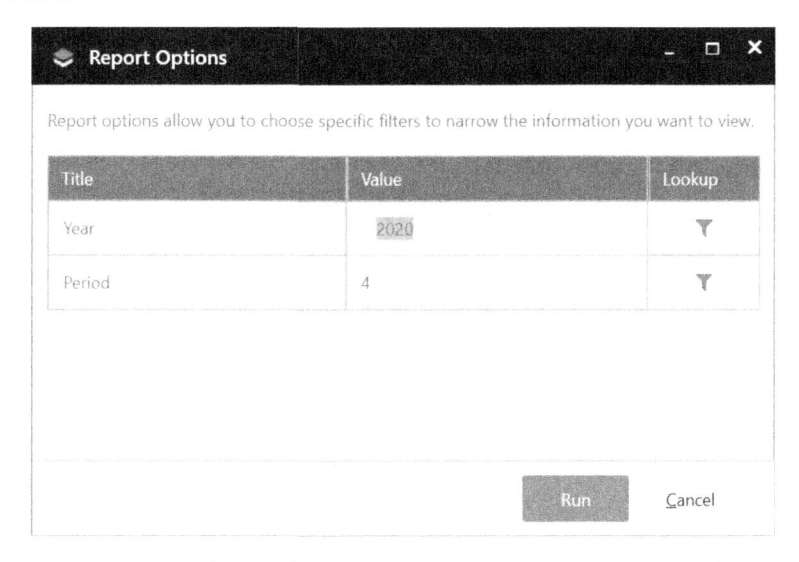

A **Report Options** page can be easily created using the **Report Options** function available from the **Tools** section of the **Jet** action pane, which will be covered in **Chapter 14, Report Creation Tools**.

Formatting

There are many ways of formatting reports, but the most important point is to be consistent in how your organization formats reports.

The approach I tend to recommend is:

- Yellow fill for hidden rows and columns.

- Blue fill for cells containing option referenced onto the report sheet from the **Options** sheet.

- Grey cells for hardcoded options on the report sheet; I recommend against hardcoded options in most circumstances, but one way they are used is to limit a report down to a specific company, vendor or customer where the user should not be able to make a change.

Adding them to the sheet as a hardcoded option, means a report designer can easily replicate the report and change the hardcoded option without needing to change every row.

- Green fill for cells with **ROWS=n** in the **What** of an **NL** function (this will be explained in *Chapter 6, Using the functions in the Excel Add-in*).

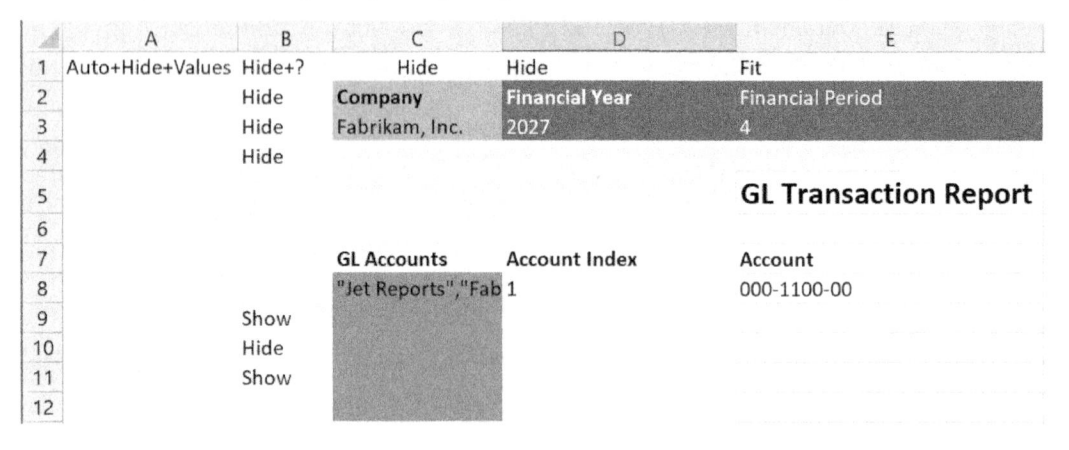

	A	B	C	D	E
1	Auto+Hide+Values	Hide+?	Hide	Hide	Fit
2		Hide	Company	Financial Year	Financial Period
3		Hide	Fabrikam, Inc.	2027	4
4		Hide			
5					**GL Transaction Report**
6					
7			GL Accounts	Account Index	Account
8			"Jet Reports","Fab	1	000-1100-00
9		Show			
10		Hide			
11		Show			
12					

Summary

In this chapter we took a look at the structure of a Jet Report. In the next chapter, we will take a look at the special **Jet Functions** which are available for use.

6

Using the functions in the Excel Add-in

In this chapter we'll take a look at the four special **Jet Functions** which the **Jet Excel Add-in** make available for the creation of reports.

Available functions

There are four **Jet Report** functions available which allows data to be read from the Microsoft Dynamics GP database and refreshed within Excel.

The **NL** function queries and returns values from any table and field in the database and supports up to 10 filters for restricting the returned data.

The **NF** Function is used in conjunction with the **NL** function. First you use the NL function to define which record is to be returned, and then use the **NF** function to retrieve fields for that record. This is a more efficient approach to creating every field with an **NL** function.

The **NP** function is a utility function which allows you to perform certain tasks such as evaluate formulas, create date filters or do array operations. The **NP** function can assist in improving the efficiency of reports.

The **GL** function combines multiple **NL** functions into one to make General Ledger reporting even easier from Microsoft Dynamics GP.

NL function

The NL function is the most used function in Jet Reports. Financial reports can generally be made with the **GL** function, but all reports can be created using the **NL** function.

Return a single record

If we have an option in cell **C3** containing a **Vendor ID**, we would use the following **NL** function to return the **Vendor Name**:

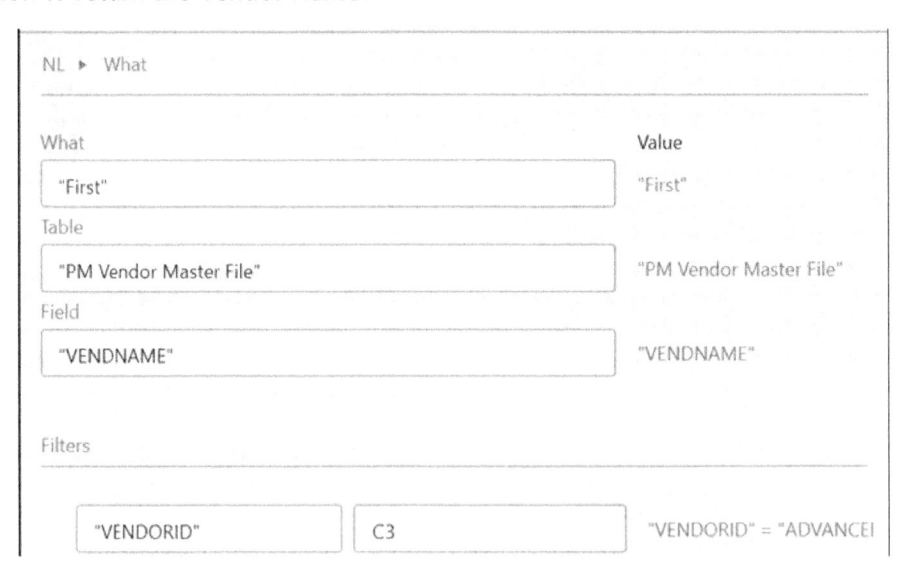

NL ▶ What		
What		Value
"First"		"First"
Table		
"PM Vendor Master File"		"PM Vendor Master File"
Field		
"VENDNAME"		"VENDNAME"
Filters		
"VENDORID"	C3	"VENDORID" = "ADVANCE|

Return all records

If we want to return a list of all vendor names, we would use the following **NL** function to return the **Vendor Name**:

NL ▶ What		
What		Value
"Rows"	▼	"Rows"
Table		
"PM Vendor Master File"		"PM Vendor Master File"
Field		
"VENDNAME"		"VENDNAME"

Return range of records

If we have an option in cell **C3** containing a range of **Vendor IDs** (for an example of all vendors with names starting **A** through **E** the range would be entered in the option as **A..E**), we would use the same NL formula as in the return a single vendor name except that the **What** would be set to **"Rows"**.

Chapter 6: Using the functions in the Jet Excel Add-in

Return field for a date range of records

To return a list of voucher numbers for a date range, the NL function would be used. This example has the vendor range in cell **C3**, start date in **D3** and end date in **E3**:

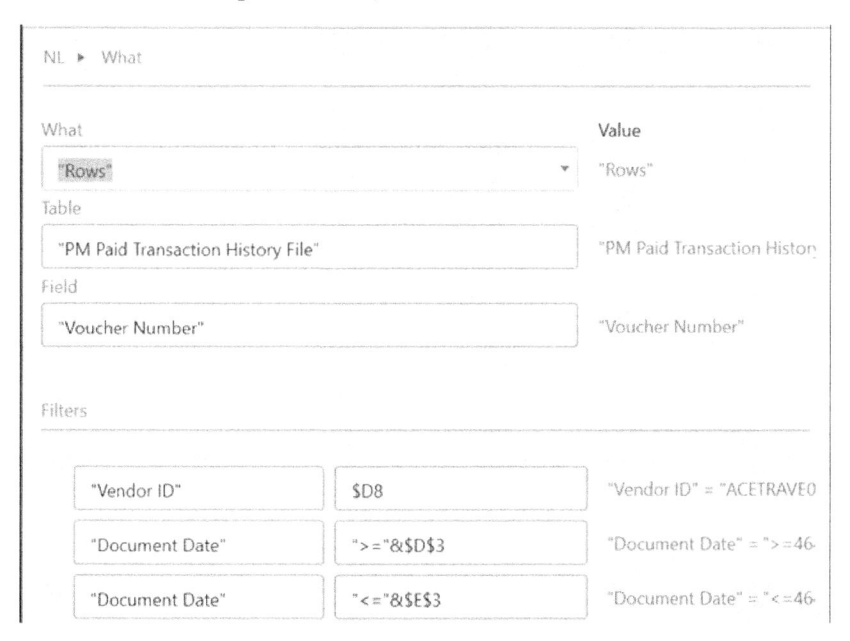

What	Value
"Rows"	"Rows"
Table	
"PM Paid Transaction History File"	"PM Paid Transaction History"
Field	
"Voucher Number"	"Voucher Number"
Filters	
"Vendor ID" — $D8	"Vendor ID" = "ACETRAVE0"
"Document Date" — ">="&$D$3	"Document Date" = ">=46
"Document Date" — "<="&$E$3	"Document Date" = "<=46

The date check is done with filters of **Document Date** greater than and less than by prefixing the cell with ">=" & and "<=" &.

You'll notice that the filter values contain **$** (such as the first filter value which is set to **$D8**); this is because I have toggled the **cell reference mode** to lock the cell reference to column **D** while allowing the replicator as it moved down the worksheet to reference each row.

The **$** can be added manually or the **F4** key can be used to toggle between the cell reference modes.

The second and third filter values are set with both the column and row locked as these are referencing the options at the top of the page and which never move.

There is an alternate method of doing the date filter using an **NP** function which I'll cover in the **NP function** section.

Handling a blank filter

When running a report you might encounter an empty filter argument error:

> The FilterField 'Vendor ID' has an empty Filter argument, which is not allowed. Use '' to filter for blank, or prefix the Filter argument with @@ if it is a cell reference.
>
> More information...

39

Jet Reports with Microsoft Dynamics GP

As the message says, you can avoid the error by prefixing "@@" & to the filter field causing the problem. Using the formula from the last example, it would be changed to this:

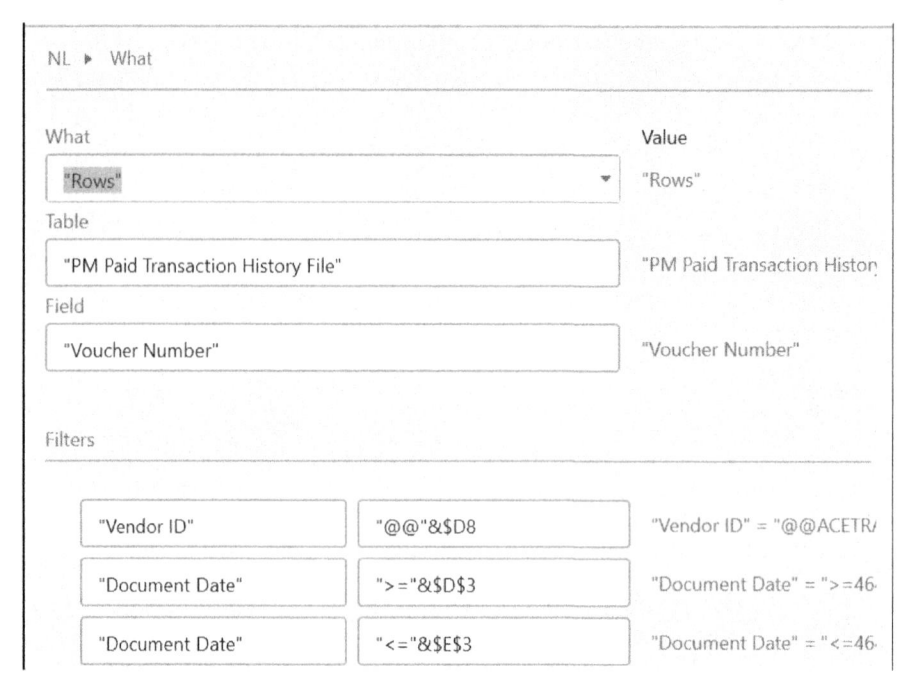

NL ▶ What		
What		**Value**
"Rows"	▼	"Rows"
Table		
"PM Paid Transaction History File"		"PM Paid Transaction History"
Field		
"Voucher Number"		"Voucher Number"
Filters		
"Vendor ID"	"@@"&$D8	"Vendor ID" = "@@ACETR/
"Document Date"	">="&$D$3	"Document Date" = ">=46
"Document Date"	"<="&$E$3	"Document Date" = "<=46

NF function

The NF function is used in conjunction with an NL function which returns a record key.

Use NL function to return a record key

To use the **NL** function to return a record key for a vendor listing from the **PM Vendor Master File**, configure the **NL** lookup like this:

NL ▶ What		
What		**Value**
"Rows"		"Rows"
Table		
"PM Vendor Master File"		"PM Vendor Master File"
Field		
Filters		
"+VendorID"	"*"	"+VendorID" = "*"

40

The difference to the previous **NL** functions we covered, is the absence of a **Field**; leaving this blank will return the record key and should be in a hidden column.

Use NF function to return a field using a record key

Once the **NL** function has been created to return the vendor list, the **NF** function can be defined to extract a field. To return the **Vendor ID** field from the replicator in cell **C8**, the **NF** function would be configured like this:

NF ▶ Key	
Key	Value
$C8	"""Jet Reports""",""Fabrikam,
Field	
"VENDORID"	"VENDORID"

One NF function is required per field to be extracted from the table for which the record key was returned. Using the **NF** function in this way is more efficient than using the **NL** function in every cell.

NP function

The NP function is a utility function which can be used to perform certain tasks such as evaluate formulas, create date filters or do array operations. I'll cover a small number of the uses below, but a full reference is available from Jet Global Support (https://azrcrv.co.uk/jetglobalsupport).

Evaluate a formula

Evaluating a formula is the most common use of the **NP** function. When using an **Options** page, it is not efficient to directly reference the options; instead the **NP** function should be used to evaluate the options and bring them to the report sheet.

This example has an **Options** page with the **Fiscal Year** in cell **C3**; the **NP** function would be a **What** of Eval:

NP ▶ What	
What	Value
"Eval"	"Eval"
Formula	
"Options!$C$3"	"Options!$C$3"

Jet Reports with Microsoft Dynamics GP

This formula would be in field **D3** and referenced from there in the **NL** or **GL** functions in the report.

Date filter

When covering the **NL** function I covered a date range where I did a greater than and less than for the Document Date and mentioned that there was an alternative. By using the **NP** function we can create a date filter:

```
NP ▸ What

What                                Value
"Datefilter"                    ▼   "Datefilter"
Start Date
$D$3                                "1/31/2027"
End Date
$E$3                                "3/31/2027"
```

While this could be a nested function, I placed it next to the options in cell **F3**; the output is 1/31/2027..3/31/2027 which can be used in the **NL** function from there and avoids the potential need to evaluate the dates more than once.

GL function

The GL function returns the account, account name, category, category name, balance, net change and budget. It cannot do the debits or credits, so a report needing these will need to use the **NL** function.

Return list of accounts

To return a list of accounts using the **GL** function, you would configure it with a **Where** of Rows like this:

```
GL ▸ Where

Where                               Value
"Rows"                              "Rows"
What
"Accounts"                          "Accounts"
```

Return Account Name

To return the name for an account in cell **G8**, the **GL** function would be used like this:

GL ▶ Where	
Where	**Value**
"Cell"	"Cell"
What	
"AccountName"	"AccountName"
Account	
$G8	"000-1100-00"

Return the YTD balance for a period

To return the year-to-date balance for a specific period, we can use the **GL** function. In this example, the **Account** is in cell **E8**, the **Fiscal Year** in cell **D3** and **Fiscal Period** in cell **E3**.

I have concatenated the **Fiscal Year** with /0 to set the **First Period**; I have then concatenated the **Fiscal year** and **Fiscal Period** to set the **End Period**.

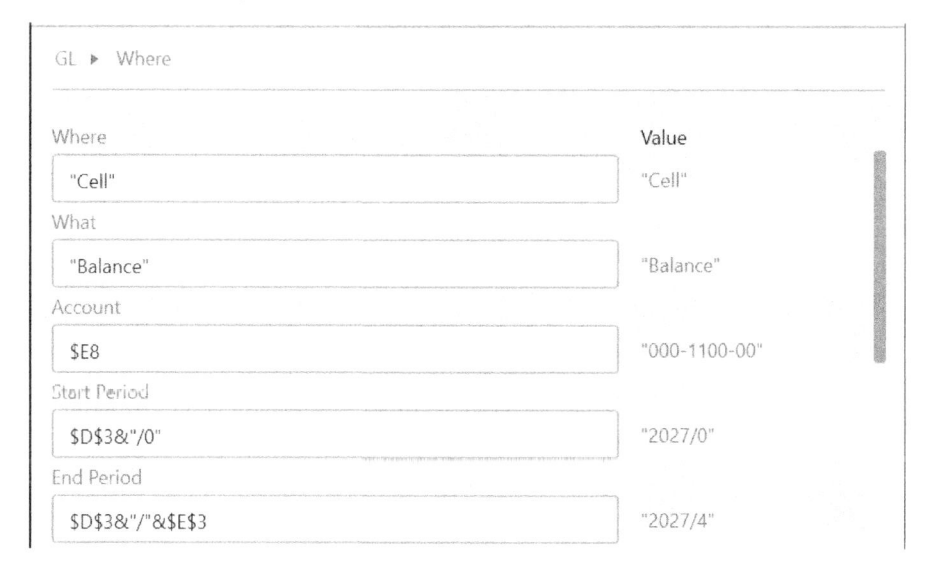

GL ▶ Where	
Where	**Value**
"Cell"	"Cell"
What	
"Balance"	"Balance"
Account	
$E8	"000-1100-00"
Start Period	
$D$3&"/0"	"2027/0"
End Period	
$D$3&"/"&$E$3	"2027/4"

Return the opening balance for period

To return the opening balance of the same period as used in the last example, we would configure a **GL** function which is exactly the same, except we would add a -1 to the End Period.

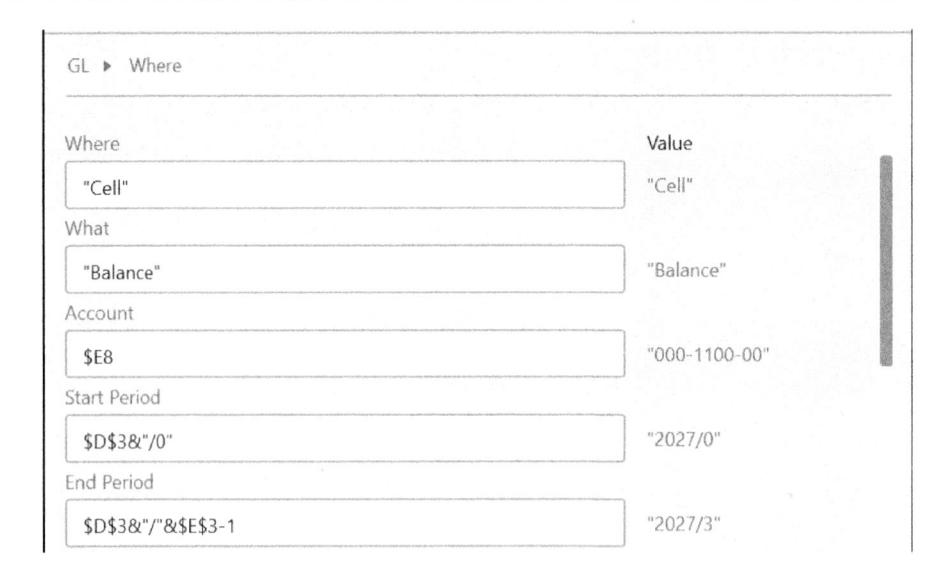

GL ▶ Where	
Where	**Value**
"Cell"	"Cell"
What	
"Balance"	"Balance"
Account	
$E8	"000-1100-00"
Start Period	
$D$3&"/0"	"2027/0"
End Period	
$D$3&"/"&$E$3-1	"2027/3"

Return the period balance for period

If you wanted to know the net change of an account, using the same data as the last two examples, we would configure the **GL** function with the same **Start Period** and **End Period**.

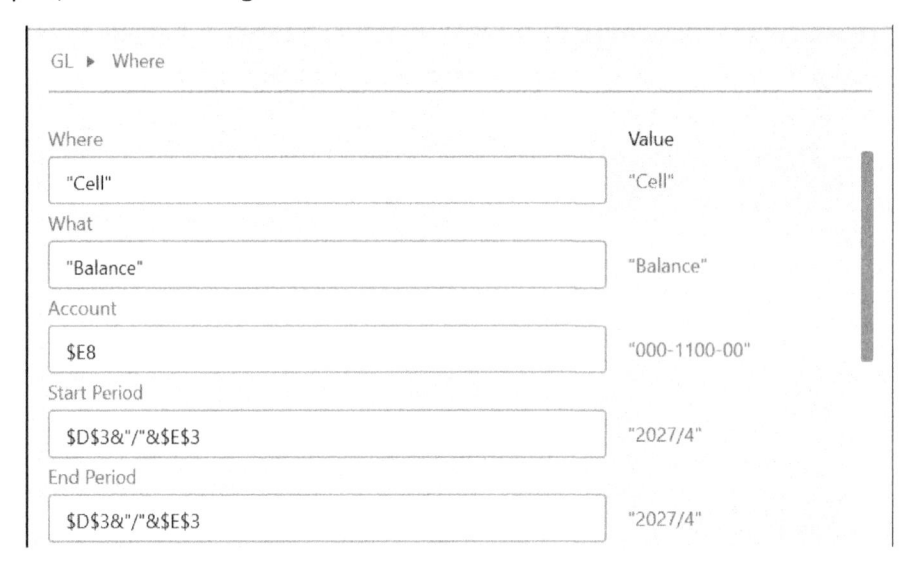

GL ▶ Where	
Where	**Value**
"Cell"	"Cell"
What	
"Balance"	"Balance"
Account	
$E8	"000-1100-00"
Start Period	
$D$3&"/"&$E$3	"2027/4"
End Period	
$D$3&"/"&$E$3	"2027/4"

Return the balance for period last year

Returning the balance for an account for the previous year, we would configure the **GL** function with -1 on the **Fiscal Year** in the **Start Period** and **End Period** fields:

GL ▶ Where	
Where	Value
"Cell"	"Cell"
What	
"Balance"	"Balance"
Account	
$E8	"000-1100-00"
Start Period	
$D$3-1&"/0"	"2026/0"
End Period	
$D$3-1&"/"&$E$3	"2026/4"

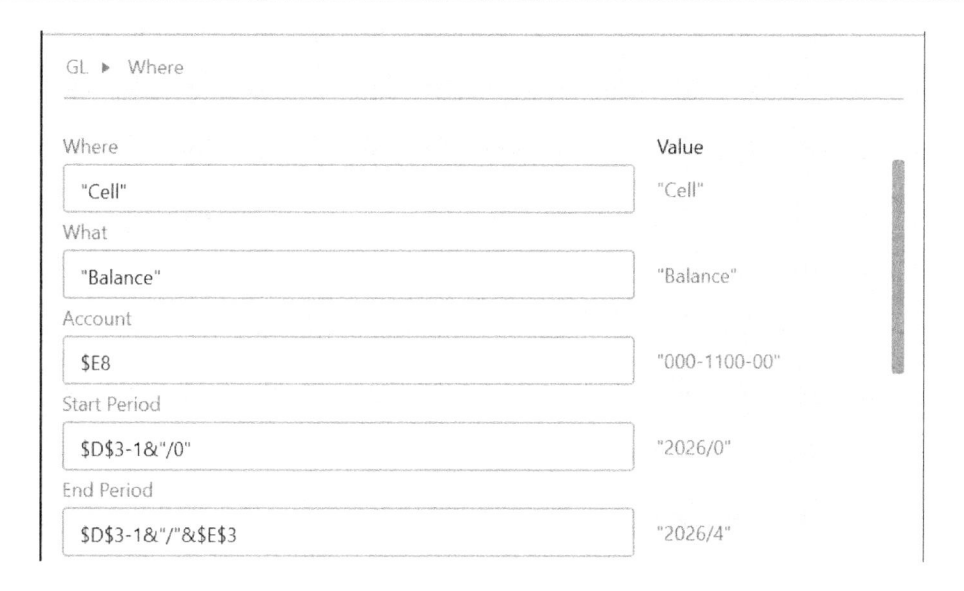

Return a budget period balance

To return a budget period balance, the **What** is set to Budget and in the **Budget** field, we can select a list of Budgets from Microsoft Dynamics GP using a dropdown.

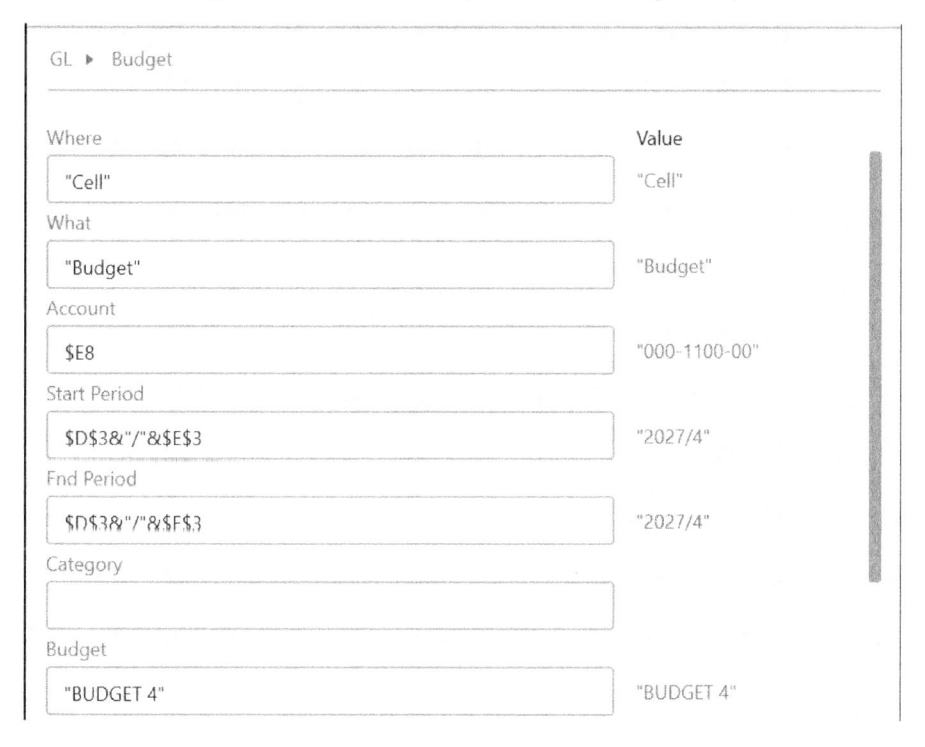

GL ▶ Budget	
Where	Value
"Cell"	"Cell"
What	
"Budget"	"Budget"
Account	
$E8	"000-1100-00"
Start Period	
$D$3&"/"&$E$3	"2027/4"
End Period	
$D$3&"/"&$E$3	"2027/4"
Category	
Budget	
"BUDGET 4"	"BUDGET 4"

Summary

In this chapter we have taken a look at the available Jet functions and how they're used to build reports. In the next chapter, we'll take a look at adding options to a report.

7

Creating and using an Options page

An **Options** page provides a standardized way of prompting users to set the options which will determine which data is included in the report. In this chapter we'll take a look at creating and using an options page.

Create a new Options page

To create an **Options** page, click **Report Options** in the **Tools** section of the **Jet** action pane. The **Title**, **Value** and **Tooltip** entries are manually entered; in the example below, I've configured options for the **Fiscal Year** and **Fiscal Period**.

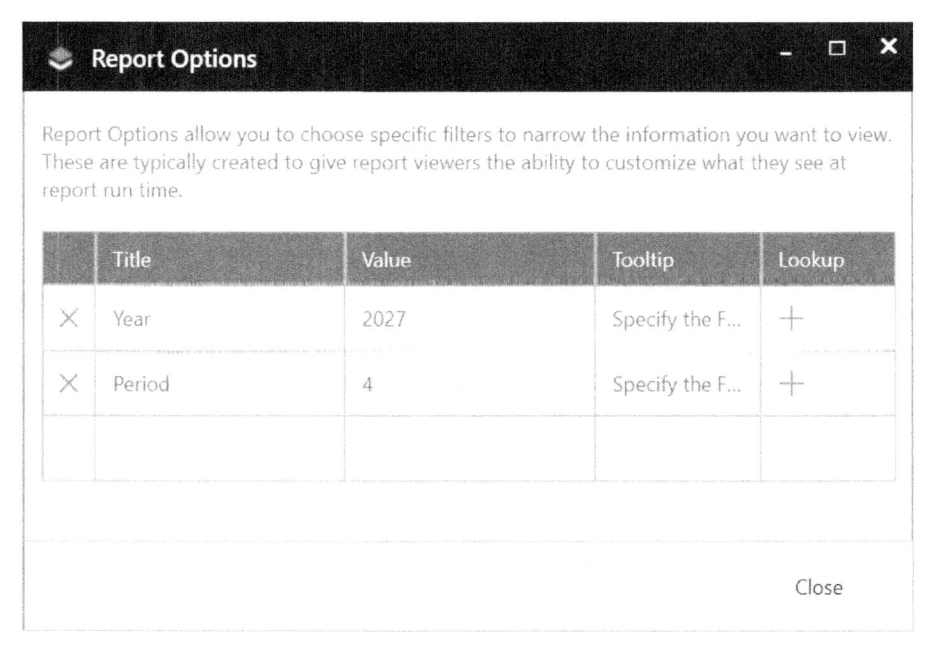

	Title	Value	Tooltip	Lookup
✕	Year	2027	Specify the F...	+
✕	Period	4	Specify the F...	+

These options will be free form entry; we can make it more user friendly by providing lookups for them to select values.

Lookup on Fiscal Year

To create a lookup for the **Fiscal Year**, click the plus icon in the **Lookup** column. The **What** will be set to Lookup automatically.

Select the **Table** Period Header (SY40101) and select the **Field** Year.

In this example, I have also set a sort order of **Year descending** and excluded **Historical Years**.

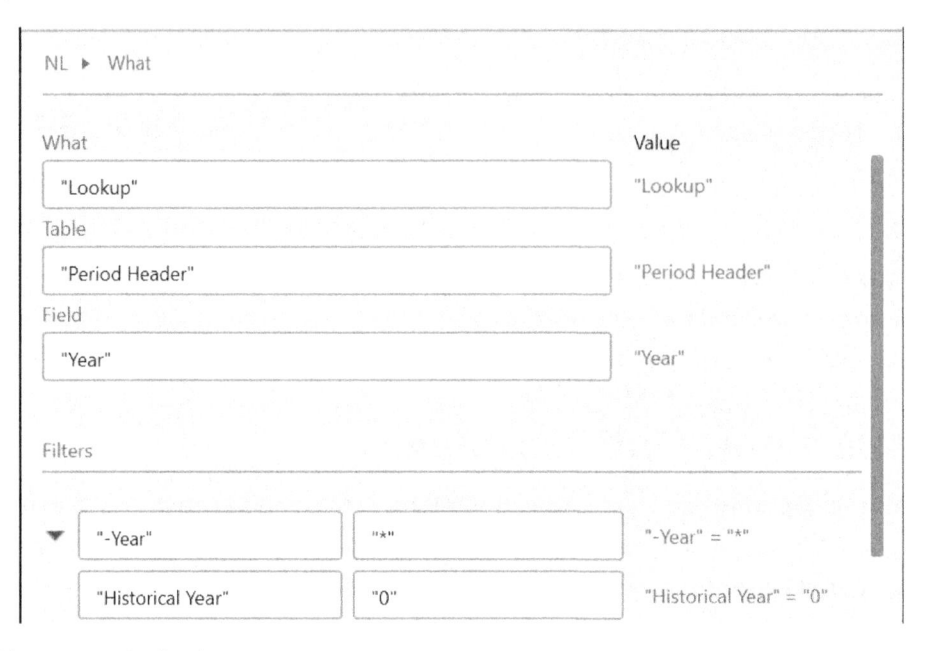

NL ▶ What		
What		**Value**
"Lookup"		"Lookup"
Table		
"Period Header"		"Period Header"
Field		
"Year"		"Year"
Filters		
"-Year"	"*"	"-Year" = "*"
"Historical Year"	"0"	"Historical Year" = "0"

Hit Ok to save the lookup.

Lookup on Fiscal Period

We can also create a lookup for the **Fiscal Period** by clicking the plus icon.

Select the **Table** Period Setup (SY40100) and select the **Field** Period ID.

In this example, I have also set a sort order of **Year descending** and excluded **Historical Years**.

I have applied filters for **Origin Description** of General Entry so that only one entry for each period is returned, for **Period ID** "<>" & 0 to exclude period 0 and **Year** equal to the selected **Fiscal Year**.

```
NL  ▶  What

What                                           Value
┌─────────────────────────────────┐             ┌─────────────┐
│ "Lookup"                        │             │ "Lookup"    │
└─────────────────────────────────┘             └─────────────┘
Table
┌─────────────────────────────────┐             "Period Setup"
│ "Period Setup"                  │
└─────────────────────────────────┘
Field
┌─────────────────────────────────┐             "Period ID"
│ "Period ID"                     │
└─────────────────────────────────┘

Filters

    ┌──────────────────────┐  ┌──────────────────────┐   "Origin Description" = "Ge
    │ "Origin Description" │  │ "General Entry"      │
    └──────────────────────┘  └──────────────────────┘

    ┌──────────────────────┐  ┌──────────────────────┐   "Period ID" = "<>0"
    │ "Period ID"          │  │ "<>"&0               │
    └──────────────────────┘  └──────────────────────┘

    ┌──────────────────────┐  ┌──────────────────────┐   "Year" = "Company"
    │ "Year"               │  │ $C$2                 │
    └──────────────────────┘  └──────────────────────┘
```

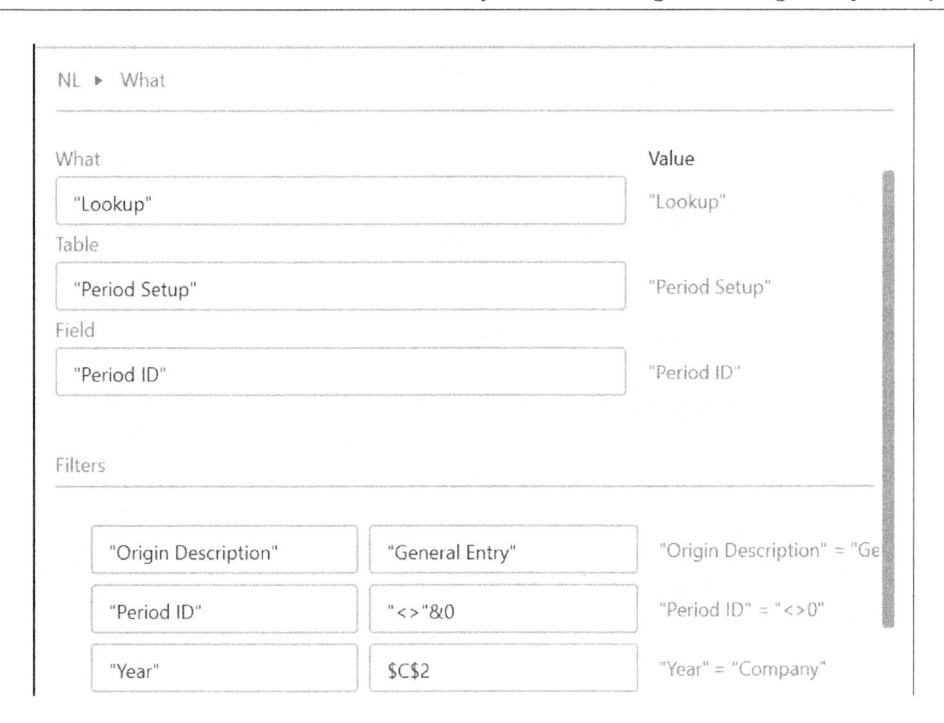

Lookup on Company

A lookup can be configured for company as well, to allow the user to select which company a report should be run against. This can be done using the **NP** utility function.

Click the **Report Options** button again to amend the **Options** and add an entry for **Company**.

Report Options allow you to choose specific filters to narrow the information you want to view. These are typically created to give report viewers the ability to customize what they see at report run time.

	Title	Value	Tooltip	Lookup
×	Year	2027	Specify the...	✏ ×
×	Period	4	Specify the...	✏ ×
×	Company	Fabrikam, Inc.	Spectify a c...	+

Click the **Lookup** icon to open the **Jet Function Wizard**; place the cursor in the **Table** field and click the **Nested Jet Functions** button on the action pane and then select **Insert NP**.

```
NL  ▶  Table

What                                           Value
┌─────────────────────────────────┐             ┌─────────────┐
│ "Lookup"                        │             │ "Lookup"    │
└─────────────────────────────────┘             └─────────────┘
```

Set **What** to Companies and click **OK**.

NL ▶ Table ▶ NP ▶ What	
What	Value
"Companies"	"Companies"

Field needs to be set to Name, but the lookup does not work, so you will need to manually enter it.

NL ▶ What	
What	Value
"Lookup"	"Lookup"
Table	
NP("Companies")	Calculation deferred.
Field	
"Name"	"Name"

Click **OK** to save the lookup.

Report Options allow you to choose specific filters to narrow the information you want to view. These are typically created to give report viewers the ability to customize what they see at report run time.

	Title	Value	Tooltip	Lookup
✕	Year	2027	Specify the...	✏ ✕
✕	Period	4	Specify the...	✏ ✕
✕	Company	Fabrikam, Inc.	Spectify a c...	✏ ✕

The Options page

When the **Report Options** window is closed, the **Options** page will be added to the workbook.

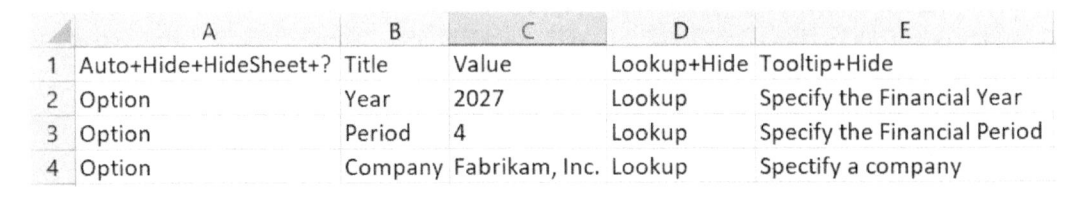

	A	B	C	D	E
1	Auto+Hide+HideSheet+?	Title	Value	Lookup+Hide	Tooltip+Hide
2	Option	Year	2027	Lookup	Specify the Financial Year
3	Option	Period	4	Lookup	Specify the Financial Period
4	Option	Company	Fabrikam, Inc.	Lookup	Spectify a company

The **Options** page can be amended either by clicking on the **Report Options** button on the action pane, or by amending it directly by editing the formula.

Using an Options page

While it is possible to use the options from the **Options** page in functions, it is not efficient to do so. Instead, it is better to use an **NP** function to evaluate the options and bring them to a field on the **Report** page and use them from there.

Below is an example of a Report page with three options from the **Options** pane. The cells with blue fill in row 2 are manually entered headings, but the three cells with blue fill on row 3 are the values from the options page.

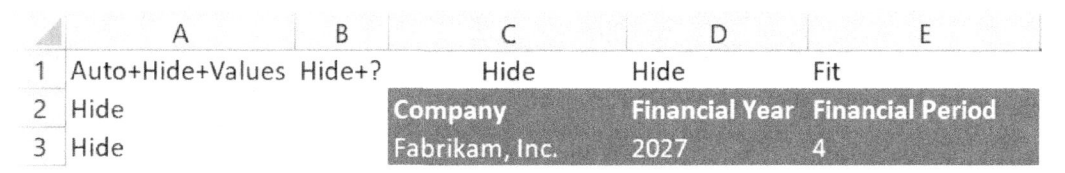

	A	B	C	D	E
1	Auto+Hide+Values	Hide+?	Hide	Hide	Fit
2	Hide		Company	Financial Year	Financial Period
3	Hide		Fabrikam, Inc.	2027	4

These have been brought through using an **NP** function where the **What** is Eval and the **Formula** is referencing the cell on the **Options** page.

```
NP ▶ What

What                                    Value
"Eval"                                  "Eval"
Formula
"Options!$C$4"                          "Options!$C$4"
```

When the report is run, the **Report Options** will be displayed for the user to change the options if required and then hit **Run** to generate the report.

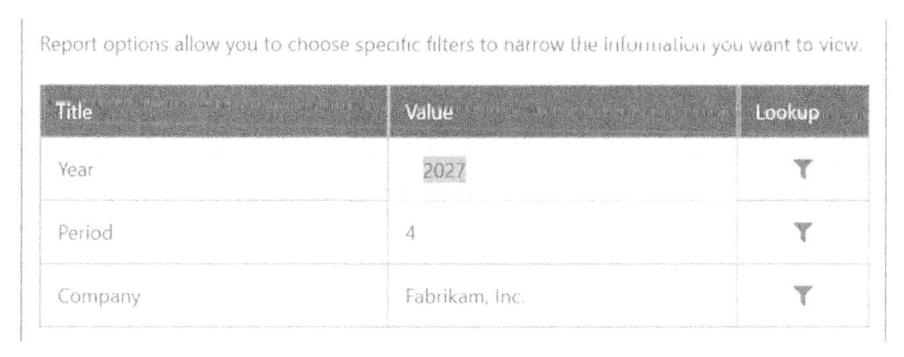

Report options allow you to choose specific filters to narrow the information you want to view.

Title	Value	Lookup
Year	2027	▼
Period	4	▼
Company	Fabrikam, Inc.	▼

Summary

In this chapter we have taken a look at how to build an Options page which prompts users when the report is run. In the next chapter, we'll take a look at using the skills learned so far to create a Summary Trial Balance.

8

Create a Summary Trial Balance

In this chapter we'll use the topics covered so far to create a General Ledger **Summary Trial Balance** report.

Design the report

The Summary Trial Balance we're going to build will:

- Include the complete chart of accounts.
- Display the Description for each account.
- For each account include:
    - Beginning Balance.
    - Debit.
    - Credit.
    - Net Change.
    - Ending Balance
- Exclude zero value rows.

The report will be laid out in this format:

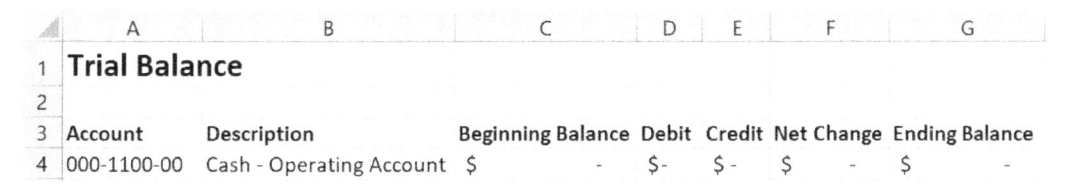

	A	B	C	D	E	F	G
1	**Trial Balance**						
2							
3	Account	Description	Beginning Balance	Debit	Credit	Net Change	Ending Balance
4	000-1100-00	Cash - Operating Account	$ -	$ -	$ -	$ -	$ -

When they run the report, users will be promoted for the **Fiscal Year**, **Fiscal Period** and **Company**.

Jet Reports with Microsoft Dynamics GP

Create the Report page

Create a new Excel workbook and change the tab name to **Report**. I have set the layout of the report up with the first four columns and rows highlighted in yellow as they will be set to **Hide**.

Column **B** has **Hide+?** added as I will use this column to control visibility of rows depending on if they are zero value or not.

The six fields for the options and their headings have had a fill of blue set and a green fill set for the field which will hold the **NL** function replicator.

The report header and column headings have all been placed and formatting applied with a **Fit** applied for the column widths in the first row.

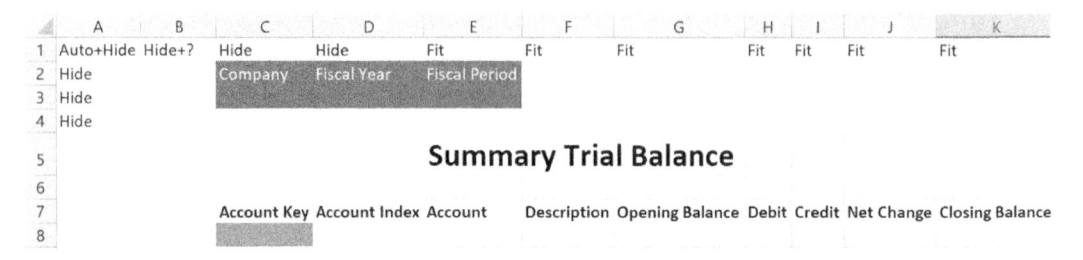

	A	B	C	D	E	F	G	H	I	J	K
1	Auto+Hide	Hide+?	Hide	Hide	Fit	Fit	Fit	Fit	Fit	Fit	Fit
2	Hide		Company	Fiscal Year	Fiscal Period						
3	Hide										
4	Hide										
5					**Summary Trial Balance**						
6											
7			Account Key	Account Index	Account	Description	Opening Balance	Debit	Credit	Net Change	Closing Balance
8											

Create the Options page

For the report we will be providing three options for the user to set. To create the options, follow these steps:

1. Click the **Report Options** button on the **Tools** tab of the **Jet** action pane.

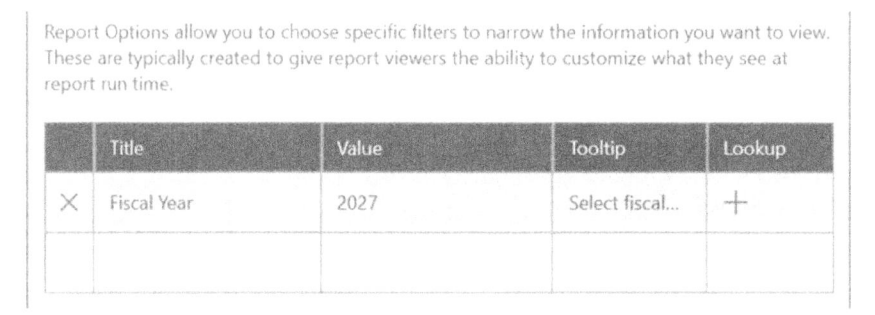

   Report Options allow you to choose specific filters to narrow the information you want to view. These are typically created to give report viewers the ability to customize what they see at report run time.

	Title	Value	Tooltip	Lookup
×	Fiscal Year	2027	Select fiscal...	+

2. Enter a **Title** of Fiscal Year.
3. Enter a **Value** of 2027.
4. Enter a **Tooltip** of Select fiscal year.
5. Click the plus icon in the **Lookup** column.
6. The **What** will default to Lookup; select the Period Header table (SY40101).

54

Chapter 8: Create a Summary Trial Balance

7. Select the **Field** of Year.

8. Enter a filter of Historical Year and value of 0.

9. To change the order to show the newest year at the top:

    a. Enter a second filter of Year and value of *.

    b. Click the arrow at the left filter changes to a down arrow.

10. Click **OK** to save the **Fiscal Year** lookup.

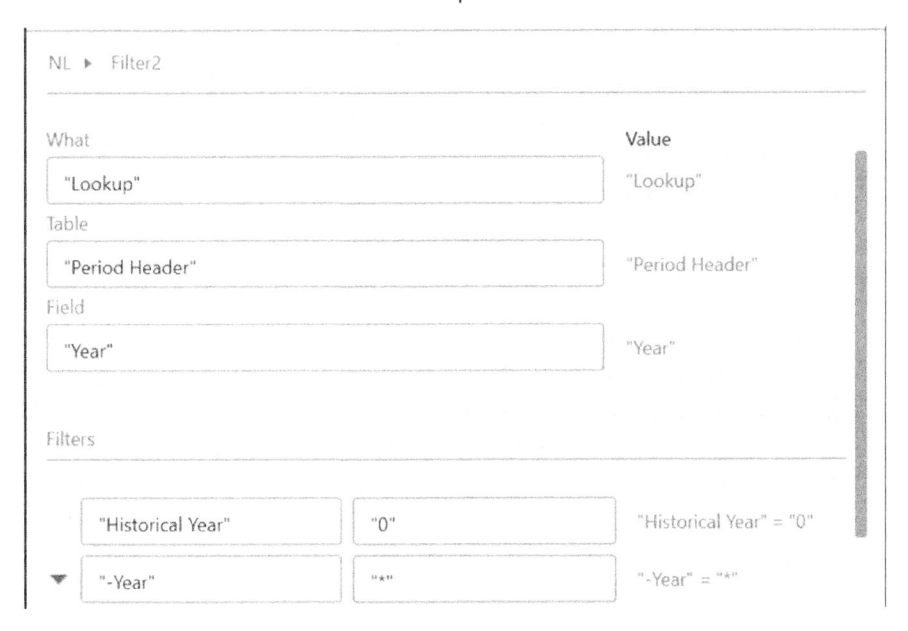

What	Value
"Lookup"	"Lookup"
Table	
"Period Header"	"Period Header"
Field	
"Year"	"Year"

    Filters

"Historical Year"	"0"	"Historical Year" = "0"
"-Year"	"*"	"-Year" = "*"

    NL ▸ Filter2

11. Enter a **Title** of Fiscal Period.

12. Enter a **Value** of 4.

13. Enter a **Tooltip** of Select fiscal period.

14. Click the plus icon in the **Lookup** column.

15. The **What** will default to Lookup; select the Period Setup table (SY40100).

16. Hold control down and select the **Field** of Period ID and Period Name.

17. Enter a filter of Year and value of $C$2 (this is the field on the options page which will contain the Fiscal Year option).

18. Exclude period 0 by adding a filter of Period ID and value of "<>" & 0.

19. To limit the return down only to one entry per period, enter a filter of Origin Description and value of General Entry.

55

Jet Reports with Microsoft Dynamics GP

NL ▸ Filter3	
What	**Value**
"Lookup"	"Lookup"
Table	
"Period Setup"	"Period Setup"
Field	
{"Period ID", "Period Name"}	{"Period ID","Period Name"}

Filters

"Year"	$C$2	"Year" =
"Period ID"	"<>" & 0	"Period ID" = "<>0"
"Origin Description"	"General Entry"	"Origin Description" = "Ge

20. Click **OK** to save the **Fiscal Period** lookup.

21. Enter a **Title** of Company.

22. Enter a **Value** of Fabrikam, Inc..

23. Enter a **Tooltip** of Select company.

24. Click the plus icon in the **Lookup** column.

25. The **What** will default to Lookup; click the **Nested Jet Function** button on the action pane and click **Insert NP**.

26. Set the **What** to Companies.

27. Click **Back** to save the function.

NL ▸ Table ▸ NP ▸ What	
What	**Value**
"Companies"	"Companies"

28. Enter Name in **Field** (this must be done manually as the lookup is blank).

	NL ▶ Field	
	What	**Value**
	"Lookup"	"Lookup"
	Table	
	NP("Companies")	"|""Companies""," """," """"
	Field	
	"Name"	"Name"

29. Click **OK** to save the **Company** lookup.

30. Review the added lookups and ensure they are correct.

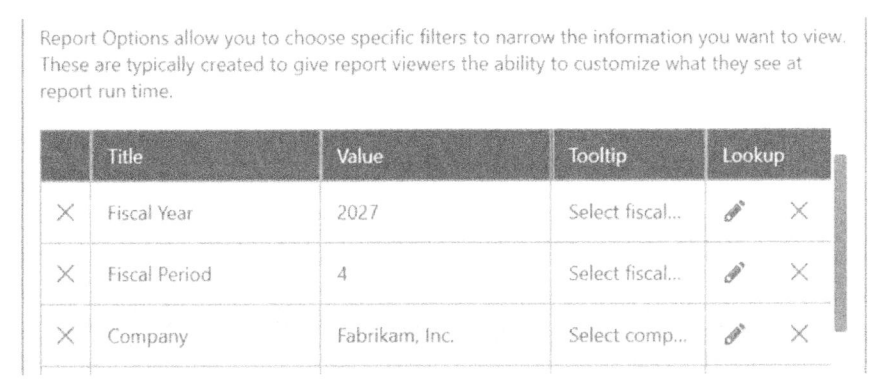

Report Options allow you to choose specific filters to narrow the information you want to view. These are typically created to give report viewers the ability to customize what they see at report run time.

	Title	Value	Tooltip	Lookup
X	Fiscal Year	2027	Select fiscal...	✏ X
X	Fiscal Period	4	Select fiscal...	✏ X
X	Company	Fabrikam, Inc.	Select comp...	✏ X

31. Click **Close** to close the **Report Options** window and generate the **Options** page.

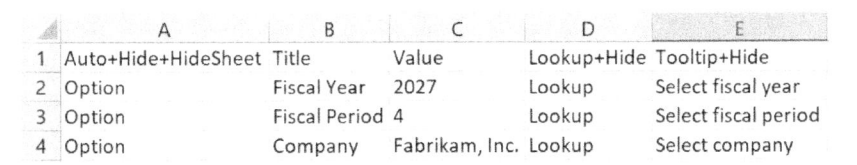

	A	B	C	D	E
1	Auto+Hide+HideSheet	Title	Value	Lookup+Hide	Tooltip+Hide
2	Option	Fiscal Year	2027	Lookup	Select fiscal year
3	Option	Fiscal Period	4	Lookup	Select fiscal period
4	Option	Company	Fabrikam, Inc.	Lookup	Select company

The options can be edited by clicking the **Report Options** button again or by editing directly through the **Options** page; the **Lookup** can be amended by selecting an entry in column **D** and clicking the **Jet Function** button.

Set Options on Report page

With the **Options** page created, we need to use an **NP** function to bring them to the **Reports** page to use. Do that by following these steps:

1. Place the cursor in cell **C3** and click the **NP** function button.

2. Set the **What** to Eval.

3. Place the cursor in the **Formula** field and select the cell on the **Options** page containing the company value (which is cell **C4**).

4. Click **OK** to save the function.

```
NP ▶ What

What                                    Value
"Eval"                                   "Eval"
Formula
"='Options'!$C$4"                        "='Options'!$C$4"
```

5. Repeat steps 1 through 4 for the **Fiscal Year** and **Fiscal Period**.

The **Report** page should now be showing the values of the **Options** in the blue filled cells.

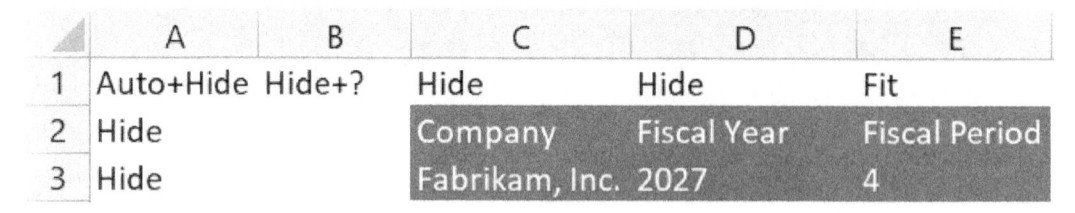

	A	B	C	D	E
1	Auto+Hide	Hide+?	Hide	Hide	Fit
2	Hide		Company	Fiscal Year	Fiscal Period
3	Hide		Fabrikam, Inc.	2027	4

Add Record Key for Account Master

The first field to add is the record key replicator from the **Account Index Master** table (**GL00105**). Do this by performing these steps:

1. Place the cursor in cell **C8** and click the **NL** function button.

2. Set **What** to Rows.

3. In **Table** select the **Account Index Master** table (**GL00105**).

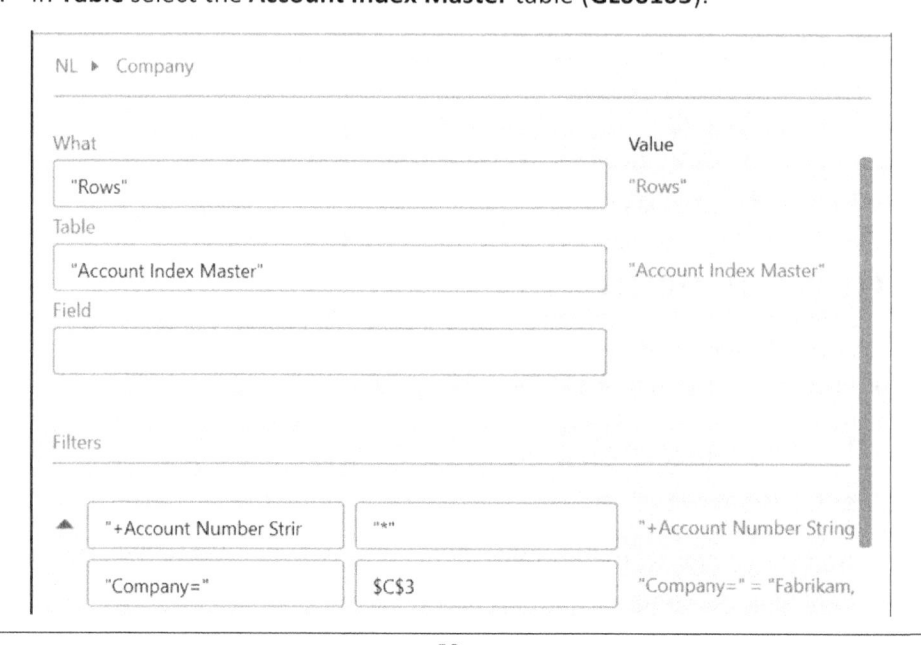

```
NL ▶ Company

What                                    Value
"Rows"                                   "Rows"
Table
"Account Index Master"                   "Account Index Master"
Field


Filters

   "+Account Number Strir"    "*"        "+Account Number String
   "Company="                 $C$3       "Company=" = "Fabrikam,
```

Chapter 8: Create a Summary Trial Balance

4. Leave **Field** blank as this is to be a record key replicator.

5. To order the accounts in ascending order, set the first filter to Account Number String and the value to *.

6. Click the arrow button until it changes to an arrow pointing upwards.

7. Add a second filter to **Company=** and the value to a locked cell **C3**.

8. Click **OK** to save the function.

Add Account Index and Account

There are two fields, **Account Index** and **Account** which we can extract using the record key. Do this by performing these steps:

1. To add the **Account Index**, place the cursor in cell **D8** and click the **NP** function button.

```
NF ▸ Field

Key                                    Value
$C8                                    """Jet Reports""",""Fabrikam,
Field
"Account Index"                        "Account Index"
```

2. In the **Key** select the record key replicator which is in cell **C8** and switch it to lock by the column.

3. In the **Field** select Account Index.

4. Click **OK** to save the function.

5. Repeat steps 1 through 4 in cell **E8** and select the **Account Number String**.

Add Account Description

The **Account Description** can be retrieved using a **GL** function. Do this by following these steps:

1. Place the cursor in cell **F8** and click the **GL** function button.

2. Set **Where** to Cell.

3. Set **What** to AccountName.

4. Set Account to the cell containing the **Account Index** (which is cell **E8**) and lock the column.

5. Set **Company** to the cell containing the **Company** option (which is cell **C3**) and lock both the column and row.

GL ▸ Company

Where	Value
"Cell"	"Cell"

What

"AccountName" | "AccountName"

Account

$E8 | "000-1100-00"

Company

$C$3 | "Fabrikam, Inc."

6. Click **OK** to save the function

Add Opening Balance

Opening Balance is a field available through the **GL** function. To add the opening balance, perform these steps:

1. Place the cursor in cell **H8** and click the **NL** function button.

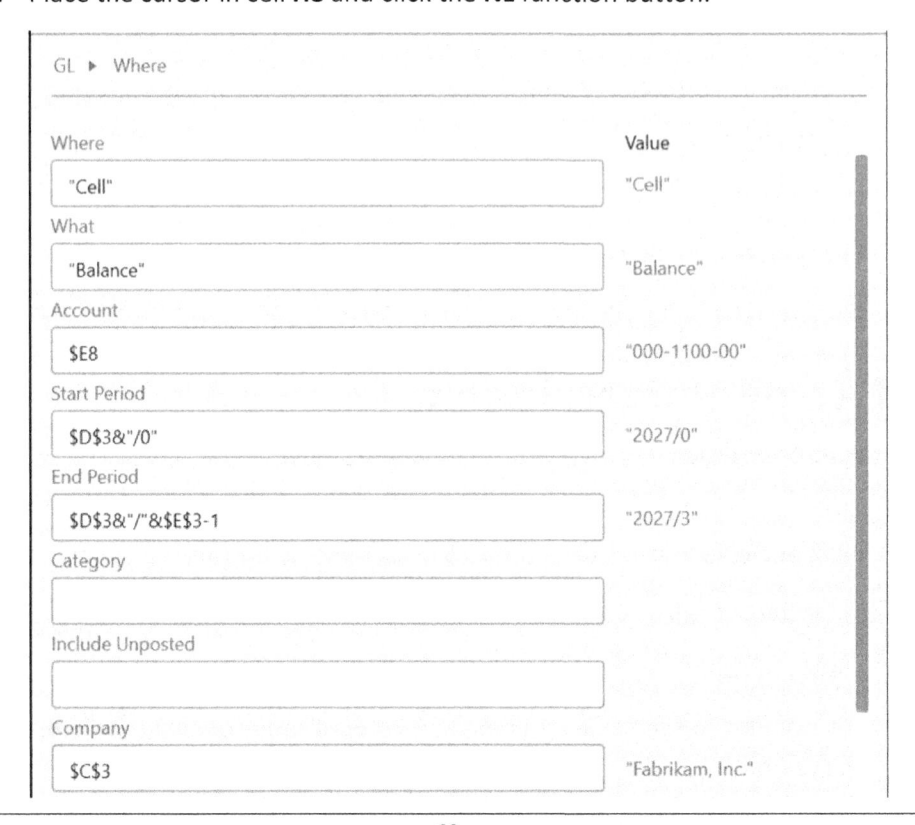

GL ▸ Where

Where	Value
"Cell"	"Cell"

What

"Balance" | "Balance"

Account

$E8 | "000-1100-00"

Start Period

$D$3&"/0" | "2027/0"

End Period

$D$3&"/"&$E$3-1 | "2027/3"

Category

Include Unposted

Company

$C$3 | "Fabrikam, Inc."

Chapter 8: Create a Summary Trial Balance

2. Set the **Where** to Cell.

3. Set the **What** to Balance.

4. Set the **Account** field to cell E8 and lock the column.

5. Set the **Start Period** to column D3, locking both column and row, and concatenate "/0" to get period 0.

6. Set the **End Period** to column D3, locking both column and row, and concatenate "/" and cell E3-1, locking column and row.

7. Set **Company** to cell C3, locking the column and row.

Add Debit and Credit

Debits and **Credits** are not available using the **GL** function, so for these two columns I'll need to use an **NL** function.

1. Place the cursor in cell **G8** and click the **NL** function button.

2. Set the **Where** to First.

3. Set the **Table** to Account Current Summary Master (**GL10110**).

4. Set the **Field** to Debit Amount.

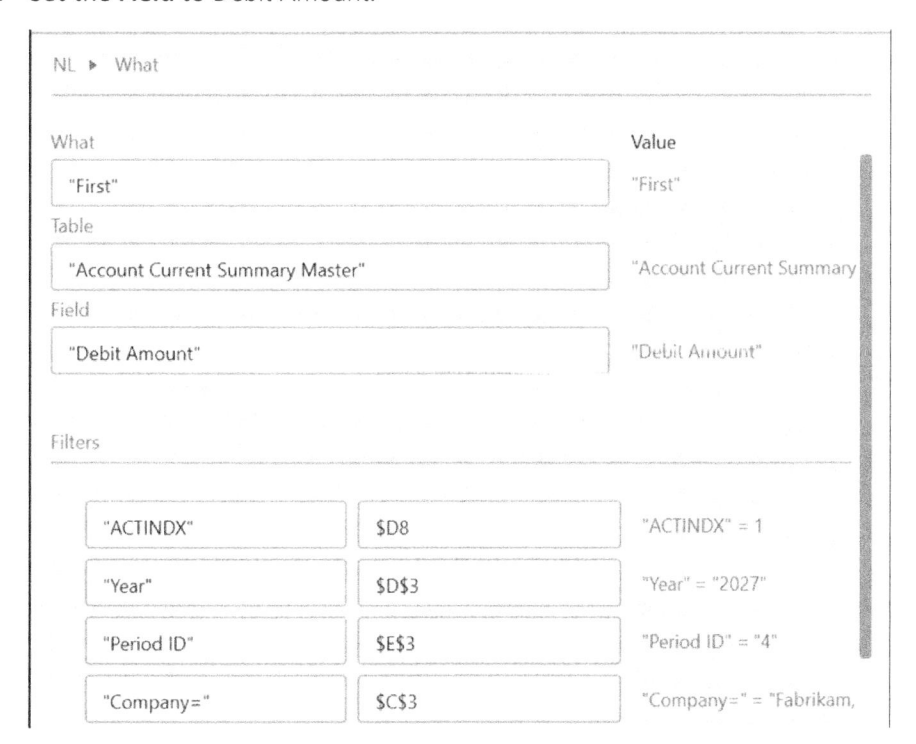

```
NL ▶ What

What                                          Value
  "First"                                       "First"
Table
  "Account Current Summary Master"              "Account Current Summary
Field
  "Debit Amount"                                "Debit Amount"

Filters

  "ACTINDX"          $D8                        "ACTINDX" = 1
  "Year"             $D$3                       "Year" = "2027"
  "Period ID"        $E$3                       "Period ID" = "4"
  "Company="         $C$3                       "Company=" = "Fabrikam,
```

5. Set the first filter to cell Account Index and set the filter value to cell D8, locking

61

the column.

6. Set the second filter to **Year** and the filter value to D3, locking both column and row.

7. Set the third filter to **Period** and the filter value to D3, locking both column and row.

8. Set third filter to **Company** and set the filter value to C3, locking the column and row.

9. Unfortunately, when there is no movement in a period, there is a null value returned which will leave the Excel field blank. If, as I do, you want zero values to show, the solution is to set the **Debit Amount** column to hidden and add an extra column using a standard Excel formula to check for a length of 0 and output 0 otherwise output the value from the hidden column:

> I8   fx   =IF(LEN($H8)=0,0,$H8)

10. Repeat steps 1 through 9 in cell J8 and select the Credit Amount in **Field.**

Add Net Change

While we could use the **GL** function to get the **Net Change,** this would be an unnecessary function call as we can use a standard Excel formula in cell **L8** subtracting the **Debt Amount** column from the **Credit Amount** one:

> L8   fx   =I8-K8

Add Closing Balance

As with the **Net Change**, we can use a standard Excel formula for the **Closing Balance** in cell **M8**, adding together the **Opening Balance** and **Net Change** columns:

> M8   fx   =G8+L8

Hide zero value rows

The final step is to hide the rows with zero values which we can do using a standard Excel **IF** with an **AND** checking if the **Opening Balance**, **Debit Amount** and **Credit Amount** are all equal to 0:

> B8   fx   =IF(AND($G8=0,$I8=0,$K8=0),"Hide","Show")

Chapter 8: Create a Summary Trial Balance

Report ready for testing

If you have followed the instructions the report should look like the example below, and is now ready for testing.

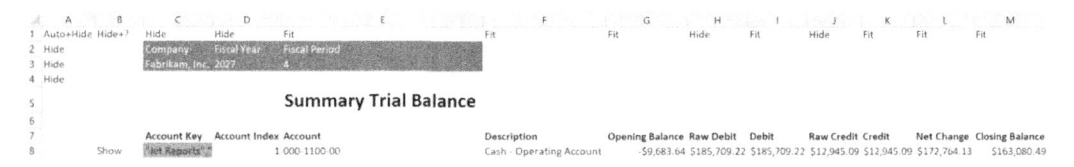

Run report

Run the report by following these steps:

1. Click the **Run** button on the action pane.

2. This will take the Jet Reports out of **Design Mode** and prompt with the **Report Options**:

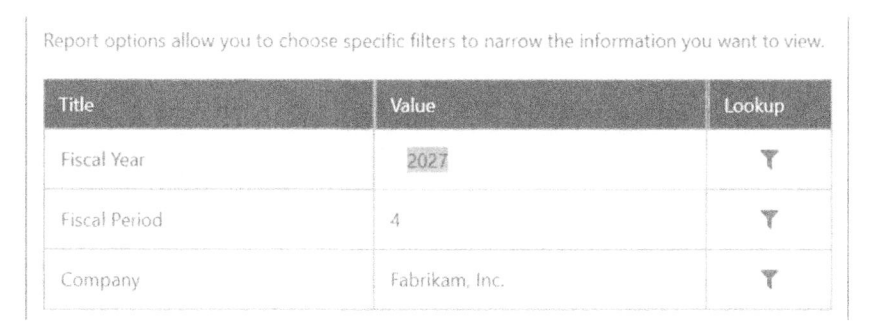

3. Enter your criteria and click **Run**.

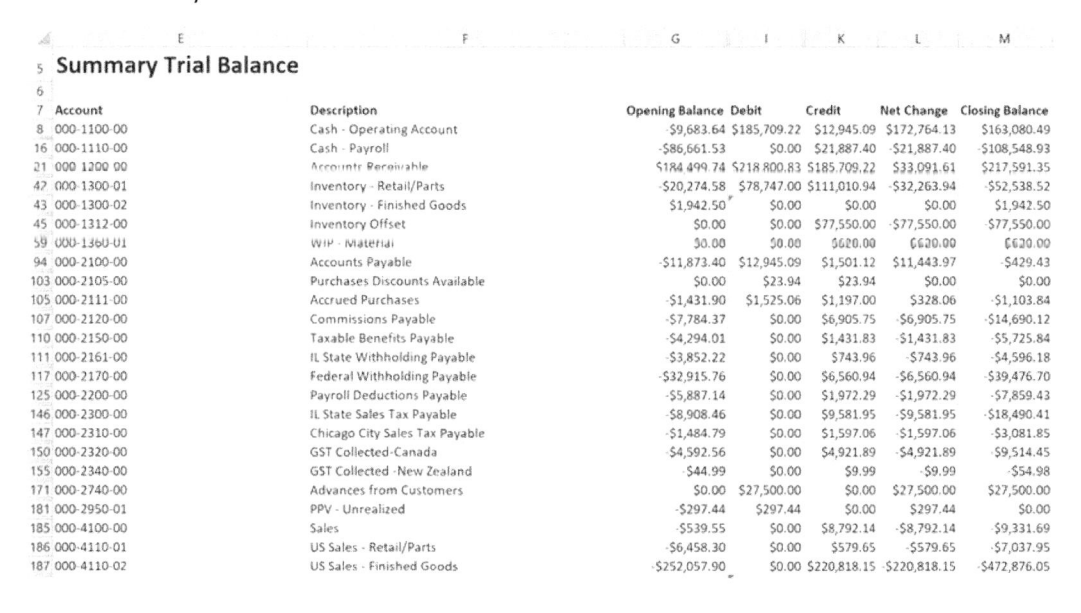

Summary

In this chapter we have taken a look at creating a **Summary Trial Balance**. In the next chapter, we're going to create a **Detailed Trial Balance** by using the **Summary Trial Balance** we have just created as the basis.

9

Create a Detailed Trial Balance

In the last chapter, we built a **Summary Trial Balance**; in this chapter we're going to make a copy of that report to create a **Detailed Trial Balance**.

Design the report

The Detailed Trial Balance we're going to build will be a copy of the Summary Trial Balance, but with transaction data added:

- Journal Entry.
- Reference.
- Transaction Date.
- Currency.
- Source Document.
- Debit.
- Credit.
- Description.

The report will be laid out in this format:

	A	B	C	D	E	F	G	H	I
1	**Detailed Trial Balance**								
2									
3	Account	Description	Opening Balance	Debit	Credit	Net Change	Closing Balance		
4	000-1100-00	Cash - Operating Account	$ -	$ -	$ -	$ -	$ -		
5		Journal Entry	Reference	Transaction Date	Currency	Source Document	Debit	Credit	Description
6		1	Adjustment	4/12/2027	Z-US$	GJ	$ -	$ -	Adjustment

65

Add transaction detail column headers

The first change to make is to add the column headers for the transactions. Add the following column headers and make bold starting in cell **D9** and skip cells **E9, H9** and **J9** while working across to cell **O9**:

- Journal Key
- Journal Entry.
- Reference.
- Transaction Date.
- Currency.
- Source Document.
- Debit.
- Credit.
- Description.

Update Record Key for Account Master

To ensure that the journals for a particular account are listed below that account, we need to change the **Account Index Master** (GL00105) record key replicator:

1. Place the cursor in cell **C8** and click the **NL** function button on the action pane.
2. Edit the **What** to Rows=4.
3. Click **OK** to save the change.

```
NL ▶ What

What                                    Value
"Rows=4"                                "Rows=4"

Table
"Account Index Master"                  "Account Index Master"
```

Add Record Key for Year-to-Date Transaction Open

We need to add a record key replicator for the **Year-to-Date Transaction Open** (GL20000) table which we can then extract fields from using the **NF** function. To add the record key,

Chapter 9: Create a Detailed Trial Balance

perform these steps

1. Place the cursor in cell **D10** and click the **NL** function button on the action pane.
2. Set the **Where** to Rows.
3. In **Table** select Year-to-Date Transaction Open (**GL20000**).

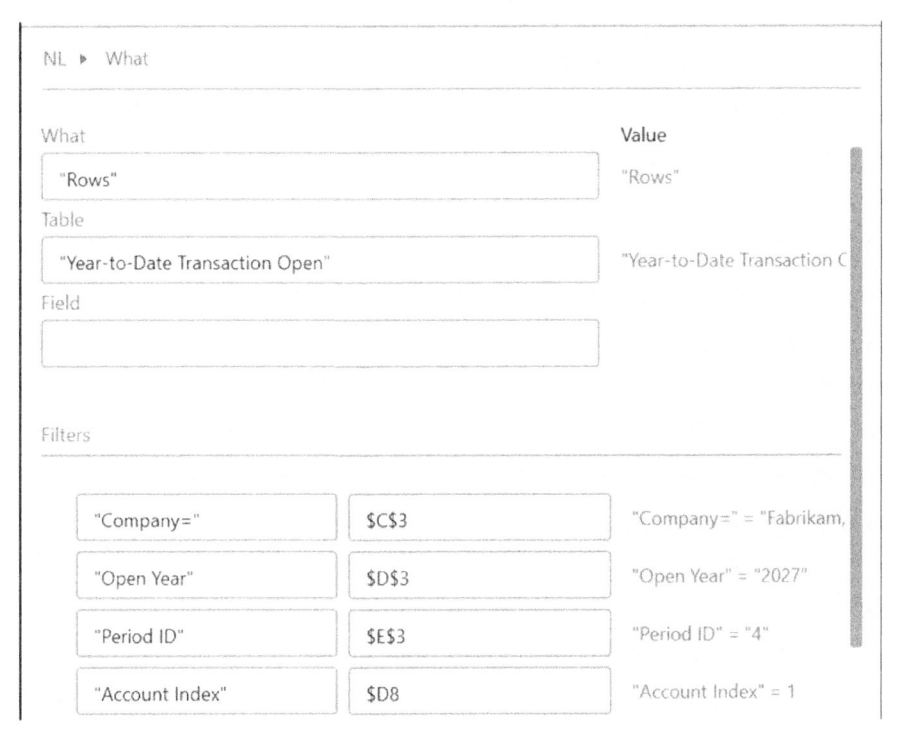

What	Value
"Rows"	"Rows"
Table	
"Year-to-Date Transaction Open"	"Year-to-Date Transaction O
Field	

Filters

"Company="	$C$3	"Company=" = "Fabrikam,
"Open Year"	$D$3	"Open Year" = "2027"
"Period ID"	$E$3	"Period ID" = "4"
"Account Index"	$D8	"Account Index" = 1

4. Leave the **Field** blank.
5. In the first filter, select Company= and set the filter value to cell **C3**, locking both the column and row.
6. In the second filter, select Open year and set the filter value to cell **D3**, locking both the column and row.
7. In the third filter, select Period ID and set the filter value to cell **E3**, locking both the column and row.
8. In the fourth filter, select Account Index and set the filter value to cell **D8**, locking the column.
9. Click **OK** to save the function.

Add Journal Entry

The **Journal Entry** can be retrieved using the **NF** function:

1. Place the cursor in cell **F10** and click the **NF** function button on the action pane.

NF ▸ Key	
Key	Value
$D10	"""Jet Reports""",""Fabrikam,
Field	
"Journal Entry"	"Journal Entry"

2. Set the **Key** to cell **D10** which contains the record key, locking the column.
3. Select Journal Entry in the **Field.**
4. Click **OK** to save the function.

Add Reference

The **Reference** can be retrieved using the **NF** function:

1. Place the cursor in cell **G10** and click the **NF** function button on the action pane.
2. Set the **Key** to cell **D10** which contains the record key, locking the column.
3. Select Reference in the **Field.**
4. Click **OK** to save the function.

Add Transaction Date

The **Transaction Date** can be retrieved using the **NF** function:

1. Place the cursor in cell **I10** and click the **NF** function button on the action pane.
2. Set the **Key** to cell **D10** which contains the record key, locking the column.
3. Select Trx Date in the **Field.**
4. Click **OK** to save the function.

Add Currency

The **Reference** can be retrieved using the **NF** function:

1. Place the cursor in cell **K10** and click the **NF** function button on the action pane.
2. Set the **Key** to cell **D10** which contains the record key, locking the column.
3. Select Currency ID in the **Field.**
4. Click **OK** to save the function.

Chapter 9: Create a Detailed Trial Balance

Add Source Document

The **Reference** can be retrieved using the **NF** function:

1. Place the cursor in cell **L10** and click the **NF** function button on the action pane.
2. Set the **Key** to cell **D10** which contains the record key, locking the column.
3. Select Source Document in the **Field.**
4. Click **OK** to save the function.

Add Debit

The **Reference** can be retrieved using the **NF** function:

1. Place the cursor in cell **M10** and click the **NF** function button on the action pane.
2. Set the **Key** to cell **D10** which contains the record key, locking the column.
3. Select Debit Amount in the **Field.**
4. Click **OK** to save the function.

Add Credit

The **Reference** can be retrieved using the **NF** function:

1. Place the cursor in cell **N10** and click the **NF** function button on the action pane.
2. Set the **Key** to cell **D10** which contains the record key, locking the column.
3. Select Credit Amount in the **Field.**
4. Click **OK** to save the function.

Add Description

The **Reference** can be retrieved using the **NF** function:

1. Place the cursor in cell **O10** and click the **NF** function button on the action pane.
2. Set the **Key** to cell **D10** which contains the record key, locking the column.
3. Select Description in the **Field.**
4. Click **OK** to save the function.

Run report

Run the report by following these steps:

1. Click the **Run** button on the action pane.

2. This will take the Jet Reports out of **Design Mode** and prompt with the **Report Options**:

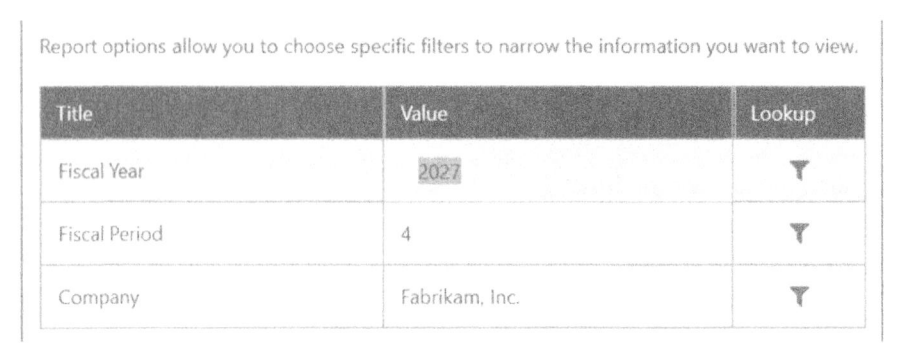

Report options allow you to choose specific filters to narrow the information you want to view.

Title	Value	Lookup
Fiscal Year	2027	▼
Fiscal Period	4	▼
Company	Fabrikam, Inc.	▼

3. Enter your criteria and click **Run**.

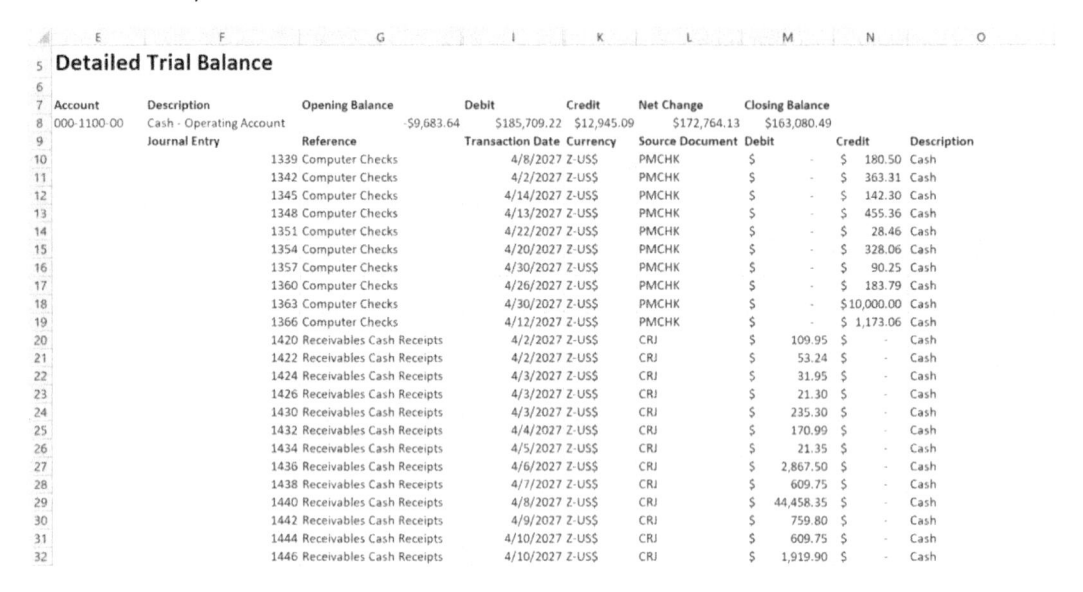

Detailed Trial Balance

Account	Description	Opening Balance	Debit	Credit	Net Change	Closing Balance		
000-1100-00	Cash - Operating Account	-$9,683.64	$185,709.22	$12,945.09	$172,764.13	$163,080.49		
	Journal Entry	Reference	Transaction Date	Currency	Source Document	Debit	Credit	Description
	1339	Computer Checks	4/8/2027	Z-US$	PMCHK	$ -	$ 180.50	Cash
	1342	Computer Checks	4/2/2027	Z-US$	PMCHK	$ -	$ 363.31	Cash
	1345	Computer Checks	4/14/2027	Z-US$	PMCHK	$ -	$ 142.30	Cash
	1348	Computer Checks	4/13/2027	Z-US$	PMCHK	$ -	$ 455.36	Cash
	1351	Computer Checks	4/22/2027	Z-US$	PMCHK	$ -	$ 28.46	Cash
	1354	Computer Checks	4/20/2027	Z-US$	PMCHK	$ -	$ 328.06	Cash
	1357	Computer Checks	4/30/2027	Z-US$	PMCHK	$ -	$ 90.25	Cash
	1360	Computer Checks	4/26/2027	Z-US$	PMCHK	$ -	$ 183.79	Cash
	1363	Computer Checks	4/30/2027	Z-US$	PMCHK	$ -	$10,000.00	Cash
	1366	Computer Checks	4/12/2027	Z-US$	PMCHK	$ -	$ 1,173.06	Cash
	1420	Receivables Cash Receipts	4/2/2027	Z-US$	CRJ	$ 109.95	$ -	Cash
	1422	Receivables Cash Receipts	4/2/2027	Z-US$	CRJ	$ 53.24	$ -	Cash
	1424	Receivables Cash Receipts	4/3/2027	Z-US$	CRJ	$ 31.95	$ -	Cash
	1426	Receivables Cash Receipts	4/3/2027	Z-US$	CRJ	$ 21.30	$ -	Cash
	1430	Receivables Cash Receipts	4/3/2027	Z-US$	CRJ	$ 235.30	$ -	Cash
	1432	Receivables Cash Receipts	4/4/2027	Z-US$	CRJ	$ 170.99	$ -	Cash
	1434	Receivables Cash Receipts	4/5/2027	Z-US$	CRJ	$ 21.35	$ -	Cash
	1436	Receivables Cash Receipts	4/6/2027	Z-US$	CRJ	$ 2,867.50	$ -	Cash
	1438	Receivables Cash Receipts	4/7/2027	Z-US$	CRJ	$ 609.75	$ -	Cash
	1440	Receivables Cash Receipts	4/8/2027	Z-US$	CRJ	$ 44,458.35	$ -	Cash
	1442	Receivables Cash Receipts	4/9/2027	Z-US$	CRJ	$ 759.80	$ -	Cash
	1444	Receivables Cash Receipts	4/10/2027	Z-US$	CRJ	$ 609.75	$ -	Cash
	1446	Receivables Cash Receipts	4/10/2027	Z-US$	CRJ	$ 1,919.90	$ -	Cash

Summary

In this chapter we have taken a look at using the **Summary Trial Balance** as the basis for a **Detailed Trial Balance**. In the next chapter, I'm going to create a **Balance Sheet** report.

10

Create a Balance Sheet

In this chapter, we're going to create a **Balance Sheet** report using the **Account Categories** to control the layout.

Design the report

All of the reports created in this book are used to demonstrate different Jet functions or ways of building reports. The **Summary** and **Detailed Trial Balances** created in the last two chapters show ways data can be loaded using the **NL** replicator function.

The **Balance Sheet** report being created in this chapter, will use **Account Categories** rather than a replicator as a **Balance Sheet** report is a much more structured report than a **Trial Balance** which is a relatively simple listing of accounts and, for the detailed version, accounts and their transactions.

The **Balance Sheet** will allow users to select three criteria at runtime:

- Company.
- Fiscal year.
- Fiscal period.

The report is then broken down into Assets and Liabilities, each with sub-sections for the different types. We'll include the current and previous years balances as columns, along with a variance column.

The report is the most formatted report covered in the book, with sections identified with colored headings and fields formatted as numbers or currencies.

The report will be laid out in this format:

Balance Sheet

Company	Fabrikam, Inc.
Fiscal year	2027
Period	4

Assets		2027		2026		Variance
Current Assets						
Cash		-		-		-
Accounts Receivable		-		-		-
Inventory		-		-		-
Work in Process		-		-		-
Prepaid Expenses		-		-		-
Short-Term Investments		-		-		-
Total current assets	$	-	$	-	$	-
Fixed (Long-Term) Assets						
Long-Term Investments		-		-		-
Property, Plant and Equipment		-		-		-
Accumulated Depreciation		-		-		-
Intangible Assets		-		-		-
Total fixed assets	$	-	$	-	$	-
Other Assets						
Other Assets		-		-		-
Total Other Assets	$	-	$	-	$	-
Total Assets	$	-	$	-	$	-

Liabilities and Shareholder's Equity						
Current Liabilities						
Accounts Payable		-		-		-
Taxes Payable		-		-		-
Other Current Liabilities		-		-		-
Total current liabilities	$	-	$	-	$	-
Long-Term Liabilities						
Long-Term Debt		-		-		-
Notes Payable		-		-		-
Interest Payable		-		-		-
Total long-term liabilities	$	-	$	-	$	-
Shareholder's Equity						
Common Stock		-		-		-
Additional Paid-in Capital - Common		-		-		-
Dividends Payable		-		-		-
Other Income		-		-		-
Retained Earnings		-		-		-
Total Shareholder's equity	$	-	$	-	$	-
Total Liabilities and Shareholder's Equity	$	-	$	-	$	-

Chapter 10: Create a Balance Sheet

Create the Report page

Create a new Excel workbook and change the tab name to **Report**. I have set the layout of the report up with the first two columns and first five rows highlighted in yellow as they will be set to **Hide**.

To keep columns **D** through **F** a consistent width >--- min width ---< has been entered in row **2** to force a minimum width to the **fit**.

The three fields for the options and their headings in cells **B3** to **D4** have had a fill of blue set; calculated start and end periods for the current and previous year in cells **E3** to **H4** have had a grey fill applied.

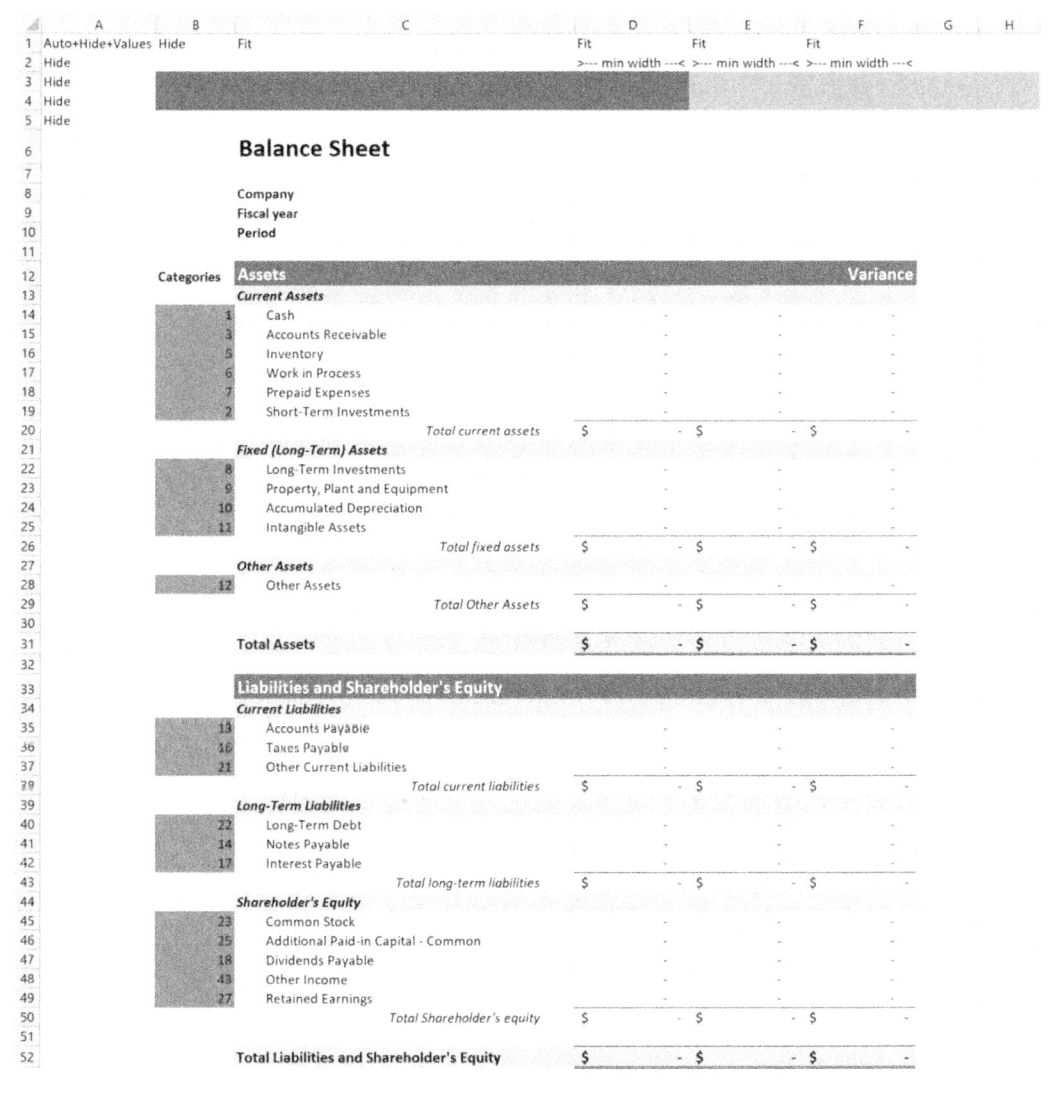

A green fill has been applied to the cells in column **B** which can be used to control which category will be on each row.

73

Unlike the previous reports covered, the Balance Sheet will have some formatting applied to enhance the output. Blue fills have been applied to rows **12**, **33** and **54** between columns **C** and **F**; a light blue fill has been applied in the same columns on rows **13**, **21**, **27**, **31**, **34**, **39**, **44** and **52**.

Certain report and field headings have also been defined on the report; the current and previous year column headings have been deliberately left blank as these will be calculated fields.

Create the Options page

For the report we will be providing three options for the user to set. To create the options, follow these steps:

1. Click the **Report Options** button on the **Tools** tab of the **Jet** action pane.

	Title	Value	Tooltip	Lookup
×	Company	Fabrikam, Inc.	Select comp...	+

2. Enter a **Title** of Company.

3. Enter a **Value** of Fabrikam, Inc..

4. Enter a **Tooltip** of Select company.

5. Click the plus icon in the **Lookup** column.

6. The **What** will default to Lookup; click the **Nested Jet Function** button on the action pane and click **Insert NP**.

7. Set the **What** to Companies.

   NL ▶ Table ▶ NP ▶ What

What	Value
"Companies"	"Companies"

8. Click **Back** to save the function.

9. Enter Name in **Field** (this must be done manually as the lookup is blank).

Chapter 10: Create a Balance Sheet

```
NL ▶ Field

What                                    Value
[ "Lookup" ]                            "Lookup"
Table
[ NP("Companies") ]                     "||""Companies"","""","""""
Field
[ "Name" ]                              "Name"
```

10. Click **OK** to save the **Company** lookup.

11. Enter a **Title** of Fiscal Year.

12. Enter a **Value** of 2027.

13. Enter a **Tooltip** of Select fiscal year.

14. Click the plus icon in the **Lookup** column.

15. The **What** will default to Lookup; select the Period Header table (SY40101).

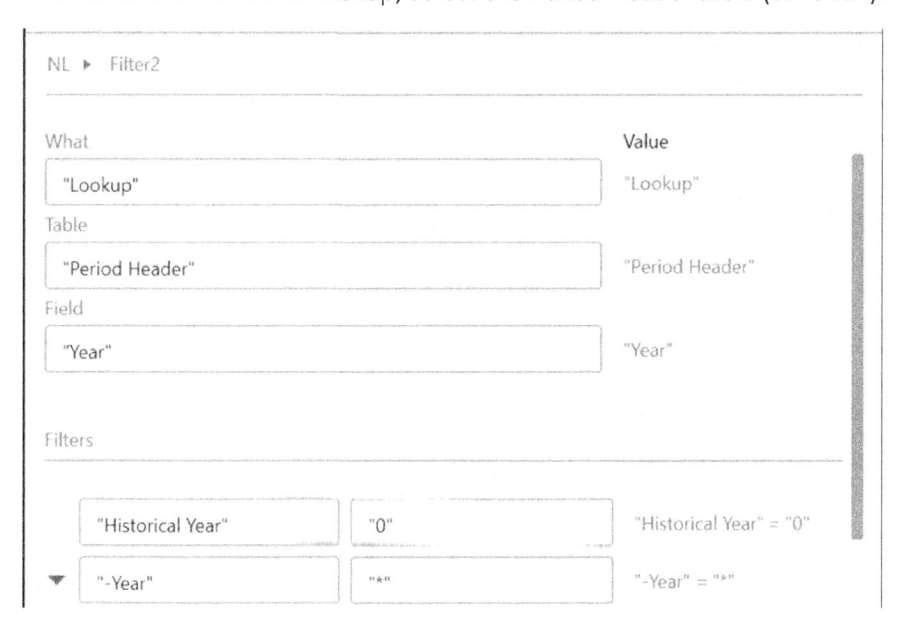

```
NL ▶ Filter2

What                                    Value
[ "Lookup" ]                            "Lookup"
Table
[ "Period Header" ]                     "Period Header"
Field
[ "Year" ]                              "Year"

Filters
    [ "Historical Year" ]  [ "0" ]      "Historical Year" = "0"
  ▼ [ "-Year" ]            [ "*" ]      "-Year" = "*"
```

16. Select the **Field** of Year.

17. Enter a filter of Historical Year and value of 0.

18. To change the order to show the newest year at the top:

    a. Enter a second filter of Year and value of *.

    b. Click the arrow at the left filter changes to a down arrow.

19. Click **OK** to save the **Fiscal Year** lookup.

20. Enter a **Title** of Fiscal Period.

21. Enter a **Value** of 4.

22. Enter a **Tooltip** of Select fiscal period.

23. Click the plus icon in the **Lookup** column.

24. The **What** will default to Lookup; select the Period Setup table (SY40100).

25. Hold control down and select the **Field** of Period ID and Period Name.

```
NL ▶ Filter3

What                                            Value
  "Lookup"                                        "Lookup"
Table
  "Period Setup"                                  "Period Setup"
Field
  {"Period ID", "Period Name"}                    {"Period ID","Period Name"}

Filters
    "Year"              $C$2                      "Year" =
    "Period ID"         "<>" & 0                  "Period ID" = "<>0"
    "Origin Description" "General Entry"          "Origin Description" = "Ge
```

26. Enter a filter of Year and value of $C$2 (this is the field on the options page which will contain the Fiscal Year option).

27. Exclude period 0 by adding a filter of Period ID and value of "<>" & 0.

28. Enter a filter of Year and value of $C$2 (this is the field on the options page which will contain the Fiscal Year option).

29. To limit the return down only to one entry per period, enter a filter of Origin Description and value of General Entry.

30. Click **OK** to save the **Fiscal Period** lookup.

31. Review the added lookups and ensure they are correct.

Chapter 10: Create a Balance Sheet

Report Options allow you to choose specific filters to narrow the information you want to view. These are typically created to give report viewers the ability to customize what they see at report run time.

	Title	Value	Tooltip	Lookup
X	Company	Fabrikam, Inc.	Select comp...	✏️ X
X	Fiscal Year	2027	Select fiscal...	✏️ X
X	Fiscal Period	4	Select fiscal...	✏️ X

32. Click **Close** to close the **Report Options** window and generate the **Options** page.

Set Options on Report page

With the **Options** page created, we need to use an **NP** function to bring them to the **Reports** page to use. Do that by following these steps:

1. Place the cursor in cell **B4** and click the **NP** function button.

2. Set the **What** to Eval.

3. Place the cursor in the **Formula** field and select the cell on the **Options** page containing the company value (which is cell **C2**).

```
NP ▶ What

What                                    Value
"Eval"                                  "Eval"

Formula
"='Options'!$C$2"                       "='Options'!$C$2"
```

4. Click **OK** to save the function.

5. Repeat steps 1 through 4 for the **Fiscal Year** and **Fiscal Period**.

6. In cell **E4** enter a formula to concatenate the fiscal year in cell3 **C4** with **/0**.

    E4   fx =CONCAT($C$4,"/0")

7. In cell **F4** enter a formula to concatenate the fiscal year in cell **C4** with the fiscal period in cell D4 separated with a **/**.

    F4   fx =CONCAT($C$4,"/",$D$4)

8. In cell **G4** enter a formula to concatenate the fiscal year in cell **C4 -1** with **/0**.

    G4   fx =CONCAT($C$4-1,"/0")

77

9. In cell **H4** enter a formula to concatenate the fiscal year in cell **C4 -1** with the fiscal period in cell D4 separated with a **/**.

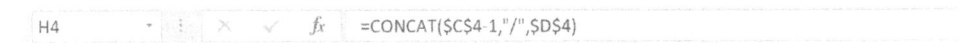

```
H4    fx  =CONCAT($C$4-1,"/",$D$4)
```

The **Report** page should now be showing the values of the **Options** in the blue filled cells and calculated fields in the grey.

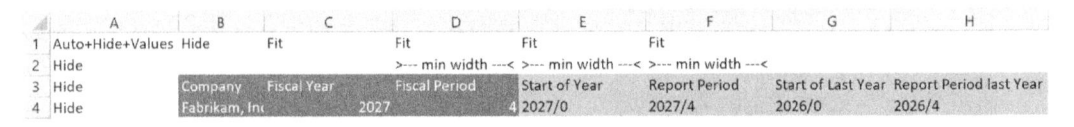

	A	B	C	D	E	F	G	H
1	Auto+Hide+Values	Hide	Fit	Fit	Fit	Fit		
2	Hide			>--- min width ---<	>--- min width ---<	>--- min width ---<		
3	Hide	Company	Fiscal Year	Fiscal Period	Start of Year	Report Period	Start of Last Year	Report Period last Year
4	Hide	Fabrikam, Inc	2027	4	2027/0	2027/4	2026/0	2026/4

Output options

There are several of the options which will be output on the report so users consuming the report know the source of the data:

1. Use a formula to bring the **Company** from cell **B4** to **D8**.
2. Use a formula to bring the **Fiscal Year** from cell **C4** to **D9**.
3. Use a formula to bring the **Fiscal Period** from cell **D4** to **D10**.
4. Use a formula to bring the **Fiscal Year** from cell **B4** to **D12**.
5. Use a formula to bring the **Fiscal Year** from cell **B4 -1** to **D13**.

Add categories

So that the Balance Sheet is produced correctly, the Account Categories will be hardcoded to appear in certain cells.

It is the account category which needs to be used for this. These numbers can be found via the Account Category Maintenance window in Microsoft Dynamics GP (Financial area page » Setup » Account Categories).

The Account Category Codes will be added in column **B** starting in row **14**; the table below includes the row reference and the **Account Category Number** to place in it.

For example, the first pair of cells means that cell **B14** will contain account category number **1**.

Chapter 10: Create a Balance Sheet

Row	Cat	Row	Cat	Row	Cat	Row	Cat	Row	Cat
14	1	19	2	28	12	41	14	48	43
15	3	22	8	35	13	42	17	49	27
16	5	23	9	36	16	45	23		
17	6	24	10	37	21	46	25		
18	7	25	11	40	22	47	18		

Alongside each of these cells, we need to use the **GL** function to get the **Account Category Description**:

1. Set the **Where** to Cell.
2. Set the **What** to CategoryName.
3. The **Category** field should be set to the cell containing the Account Category Number, which for cell **C14** is cell **B14**, with a locked column.
4. Set the **Company** to cell **B4**, with locked column and row.

5. Click **OK** to save the formula.
6. Repeat steps **1** through **5** for the other 21 categories using the table above for the category numbers.

Add current year

The current year for each row category is calculated in the same way with only the account category itself changing. To add the required function, perform the following

79

steps:

1. Place the cursor in cell **D14** and click the **GL** function button on the Tools section of the **Jet** action pane.
2. Set the **Where** to Cell.
3. Set the **What** to Balance.
4. Set the **Start Period** to cell **E4**, with column and row both locked.
5. Set the **End Period** to cell **F4**, with column and row both locked.
6. The **Category** field should be set to the cell containing the Account Category Number, which for cell **C14** is cell **B14**, with a locked column.
7. Set the **Company** to cell **B4**, with locked column and row.

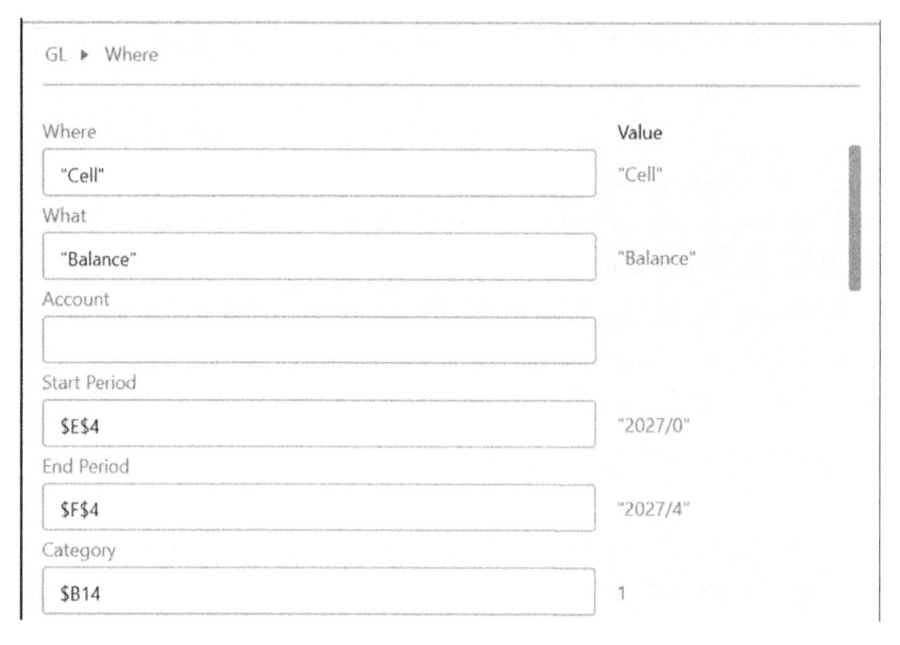

```
GL ▶ Where

Where                               Value
"Cell"                              "Cell"
What
"Balance"                           "Balance"
Account

Start Period
$E$4                                "2027/0"
End Period
$F$4                                "2027/4"
Category
$B14                                1
```

5. Click **OK** to save the function.
6. Repeat steps **1** through **5** for the remaining category rows changing the **B14** cell reference accordingly.

Add previous year

The current year for each row category is calculated in the same way with only the account category itself changing. To add the required function, perform the following steps:

1. Place the cursor in cell **D14** and click the **GL** function button on the Tools section of the **Jet** action pane.

2. Set the **Where** to Cell.

3. Set the **What** to Balance.

4. Set the **Start Period** to cell **G4**, with column and row both locked.

5. Set the **End Period** to cell **H4**, with column and row both locked.

6. The **Category** field should be set to the cell containing the Account Category Number, which for cell **D14** is cell **B14**, with a locked column.

7. Set the **Company** to cell **B4**, with locked column and row.

8. Click **OK** to save the function.

9. Repeat steps **1** through **8** for the remaining category rows changing the **B14** cell reference accordingly.

Add variance

The variance can be calculated using a standard Excel formula:

1. In cell **F14** enter =E14-D14.

2. Repeat step **1** for the remaining category rows changing the **B14** cell reference accordingly.

Add section totals

The section totals on rows **20**, **26**, **29**, **38**, **43** and **50** are standard Excel sums of the rows of the section above. For example, the formula for cell **D20** is =SUM(D14:D19). Repeat across columns **E** and **F** for all sections.

Add Total Assets

The **Total Asset** are also accomplished using standard Excel formula; for the current year column it is the sum of cells D20+D26+D29. Repeat across for the previous year and variance columns.

Add Total Liabilities and Shareholders's Equity

The **Total Liabilities and Shareholder's Equity** are also accomplished using standard Excel formula; for the current year column it is the sum of cells D38+D43+D50. Repeat across for the previous year and variance columns.

Run report

Run the report by following these steps:

1. Click the **Run** button on the action pane.

2. This will take the Jet Reports out of **Design Mode** and prompt with the **Report Options**:

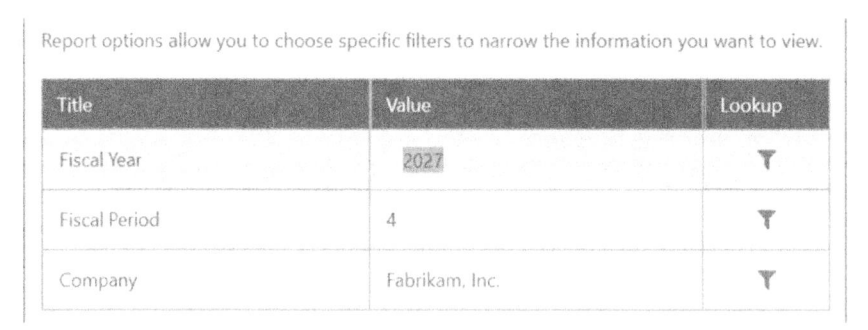

   Report options allow you to choose specific filters to narrow the information you want to view.

Title	Value	Lookup
Fiscal Year	2027	▼
Fiscal Period	4	▼
Company	Fabrikam, Inc.	▼

3. Enter your criteria and click **Run**.

Balance Sheet

Company	Fabrikam, Inc.	
Fiscal year	2027	
Period	4	

Assets	2027	2026	Variance
Current Assets			
Cash	54,531.56	161,466.09	106,934.53
Accounts Receivable	217,591.35	4,444.58	(213,146.77)
Inventory	(128,146.02)	(37,950.39)	90,195.63
Work in Process	(620.00)	-	620.00
Prepaid Expenses	-	-	-
Short-Term Investments	-	-	-
Total current assets	$ 143,356.89	$ 127,960.28	$ (15,396.61)
Fixed (Long-Term) Assets			
Long-Term Investments	-	-	-
Property, Plant and Equipment	-	-	-
Accumulated Depreciation	-	-	-
Intangible Assets	-	-	-
Total fixed assets	$ -	$ -	$ -
Other Assets			
Other Assets	-	-	-
Total Other Assets	$ -	$ -	$ -
Total Assets	$ 143,356.89	$ 127,960.28	$ (15,396.61)
Liabilities and Shareholder's Equity			
Current Liabilities			
Accounts Payable	30,998.42	26,711.01	(4,287.41)
Taxes Payable	75,214.57	46,792.10	(28,422.47)
Other Current Liabilities	(27,500.00)	-	27,500.00
Total current liabilities	$ 78,712.99	$ 73,503.11	$ (5,209.88)

Summary

In this chapter we have taken a look at a **Balance Sheet** report using the **Account Categories** to control the layout. In the next chapter, I'm going to create an **Income Statement** report.

11

Create an Income Statement

In this chapter, we're going to create an **Income Statement** report using the **Account Categories** to control the layout.

Design the report

All of the reports created in this book are used to demonstrate different Jet functions or ways of building reports. The **Income Statement**, like the **Balance Sheet** created in the previous chapter, predominantly uses the **GL** function.

The **Income Statement** report being created in this chapter, will use **Account Categories** in the same was as the **Balance Sheet** report as it is a much more structured report than the **Trial Balance** reports which are relatively simple listing of accounts or, for the detailed version, accounts and their transactions.

The **Income Statement** will allow users to select criteria at runtime:

- Fiscal year
- Fiscal period.

The **Income Statement** is going to be a multicompany report with a summary sheet, so there will be no company selection at runtime.

The report is then broken down into Revenues and Expenses, each with sub-sections for the different types. We'll include the period and year to date amounts for both the current and previous year as columns, along with variance columns.

The report is one of the most formatted report covered in the book, with sections identified with colored headings and fields formatted as numbers or currencies.

Jet Reports with Microsoft Dynamics GP

The report for a company will be laid out in this format:

Income Statement

Company		Fabrikam, Inc.					
Fiscal year		2027					
Period		4					

	2027 Period 3	2027 YTD	2026 Period 3	2026 YTD	Variance Period 3	Variance YTD
Revenues						
Sales	-	-	-	-	-	-
Sales Returns and Discounts	-	-	-	-	-	-
Other Income	-	-	-	-	-	-
Total Revenues	$ -	$ -	$ -	$ -	$ -	$ -
Cost of Goods Sold	-	-	-	-	-	-
Gross Profit	$ -	$ -	$ -	$ -	$ -	$ -
Expenses						
Selling Expense	-	-	-	-	-	-
Salaries Expense	-	-	-	-	-	-
Other Employee Expenses	-	-	-	-	-	-
Administrative Expense	-	-	-	-	-	-
Depreciation Expense	-	-	-	-	-	-
Tax Expense	-	-	-	-	-	-
Other Expenses	-	-	-	-	-	-
Total Operating Expenses	$ -	$ -	$ -	$ -	$ -	$ -
Interest Payable	-	-	-	-	-	-
Gain/Loss on Asset Disposal	-	-	-	-	-	-
Net Operating Income	$ -	$ -	$ -	$ -	$ -	$ -
Interest Expense	-	-	-	-	-	-
Income Tax Expense	-	-	-	-	-	-
Net Income	$ -	$ -	$ -	$ -	$ -	$ -

Once complete this page will be replicated for each company and then a consolidation page created.

Create the Report page

Create a new Excel workbook and change the tab name to **Report**. I have set the layout of the report up with the first two columns and first five rows highlighted in yellow as they will be set to **Hide**.

To keep columns **D**, **E**, **G**, **H**, **J** and **K** a consistent width >--- min width ---< has been entered in row **2** to force a minimum width to the **fit**; columns **F** and **I** have a smaller consistent width set using >---<.

Grey formatted fields in **B3** and **B4** will hold the company and heading for the page; the three fields for the options and their headings in cells **C3** to **D4** have had a fill of blue set; calculated start and end periods for the current and previous year in cells **G3** to **H4** and **J3** to **K4** have had a grey fill applied.

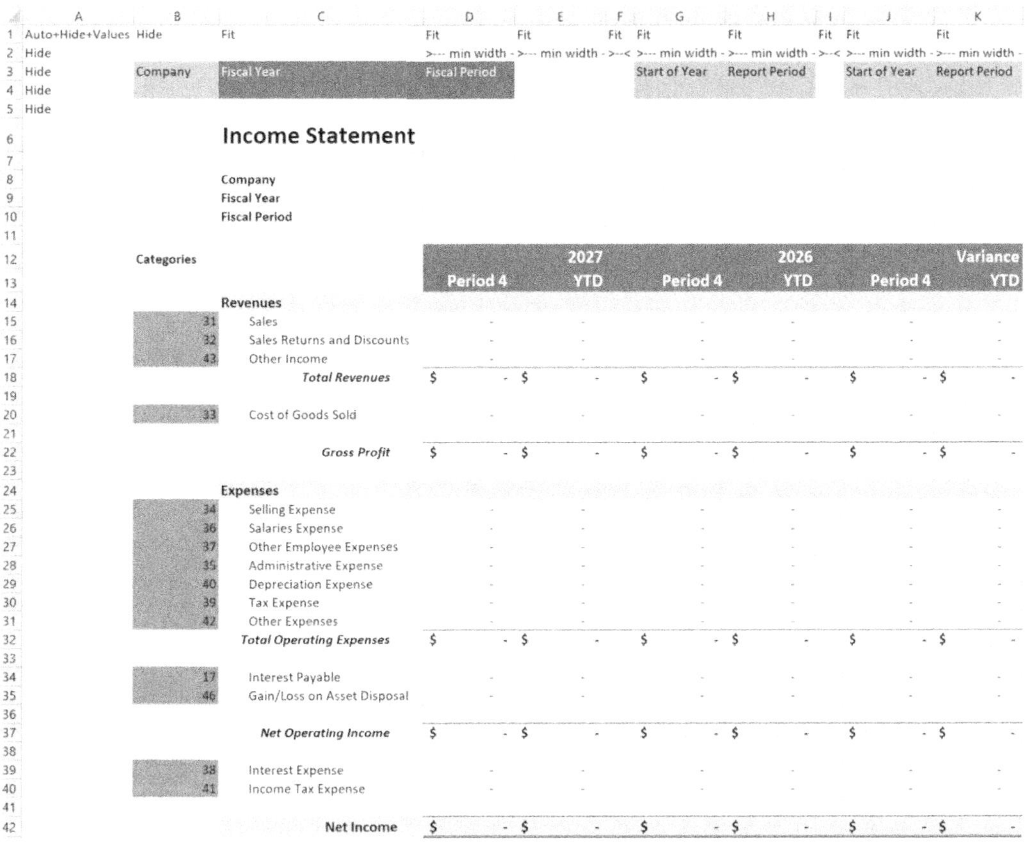

	A	B	C	D	E	F	G	H	I	J	K
1	Auto+Hide+Values	Hide	Fit	Fit	Fit	Fit	Fit	Fit	Fit	Fit	Fit
2	Hide			>--- min width -	>--- min width -	>--<	>--- min width -	>--- min width -	>--<	>--- min width -	>--- min width -
3	Hide	Company	Fiscal Year	Fiscal Period			Start of Year	Report Period		Start of Year	Report Period
4	Hide										
5	Hide										
6			**Income Statement**								
7											
8			Company								
9			Fiscal Year								
10			Fiscal Period								
11											
12		Categories			2027			2026			Variance
13				Period 4	YTD		Period 4	YTD		Period 4	YTD
14			**Revenues**								
15		31	Sales	-	-		-	-		-	-
16		32	Sales Returns and Discounts	-	-		-	-		-	-
17		43	Other Income	-	-		-	-		-	-
18			*Total Revenues*	$ -	$ -		$ -	$ -		$ -	$ -
19											
20		33	Cost of Goods Sold	-	-		-	-		-	-
21											
22			*Gross Profit*	$ -	$ -		$ -	$ -		$ -	$ -
23											
24			**Expenses**								
25		34	Selling Expense	-	-		-	-		-	-
26		36	Salaries Expense	-	-		-	-		-	-
27		37	Other Employee Expenses	-	-		-	-		-	-
28		35	Administrative Expense	-	-		-	-		-	-
29		40	Depreciation Expense	-	-		-	-		-	-
30		39	Tax Expense	-	-		-	-		-	-
31		42	Other Expenses	-	-		-	-		-	-
32			*Total Operating Expenses*	$ -	$ -		$ -	$ -		$ -	$ -
33											
34		17	Interest Payable	-	-		-	-		-	-
35		46	Gain/Loss on Asset Disposal	-	-		-	-		-	-
36											
37			*Net Operating Income*	$ -	$ -		$ -	$ -		$ -	$ -
38											
39		38	Interest Expense	-	-		-	-		-	-
40		41	Income Tax Expense	-	-		-	-		-	-
41											
42			**Net Income**	$ -	$ -		$ -	$ -		$ -	$ -

A green fill has been applied to the cells in column **B** which can be used to control which category will be on each row.

Unlike the previous reports covered, the Balance Sheet will have some formatting applied to enhance the output. Blue fills have been applied to rows **14**, **24** and **42** between columns **C** and **K**; a light grey fill has been applied in the same columns on rows **18**, **22**, **32** and **37**.

Certain report and field headings have also been defined on the report; the period and year headings will be derived from the report options rather than hardcoded.

Create the Options page

For the report we will be providing three options for the user to set. To create the options, follow these steps:

1. Click the **Report Options** button on the **Tools** tab of the **Jet** action pane.
2. Enter a **Title** of Fiscal Year.
3. Enter a **Value** of 2027.

4. Enter a **Tooltip** of Select fiscal year.

Report Options allow you to choose specific filters to narrow the information you want to view. These are typically created to give report viewers the ability to customize what they see at report run time.

	Title	Value	Tooltip	Lookup
X	Fiscal Year	2027	Select fiscal year	+

5. Click the plus icon in the **Lookup** column.

6. The **What** will default to Lookup; select the Period Header table (SY40101).

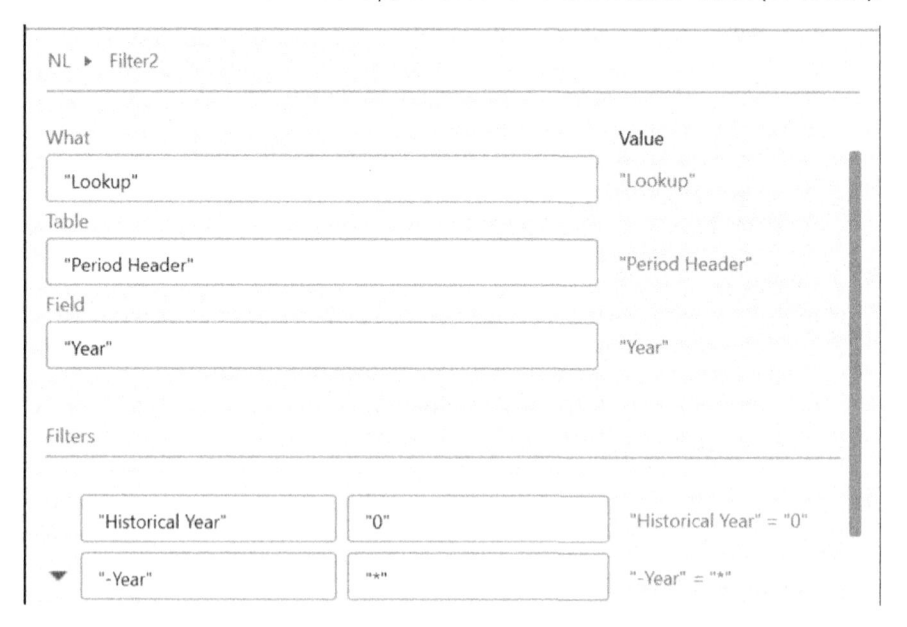

NL ▶ Filter2

What: "Lookup" Value: "Lookup"
Table: "Period Header" "Period Header"
Field: "Year" "Year"

Filters:
"Historical Year" "0" "Historical Year" = "0"
"-Year" "*" "-Year" = "*"

7. Select the **Field** of Year.

8. Enter a filter of Historical Year and value of 0.

9. To change the order to show the newest year at the top:

    a. Enter a second filter of Year and value of *.

    b. Click the arrow at the left filter changes to a down arrow.

10. Click **OK** to save the **Fiscal Year** lookup.

11. Enter a **Title** of Fiscal Period.

12. Enter a **Value** of 4.

13. Enter a **Tooltip** of Select fiscal period.

Chapter 11: Create an Income Statement

14. Click the plus icon in the **Lookup** column.

15. The **What** will default to Lookup; select the Period Setup table (SY40100).

16. Hold control down and select the **Field** of Period ID and Period Name.

```
NL ▶ Filter3

What                                              Value
  "Lookup"                                          "Lookup"
Table
  "Period Setup"                                    "Period Setup"
Field
  {"Period ID", "Period Name"}                      {"Period ID","Period Name"}

Filters

  "Year"              $C$2              "Year" =
  "Period ID"         "<>" & 0          "Period ID" = "<>0"
  "Origin Description"  "General Entry"  "Origin Description" = "Ge
```

17. Enter a filter of Year and value of $C$2 (this is the field on the options page which will contain the Fiscal Year option).

18. Exclude period 0 by adding a filter of Period ID and value of "<>" & 0.

19. Enter a filter of Year and value of $C$2 (this is the field on the options page which will contain the Fiscal Year option).

20. To limit the return down only to one entry per period, enter a filter of Origin Description and value of General Entry.

21. Click **OK** to save the **Fiscal Period** lookup.

22. Review the added lookups and ensure they are correct.

Report Options allow you to choose specific filters to narrow the information you want to view. These are typically created to give report viewers the ability to customize what they see at report run time.

	Title	Value	Tooltip	Lookup	
×	Fiscal Year	2027	Select fiscal...	✏	×
×	Fiscal Period	3	Select fiscal...	✏	×

23. Click **Close** to close the **Report Options** window and generate the **Options** page.

Set Options on Report page

With the **Options** page created, we need to use an **NP** function to bring them to the **Reports** page to use. Do that by following these steps:

1. In cell **B4** enter the name of the company to be used on this page.

2. Place the cursor in cell **C4** and click the **NP** function button.

3. Set the **What** to Eval.

4. Place the cursor in the **Formula** field and select the cell on the **Options** page containing the fiscal year value (which is cell **C2**).

What	Value
"Eval"	"Eval"
Formula	
"='Options'!$C$2"	"='Options'!$C$2"

5. Click **OK** to save the function.

6. Repeat steps 2 through 5 for the **Fiscal Period**.

7. In cell **G4** enter a formula to concatenate the fiscal year in cell3 **C4** with **/0**.

    `G4    fx    =CONCATENATE($C$4,"/0")`

8. In cell **H4** enter a formula to concatenate the fiscal year in cell **C4** with the fiscal period in cell **D4** separated with a **/**.

    `H4    fx    =CONCATENATE($C$4,"/",$D$4)`

9. In cell **J4** enter a formula to concatenate the fiscal year in cell **C4 -1** with **/0**.

    `J4    fx    =CONCATENATE($C$4-1,"/0")`

10. In cell **K4** enter a formula to concatenate the fiscal year in cell **C4 -1** with the fiscal period in cell D4 separated with a **/**.

    `K4    fx    =CONCATENATE($C$4-1,"/",$D$4)`

The **Report** page should now be showing the values of the **Options** in the blue filled cells and calculated fields in the grey.

Chapter 11: Create an Income Statement

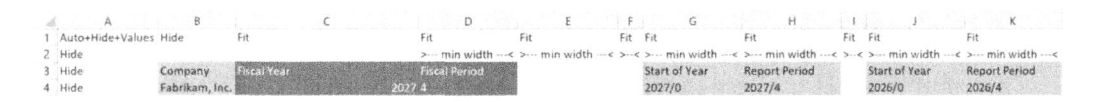

	A	B	C	D	E	F	G	H	I	J	K
1	Auto+Hide+Values	Hide	Fit	Fit	Fit	Fit	Fit	Fit	Fit	Fit	Fit
2	Hide			>--- min width ---<	>--- min width ---<	>--- min width ---<	>--- min width ---<	>--- min width ---<	>--- min width ---<	>--- min width ---<	>--- min width ---<
3	Hide		Company	Fiscal Year		Fiscal Period		Start of Year	Report Period	Start of Year	Report Period
4	Hide		Fabrikam, Inc.	2027	4			2027/0	2027/4	2026/0	2026/4

Output options

There are several of the options which will be output on the report so users consuming the report know the source of the data:

1. Use a formula to bring the **Company** heading from cell **B3** to **C8**.
2. Use a formula to bring the **Company** value from cell **B4** to **D8**.
3. Use a formula to bring the **Fiscal Year** heading from cell **C3** to **C9**.
4. Use a formula to bring the **Fiscal Year** value from cell **C4** to **D9**.
5. Use a formula to bring the **Fiscal Period** heading from cell **D3** to **C10**.
6. Use a formula to bring the **Fiscal Period** value from cell **D4** to **C10**.

Add categories

So that the **Income Statement** is produced correctly, the **Account Categories** will be hardcoded to appear in certain cells.

It is the account category which needs to be used for this. These numbers can be found via the Account Category Maintenance window in Microsoft Dynamics GP (Financial area page » Setup » Account Categories).

The Account Category Codes will be added in column **B** starting in row **15**; the table below includes the row reference and the **Account Category Number** to place in it.

For example, the first pair of cells means that cell **B15** will contain account category number **31**.

Row	Cat	Row	Cat	Row	Cat	Row	Cat	Row	Cat
15	31	20	33	27	37	30	29	35	46
16	32	25	34	28	35	31	42	38	38
17	43	26	36	29	40	34	17	40	41

Alongside each of these cells, we need to use the **GL** function to get the **Account Category Description**:

7. Set the **Where** to Cell.

8. Set the **What** to CategoryName.

9. The **Category** field should be set to the cell containing the Account Category Number, which for cell **C15** is cell **B15**, with a locked column.

10. Set the **Company** to cell **B4**, with locked column and row.

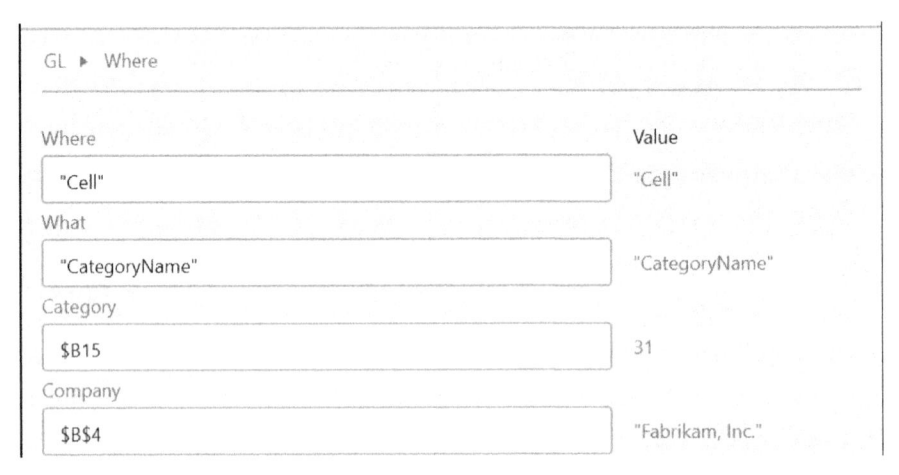

GL ▶ Where	
Where	Value
"Cell"	"Cell"
What	
"CategoryName"	"CategoryName"
Category	
$B15	31
Company	
$B$4	"Fabrikam, Inc."

11. Click **OK** to save the formula.

12. Repeat steps **1** through **5** for the other 14 categories using the table above for the category numbers (as a shortcut, you can copy and paste the cell down through the rows).

Add current period

The current period for each row category is calculated in the same way with only the account category itself changing. To add the required function, perform the following steps:

1. Place the cursor in cell **D14** and click the **GL** function button on the Tools section of the **Jet** action pane.

2. Set the **Where** to Cell.

3. Set the **What** to Balance.

4. Set the **Start Period** to cell **H4**, with column and row both locked.

5. Set the **End Period** to cell **H4**, with column and row both locked.

6. The **Category** field should be set to the cell containing the Account Category Number, which for cell **C15** is cell **B15**, with a locked column.

7. Set the **Company** to cell **B4**, with locked column and row.

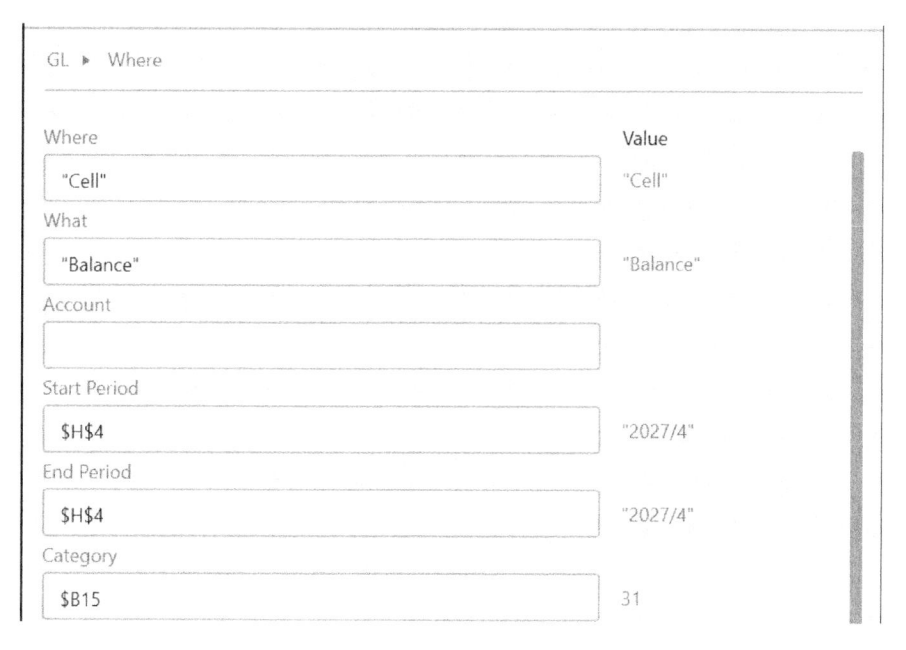

Chapter 11: Create an Income Statement

GL ▶ Where	
Where	**Value**
"Cell"	"Cell"
What	
"Balance"	"Balance"
Account	
Start Period	
$H$4	"2027/4"
End Period	
$H$4	"2027/4"
Category	
$B15	31

8. Click **OK** to save the function.

9. Repeat steps **1** through **7** for the remaining category rows changing the **B15** cell reference accordingly.

Add current year

The current year for each row category is calculated in the same way with only the account category itself changing. To add the required function, perform the following steps:

1. Place the cursor in cell **E14** and click the **GL** function button on the Tools section of the **Jet** action pane.

2. Set the **Where** to Cell.

3. Set the **What** to Balance.

4. Set the **Start Period** to cell **G4**, with column and row both locked.

5. Set the **End Period** to cell **H4**, with column and row both locked.

6. The **Category** field should be set to the cell containing the Account Category Number, which for cell **C15** is cell **B15**, with a locked column.

7. Set the **Company** to cell **B4**, with locked column and row.

```
GL ▶ Where

Where                                          Value
┌──────────────────────────────┐   ┌──────────────┐
│ "Cell"                       │   │ "Cell"       │
└──────────────────────────────┘   └──────────────┘
What
┌──────────────────────────────┐   ┌──────────────┐
│ "Balance"                    │   │ "Balance"    │
└──────────────────────────────┘   └──────────────┘
Account
┌──────────────────────────────┐
│                              │
└──────────────────────────────┘
Start Period
┌──────────────────────────────┐   ┌──────────────┐
│ $H$4                         │   │ "2027/4"     │
└──────────────────────────────┘   └──────────────┘
End Period
┌──────────────────────────────┐   ┌──────────────┐
│ $H$4                         │   │ "2027/4"     │
└──────────────────────────────┘   └──────────────┘
Category
┌──────────────────────────────┐   ┌──────────────┐
│ $B15                         │   │ 31           │
└──────────────────────────────┘   └──────────────┘
```

8. Click **OK** to save the function.

9. Repeat steps **1** through **7** for the remaining category rows changing the **B15** cell reference accordingly.

Add current period for previous year

The current period for each row category is calculated in the same way with only the account category itself changing. To add the required function, perform the following steps:

1. Place the cursor in cell **G14** and click the **GL** function button on the Tools section of the **Jet** action pane.

2. Set the **Where** to Cell.

3. Set the **What** to Balance.

4. Set the **Start Period** to cell **K4**, with column and row both locked.

5. Set the **End Period** to cell **K4**, with column and row both locked.

6. The **Category** field should be set to the cell containing the Account Category Number, which for cell **C15** is cell **B15**, with a locked column.

7. Set the **Company** to cell **B4**, with locked column and row.

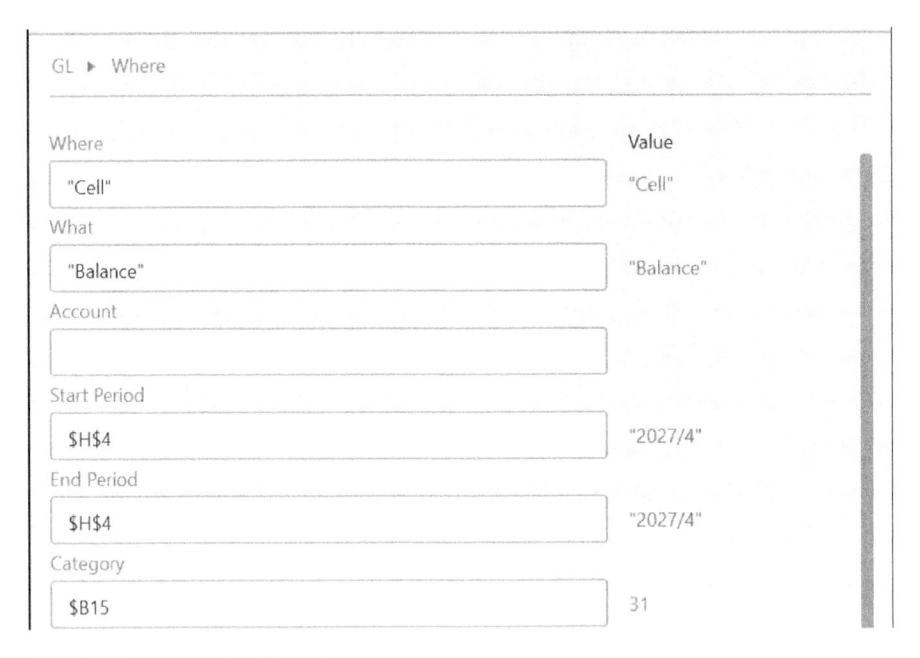

8. Click **OK** to save the function.

9. Repeat steps **1** through **7** for the remaining category rows changing the **B15** cell reference accordingly.

Add previous year

The current year for each row category is calculated in the same way with only the account category itself changing. To add the required function, perform the following steps:

1. Place the cursor in cell **H14** and click the **GL** function button on the Tools section of the **Jet** action pane.
2. Set the **Where** to Cell.
3. Set the **What** to Balance.
4. Set the **Start Period** to cell **J4**, with column and row both locked.
5. Set the **End Period** to cell **I4**, with column and row both locked.
6. The **Category** field should be set to the cell containing the Account Category Number, which for cell **D15** is cell **B15**, with a locked column.
7. Set the **Company** to cell **B4**, with locked column and row.
8. Click **OK** to save the function.
9. Repeat steps **1** through **8** for the remaining category rows changing the **B15** cell reference accordingly.

Add period variance

The variance for the period column between years, can be calculated using a standard Excel formula:

1. In cell **J14** enter =G15-D15.
2. Repeat step **1** for the remaining category rows changing the **B15** cell reference accordingly.

Add period variance for previous year

The variance for the period column between years, can be calculated using a standard Excel formula:

1. In cell **K14** enter =H15-E15.
2. Repeat step **1** for the remaining category rows changing the **B15** cell reference accordingly.

Add section totals

The section totals on rows **18**, **22** and **32** are standard Excel sums of the rows of the section above. For example, the formula for cell **D18** is =SUM(D15:D17). Repeat across columns **E**, **F**, **G**, **H**, **J** and **K** for all sections.

Add Net Operating Income

The **Net Operating Income** is accomplished using standard Excel formula; for the current year column it is the sum of cells D22+D32+D34+D37. Repeat across for the previous year and variance columns.

Add Net Income

The **Net Income** is also accomplished using standard Excel formula; for the current year column it is the sum of cells D37+D39+D40. Repeat across for the previous year and variance columns.

Run report

Run the report by following these steps:

1. Click the **Run** button on the action pane.

2. This will take the Jet Reports out of **Design Mode** and prompt with the **Report Options**:

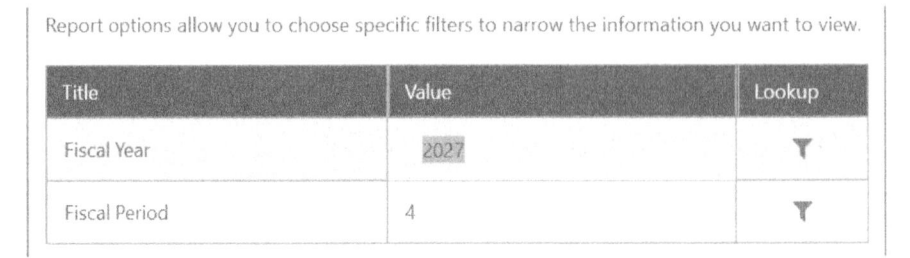

   Report options allow you to choose specific filters to narrow the information you want to view.

Title	Value	Lookup
Fiscal Year	2027	▼
Fiscal Period	4	▼

3. Enter your criteria and click **Run**.

Chapter 11: Create an Income Statement

Income Statement

Company	Fabrikam, Inc.						
Fiscal Year	2027						
Fiscal Period	4						

		2027		2026		Variance	
		Period 4	YTD	Period 4	YTD	Period 4	YTD
Revenues							
	Sales	(230,189.94)	(489,665.09)	-	(361,211.21)	230,189.94	128,453.88
	Sales Returns and Discounts	-	-	-	-	-	-
	Other Income	-	-	-	-	-	-
	Total Revenues	$ (230,189.94) $	(489,665.09)	$ - $	(361,211.21)	$ 230,189.94 $	128,453.88
	Cost of Goods Sold	111,607.00	244,108.99	(23.94)	145,538.91	(111,630.94)	(98,570.08)
	Gross Profit	$ (341,796.94) $	(733,774.08)	$ 23.94 $	(506,750.12)	$ 341,820.88 $	227,023.96
Expenses							
	Selling Expense	-	-	-	-	-	-
	Salaries Expense	35,925.14	164,044.84	29,328.24	144,743.77	(6,596.90)	(19,301.07)
	Other Employee Expenses	1,431.83	5,725.84	1,432.39	5,754.44	0.56	28.60
	Administrative Expense	-	15.00	-	15.00	-	-
	Depreciation Expense	-	-	-	-	-	-
	Tax Expense	2,145.20	11,126.52	2,168.82	9,944.80	23.62	(1,181.72)
	Other Expenses	-	-	-	757.12	-	757.12
	Total Operating Expenses	$ 39,502.17 $	180,912.20	$ 32,929.45 $	161,215.13	$ (6,572.72) $	(19,697.07)
	Interest Payable	-	-	-	-	-	-
	Gain/Loss on Asset Disposal	-	-	-	-	-	-
	Net Operating Income	$ (381,299.11) $	(914,686.28)	$ (32,905.51) $	(667,965.25)	$ 348,393.60 $	246,721.03
	Interest Expense	-	-	-	-	-	-
	Income Tax Expense	-	-	-	-	-	-
	Net Income	$ (381,299.11) $	(914,686.28)	$ (32,905.51) $	(667,965.25)	$ 348,393.60 $	246,721.03

Adding extra companies

The report page we've created for one company, can easily be replicated for other companies by making a copy of the worksheet and changing the company name in cell **B4**.

Making a consolidation page

A consolidation page can be made by duplicating one of the report pages and replacing the **GL** formula with sums of the same cell on the company pages.

To avoid problems with the category names in column **C**, there are two adjustments which need to be made to the options fields.

1. Drag (do not copy) cell **B4** to **B5**; this will update the formula in column **C** used to get the category names.

2. Add Consolidation to cell **B4**.

3. Update cell **D8** to get the name to display from cell **D4** (it automatically updated when cell **B4** was dragged to cell **B5**.

Jet Reports with Microsoft Dynamics GP

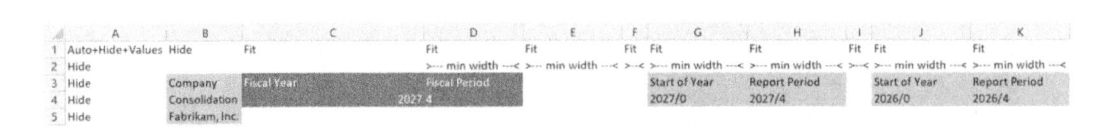

![Screenshot of spreadsheet with columns A through K showing Auto+Hide+Values, Hide, Fit settings with Company, Consolidation, Fabrikam Inc. rows and Fiscal Year 2027 4, Fiscal Period, Start of Year 2027/0, Report Period 2027/4, Start of Year 2026/0, Report Period 2026/4]

Run report

Even with the changes for multiple company pages and the consolidation page, the report is run as normal and will update all of the pages.

Summary

In this chapter we have taken a look at an **Income Statement** report using the **Account Categories** to control the layout. In the next chapter, I'm going to create a **Summary Payables Aged Trial Balance** report.

12

Create a Summary Payables Aged Trial Balance

In this chapter, we're going to create move away from the Financial series into Payables and create a **Summary Aged Trial Balance** report.

Design the report

The **Summary Payables Aged Trial Balance** report we're going to build will:

- Allow the user to specify options for:
    - Company.
    - Aging Date.
    - Vendors.
    - Vendor Class.
- Ordered the output by **Vendor ID**.
- Include only vendors with a **Due Balance**.
- Work for Aging by **Due Date** or **Document Date**.
- For each vendor include:
    - Vendor Name.
    - Vendor Class.
    - User-Defined 1.
    - Number of Vouchers.

Jet Reports with Microsoft Dynamics GP

- o Due Amount.
- o Four aging buckets.
- Include totals at the bottom.

The report will be laid out in this format:

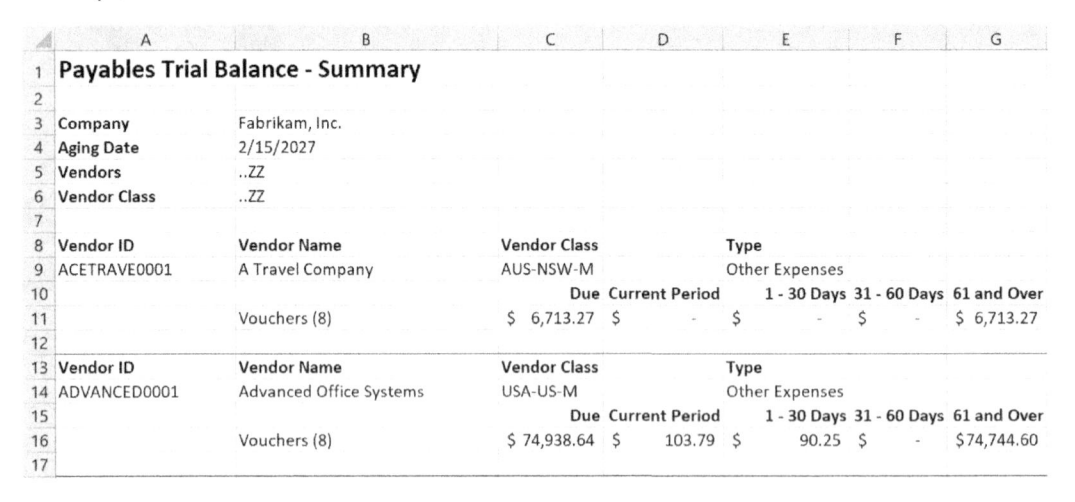

	A	B	C	D	E	F	G
1	**Payables Trial Balance - Summary**						
2							
3	Company	Fabrikam, Inc.					
4	Aging Date	2/15/2027					
5	Vendors	..ZZ					
6	Vendor Class	..ZZ					
7							
8	Vendor ID	Vendor Name	Vendor Class		Type		
9	ACETRAVE0001	A Travel Company	AUS-NSW-M		Other Expenses		
10			Due	Current Period	1 - 30 Days	31 - 60 Days	61 and Over
11		Vouchers (8)	$ 6,713.27	$ -	$ -	$ -	$ 6,713.27
12							
13	Vendor ID	Vendor Name	Vendor Class		Type		
14	ADVANCED0001	Advanced Office Systems	USA-US-M		Other Expenses		
15			Due	Current Period	1 - 30 Days	31 - 60 Days	61 and Over
16		Vouchers (8)	$ 74,938.64	$ 103.79	$ 90.25	$ -	$74,744.60
17							

Create the Report page

Create a new Excel workbook and change the tab name to **Report**. I have set the layout of the report up with the first four columns and first seven rows highlighted in yellow as they will be set to **Hide**.

Column **B** has **Hide+?** added as I will use this column to control visibility of rows depending on if they are zero value or not.

The eight fields for the options and their headings have had a fill of blue set; the grey fields will hold the settings either read from the **Payables Management Setup** tables or calculated from them.

A green fill set for the field which will hold the **NL** function replicator and the rows it covers.

The report header and column headings have all been placed and formatting applied with a **Fit** applied for the column widths in the first row. Some columns are set to hide as they will hold the formula getting the data which will be used in a calculation in the shown columns.

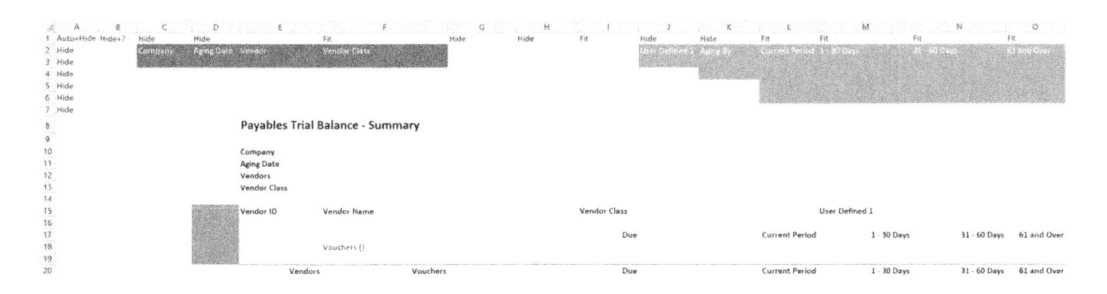

Chapter 12: Create a Summary Payables Trial Balance

Create the Options page

For the report we will be providing three options for the user to set. To create the options, follow these steps:

1. Click the **Report Options** button on the **Tools** tab of the **Jet** action pane.

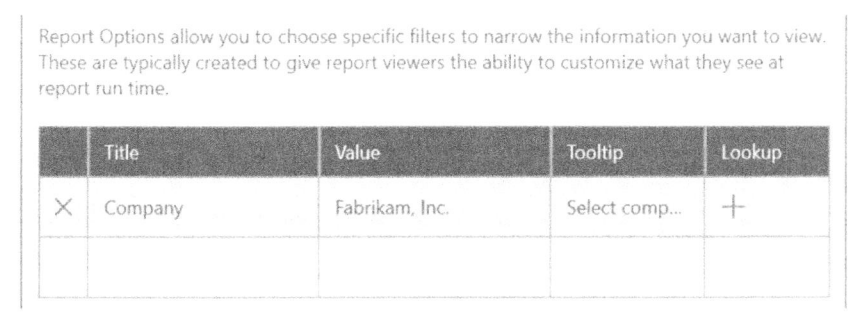

2. Enter a **Title** of Company.

3. Enter a **Value** of Fabrikam, Inc..

4. Enter a **Tooltip** of Select company.

5. Click the plus icon in the **Lookup** column.

6. The **What** will default to Lookup; click the **Nested Jet Function** button on the action pane and click **Insert NP**.

7. Set the **What** to Companies.

8. Click **Back** to save the function.

9. Enter Name in **Field** (this must be done manually as the lookup is blank).

```
NL ▶ Field

What                                          Value
┌─────────────────────────────┐                ┌─────────────────────────────┐
│ "Lookup"                    │                │ "Lookup"                    │
└─────────────────────────────┘                └─────────────────────────────┘
Table
┌─────────────────────────────┐                ┌─────────────────────────────┐
│ NP("Companies")             │                │ "||""Companies"","""",""""" │
└─────────────────────────────┘                └─────────────────────────────┘
Field
┌─────────────────────────────┐                ┌─────────────────────────────┐
│ "Name"                      │                │ "Name"                      │
└─────────────────────────────┘                └─────────────────────────────┘
```

10. Click **OK** to save the **Company** lookup.

11. On the second row, enter a **Title** of Aging Date.

12. Enter date in the **Value**.

13. Enter a **Tooltip** of Select aging date.

14. On the third row, enter a **Title** of Vendor ID.

15. Enter a **Value of** ..Z which will give us a range of all vendors.

16. Enter a **Tooltip** of Select vendor.

17. Click the plus icon in the **Lookup** column.

18. The **What** will default to Lookup; select the PM Vendor Master File table (PM00200).

19. Select the **Fields** of Vendor ID and Vendor Name.

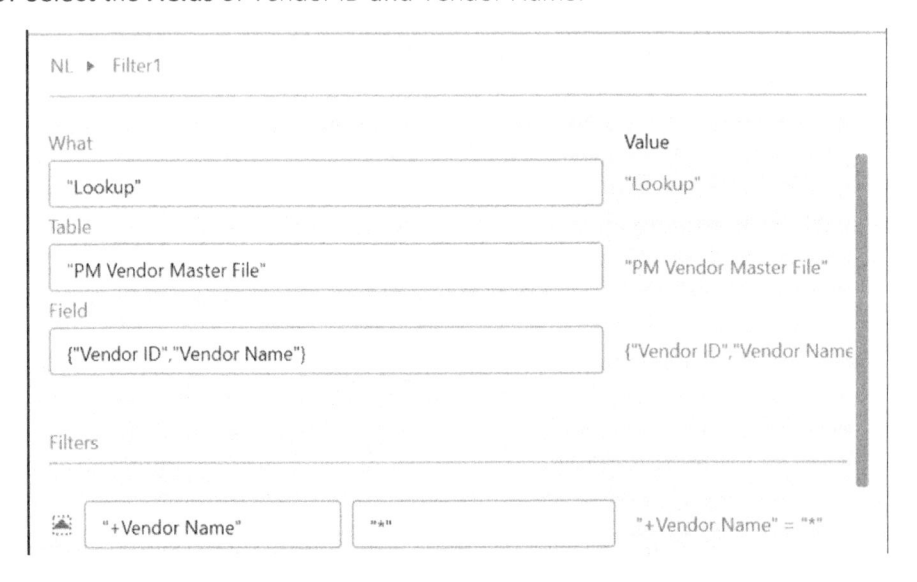

```
NL ▶ Filter1

What                                          Value
┌─────────────────────────────┐                ┌─────────────────────────────┐
│ "Lookup"                    │                │ "Lookup"                    │
└─────────────────────────────┘                └─────────────────────────────┘
Table
┌─────────────────────────────┐                ┌─────────────────────────────┐
│ "PM Vendor Master File"     │                │ "PM Vendor Master File"     │
└─────────────────────────────┘                └─────────────────────────────┘
Field
┌─────────────────────────────┐                ┌─────────────────────────────┐
│ {"Vendor ID","Vendor Name"} │                │ {"Vendor ID","Vendor Name"} │
└─────────────────────────────┘                └─────────────────────────────┘

Filters
   ┌─────────────────┐   ┌─────┐              ┌─────────────────────────────┐
🔽 │ "+Vendor Name"  │   │ "*" │              │ "+Vendor Name" = "*"        │
   └─────────────────┘   └─────┘              └─────────────────────────────┘
```

20. In the first filter select Vendor Name and in the filter add *.

Chapter 12: Create a Summary Payables Trial Balance

21. Click the arrows to the left until an up arrow is shown so that the returned vendors are in alphabetic order.

22. Click **OK** to save the **Vendor** lookup.

23. On the third row, enter a **Title** of Vendor Class.

24. Enter a **Value of** ..Z which will give us a range of all vendor classes.

25. Enter a **Tooltip** of Select vendor class.

26. Click the plus icon in the **Lookup** column.

27. The **What** will default to Lookup; select the PM Class Master File table (PM00100).

28. Select the **Fields** of Vendor Class ID and Vendor Class Description.

29. In the first filter select Vendor Class ID and in the filter add *.

30. Click the arrows to the left until an up arrow is shown so that the returned vendor classes are in alphabetic order.

31. Click **OK** to save the **Vendor Class** lookup.

NL ▶ Filter1

What: "Lookup"
Value: "Lookup"
Table: "PM Class Master File"
"PM Class Master File"
Field: {"Vendor Class ID","Vendor Class Description"}
{"Vendor Class ID","Vendor
Filters: "+Vendor Class ID" "*"   "+Vendor Class ID" = "*"

32. Review the added lookups and ensure they are correct.

33. Click **Close** to close the **Report Options** window and generate the **Options** page.

	A	B	C	D	E
1	Auto+Hide+HideSheet	Title	Value	Lookup+Hide	Tooltip+Hide
2	Option	Company	Fabrikam, Inc.	Lookup	Select company
3	Option	Aging Date	2/15/2027		Select aging date
4	Option	Vendor	..ZZ	Lookup	Select vendor
5	Option	Vendor Class	..ZZ	Lookup	Select vendor class

The options can be edited by clicking the **Report Options** button again or by editing directly through the **Options** page; the **Lookup** can be amended by selecting an entry in column **D** and clicking the **Jet Function** button.

Set Options on Report page

With the **Options** page created, we need to use an **NP** function to bring them to the **Report** page to use:

Do that by following these steps:

1. Place the cursor in cell **C3** and click the **NP** function button.

2. Set the **What** to Eval.

3. Place the cursor in the **Formula** field and select the cell on the **Options** page containing the company value (which is cell **C**), lock the rows and columns.

4. Click **OK** to save the function.

NP ▶ What		
What		Value
"Eval"		"Eval"
Formula		
"='Options'!$C$4"		"='Options'!$C$4"

5. Repeat steps 1 through 4 for the **Aging Date**, **Vendor ID** and **Vendor Class**.

The **Report** page should now be showing the values of the **Options** in the blue filled cells.

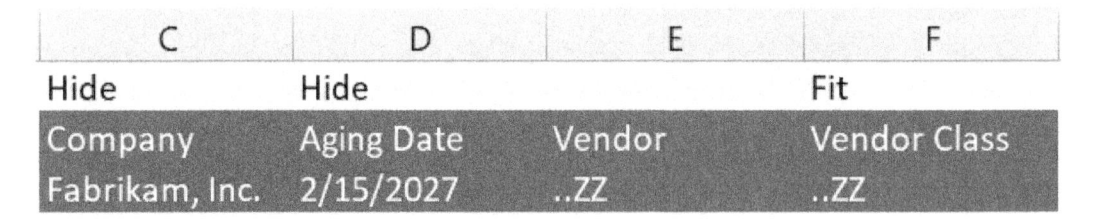

C	D	E	F
Hide	Hide		Fit
Company	Aging Date	Vendor	Vendor Class
Fabrikam, Inc.	2/15/2027	..ZZ	..ZZ

Add settings from Payables Management setup

This report includes a number of settings which are being read from **Payables Management Setup**; these include the label for **User Defined 1**, **Aging By** and four aging buckets description and number of days. These will be loaded into the cells filled grey:

1. Place the cursor in cell **J3** and click the **NL** function button on the action pane.

2. Set **What** to First.

Chapter 12: Create a Summary Payables Trial Balance

3. Set **Table** to PM Setup File.

What	Value
"First"	"First"
Table	
"PM Setup File"	"PM Setup File"
Field	
"User Defined Prompt 1"	"User Defined Prompt 1"

4. Select User Defined Prompt 1 in **Field**.

5. Click **Ok** to save the function.

6. Place the cursor in cell **K3** and click the **NL** function button on the action pane.

7. Set **What** to First.

8. Set **Table** to PM Setup File.

9. Select Age By in **Field**.

10. Click **Ok** to save the function.

What	Value
"First"	"First"
Table	
"PM Setup File"	"PM Setup File"
Field	
"Age By"	"Age By"

11. Place the cursor in cell **K4** and enter an Excel IF to set the field to **DUEDATE** when cell **K3** is 0 else set the field to **DOCDATE**.

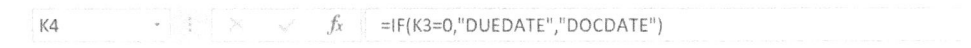

    `K4    fx   =IF(K3=0,"DUEDATE","DOCDATE")`

12. Place the cursor in cell **L3** and click the **NL** function button on the action pane.

13. Set **What** to First.

14. Set **Table** to PM Period Setup File.

15. Select Ending Period Days in **Field**.

Jet Reports with Microsoft Dynamics GP

16. Set the first filter to Index and the filter value to 1.
17. Click **Ok** to save the function.

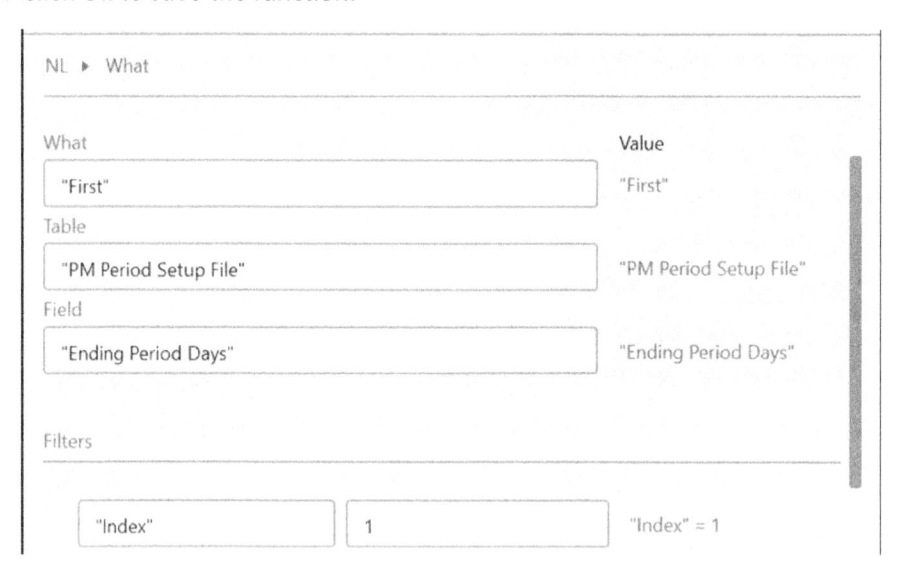

```
NL ▸ What

What                                          Value
"First"                                        "First"
Table
"PM Period Setup File"                         "PM Period Setup File"
Field
"Ending Period Days"                           "Ending Period Days"

Filters

"Index"              1                         "Index" = 1
```

18. With the aging days returned, I can use this to calculate the start date of the **Current Period** by subtracting it from the **Aging Date** in cell **D3**:

```
L5       ▾  :  ×  ✓  fx   =D3-L3
```

19. Place the cursor in cell **M3** and click the **NL** function button on the action pane.
20. Set **What** to First.
21. Set **Table** to PM Period Setup File.
22. Select Ending Period Days in **Field**.

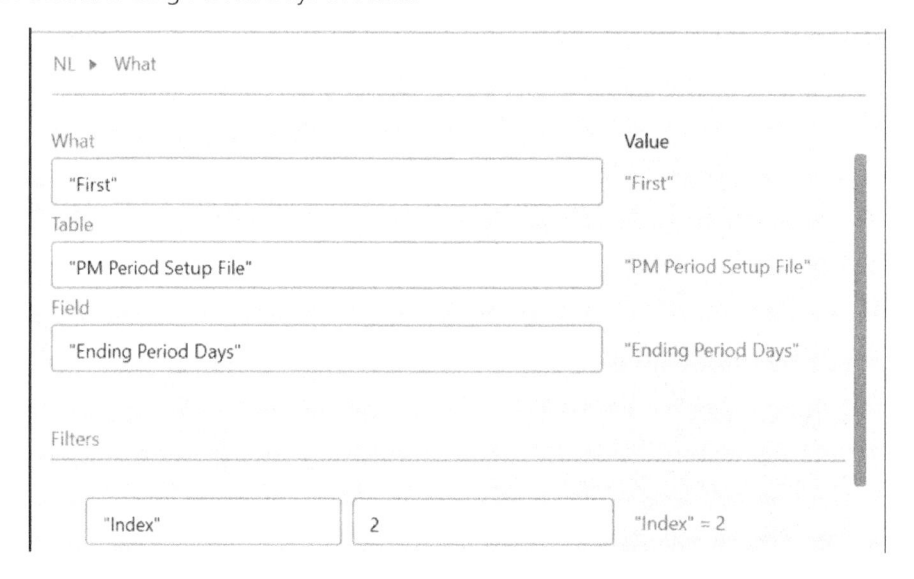

```
NL ▸ What

What                                          Value
"First"                                        "First"
Table
"PM Period Setup File"                         "PM Period Setup File"
Field
"Ending Period Days"                           "Ending Period Days"

Filters

"Index"              2                         "Index" = 2
```

106

Chapter 12: Create a Summary Payables Trial Balance

23. Set the first filter to Index and the filter value to 2.
24. Click **Ok** to save the function.
25. Place the cursor in cell **M4** and create an Excel formula taking the **Aging Date** in **D3** and subtracting the end date of **Aging Period 1** in cell **L5** and adding **1** to calculate the starting date of **Aging Period 2**:

    M4   *fx*   =D3-L3+1

26. In cell **M5**, calculate the ending period of **Aging Period 2** by subtracting the number of days in **Aging Period 2** in **M3** from the **Aging Date** in **D3**.

    M5   *fx*   =D3-M3

27. As there is both a start and end date for **Aging Period 2**, create a formula concatenating the dates in **M5** and **M4** with .. between them which gives a range of dates as used by the jet functions:

    M6   *fx*   =CONCAT(TEXT(M5,"MM/DD/YYYY"),"..",TEXT(M4,"MM/DD/YYYY"))

28. Place the cursor in cell **N3** and click the **NL** function button on the action pane.
29. Set **What** to First.
30. Set **Table** to PM Period Setup File.
31. Select Ending Period Days in **Field**.

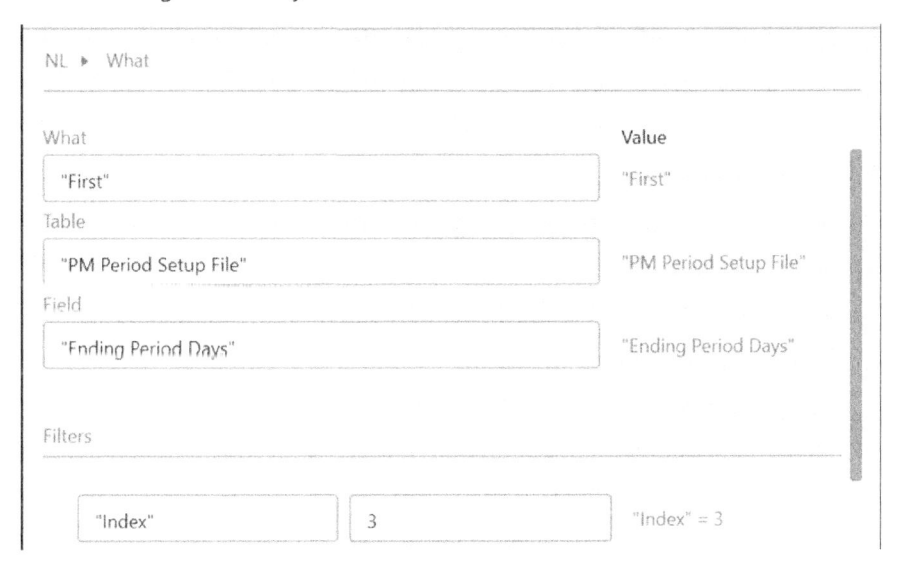

NL ▶ What	
What	Value
"First"	"First"
Table	
"PM Period Setup File"	"PM Period Setup File"
Field	
"Ending Period Days"	"Ending Period Days"
Filters	
"Index" 3	"Index" = 3

32. Set the first filter to Index and the filter value to 3.
33. Click **Ok** to save the function.
34. To set the start date for **Aging Period 3**, create a formula from the **Aging Date** in

C3 subtracting the **Aging Period 2** start date in cell **M3** plus 1:

| N4 | ▼ | : | × | ✓ | *fx* | =D3-M3+1 |

35. To set the end date, subtract the **Aging Period 3** end date in cell **N3** from the **Aging Date** in cell **C3**:

| N5 | ▼ | : | × | ✓ | *fx* | =D3-N3 |

36. As there is both a start and end date for **Aging Period 3**, create a formula concatenating the dates in **N5** and **N4** with .. between them which gives a range of dates as used by the jet functions:

| N6 | ▼ | : | × | ✓ | *fx* | =CONCAT(TEXT(N5,"MM/DD/YYYY"),"..",TEXT(N4,"MM/DD/YYYY")) |

37. **Aging Period 4** is out final aging period, so we want everything older than the **Aging Period 3** end date. To calculate this, take the **Aging Date** in cell **C3**, subtract the **Aging Period 3** end date and add 1:

| O4 | ▼ | : | × | ✓ | *fx* | =D3-N3+1 |

With the settings and calculated fields created, the grey area on the report should look like this (exact dates will depend on the **Aging Date** entered on the options page:

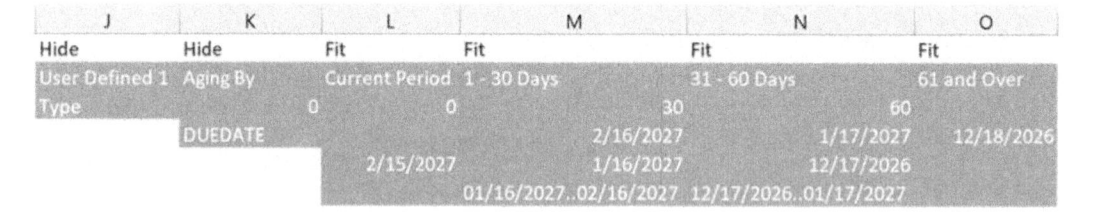

J	K	L	M	N	O
Hide	Hide	Fit	Fit	Fit	Fit
User Defined 1	Aging By	Current Period	1 - 30 Days	31 - 60 Days	61 and Over
Type		0	0	30	60
	DUEDATE		2/16/2027	1/17/2027	12/18/2026
		2/15/2027	1/16/2027	12/17/2026	
			01/16/2027..02/16/2027	12/17/2026..01/17/2027	

Add parameters to report

On this report I am going to include the report options to the output so people looking at the report will know the options used to generate it. These will be in cells **F10** to **F13**:

As we already have the report options brought through to the blue fill cells, we can use a simple Excel formula to make them visible:

1. To add the **Company**, place the cursor in cell **F10** and enter =C3.

2. To add the **Aging Date**, place the cursor in cell **F11** and enter =D3.

3. To add the **Vendors**, place the cursor in cell **F12** and enter =E3.

4. To add the **Vendor Class**, place the cursor in cell **F13** and enter =F3.

Add Record Key for PM Vendor Master File

The first field to add is the record key replicator from the **PM Vendor Master File** table (**PM00200**). Do this by performing these steps:

1. Place the cursor in cell **D15** and click the **NL** function button.

2. Set **What** to Rows=5.

3. In **Table** select the **PM Vendor Master File** table (**PM00200**).

4. Leave **Field** blank as this is to be a record key replicator.

5. To order the accounts in ascending order, set the first filter to Vendor ID, click the arrow button till it shows an arrow pointing up and set the filter value to E3, locked cell and value.

6. Set the second filter field to Vendor Class ID and the filter value to F3, with locked column and row.

7. Add a third filter to Company= and the value to a locked cell C3.

8. Click **OK** to save the function.

Add Vendor Master fields

There are four fields, **Vendor ID**, **Vendor Name**, **Vendor Class** and **User Defined 1,** which we can extract using the record key. Do this by performing these steps:

1. To add the **Vendor ID**, place the cursor in cell **E16** and click the **NF** function button.

   ```
   NF ▸ Key

   Key                                    Value
   $D15                                   """Jet Reports""",""Fabrikam,
   Field
   "Vendor ID"                            "Vendor ID"
   ```

2. In the **Key** select the record key replicator which is in cell **D15** and switch it to lock by the column.

3. In the **Field** select Vendor ID.

4. Click **OK** to save the function.

5. Repeat steps 1 through 4 in cell **F16** and select **Vendor Name**.

6. Repeat steps 1 through 4 in cell **I16** and select **Vendor Class ID**.

7. Repeat steps 1 through 4 in cell **M16** and select **User Defined 1**.

Add count of vouchers

The count of vouchers for a vendor can be retrieved using a **NL** function. Do this by following these steps:

1. Place the cursor in cell **D18** and click the **NL** function button.

2. Set **What** to Count.

3. In **Table** select the **PM Transaction Open File** table (**PM20000**).

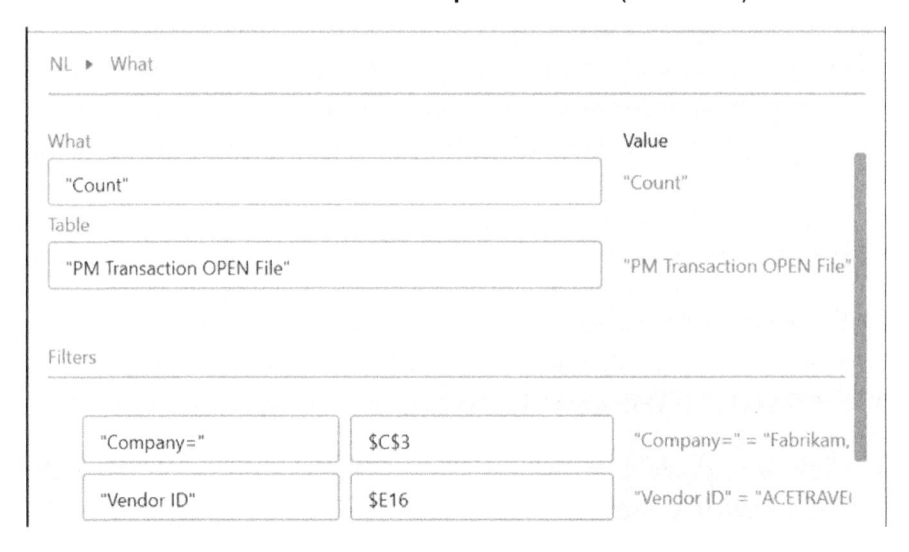

   ```
   NL ▸ What

   What                                   Value
   "Count"                                "Count"
   Table
   "PM Transaction OPEN File"             "PM Transaction OPEN File"

   Filters

   "Company="          $C$3               "Company=" = "Fabrikam,
   "Vendor ID"         $E16               "Vendor ID" = "ACETRAVEL
   ```

Chapter 12: Create a Summary Payables Trial Balance

4. Leave **Field** blank as this is not required for a count.

5. Set the first filter field to Company= and the value to a locked cell C3.

6. Set the second filter field to Vendor ID and the filter value to E16, with locked column.

7. Click **OK** to save the function.

The steps above set the count into a hidden column; this was done deliberately so that I can add some text around the number using the standard Excel **CONCATENATE** function:

F18   ▾   :   ✕   ✓   *fx*   =CONCATENATE("Vouchers (",D18,")")

For **Jet Hub** compatibility, use the **CONCATENATE** function instead of the newer **CONCAT**.

Add Due balance for a vendor

To get the due balance for a vendor we cannot simply sum all of the transactions, as Microsoft Dynamics GP stores all transactions as a positive number. In order to get an accurate due balance, we will first need to get a sum of the credit transactions and a sum of the debit transactions, before subtracting one from the other.

Add sum of credit transactions

To get a sum of all the credit transactions can be done using a **NL** function. Do this by following these steps:

1. Place the cursor in cell **G18** and click the **NL** function button.

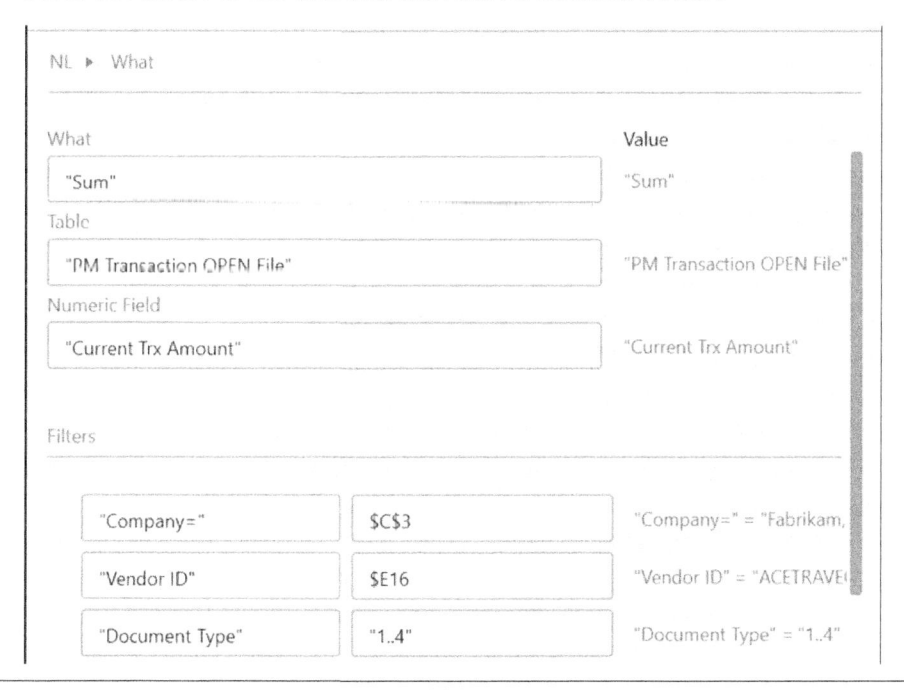

NL ▸ What	
What	**Value**
"Sum"	"Sum"
Table	
"PM Transaction OPEN File"	"PM Transaction OPEN File"
Numeric Field	
"Current Trx Amount"	"Current Trx Amount"
Filters	
"Company=" — $C$3	"Company=" = "Fabrikam,
"Vendor ID" — $E16	"Vendor ID" = "ACETRAVE(
"Document Type" — "1..4"	"Document Type" = "1..4"

Jet Reports with Microsoft Dynamics GP

2. Set **What** to Sum.

3. In **Table** select the **PM Transaction Open File** table (**PM20000**).

4. Set **Field** to Current Trx Amount.

5. Set the first filter field to Company= and the value to a locked cell C3.

6. Set the second filter field to Vendor ID and the filter value to E16, with locked column.

7. Set the third filter field to Document Type and the value 1..4 which will return all voucher types except **Credit Menu** and **Payment**.

8. Click **OK** to save the function.

Add sum of debit transactions

To get a sum of all the debit transactions can be done using a **NL** function. Do this by following these steps:

1. Place the cursor in cell **H18** and click the **NL** function button.

2. Set **What** to Sum.

3. In **Table** select the **PM Transaction Open File** table (**PM20000**).

4. Set **Field** to Current Trx Amount.

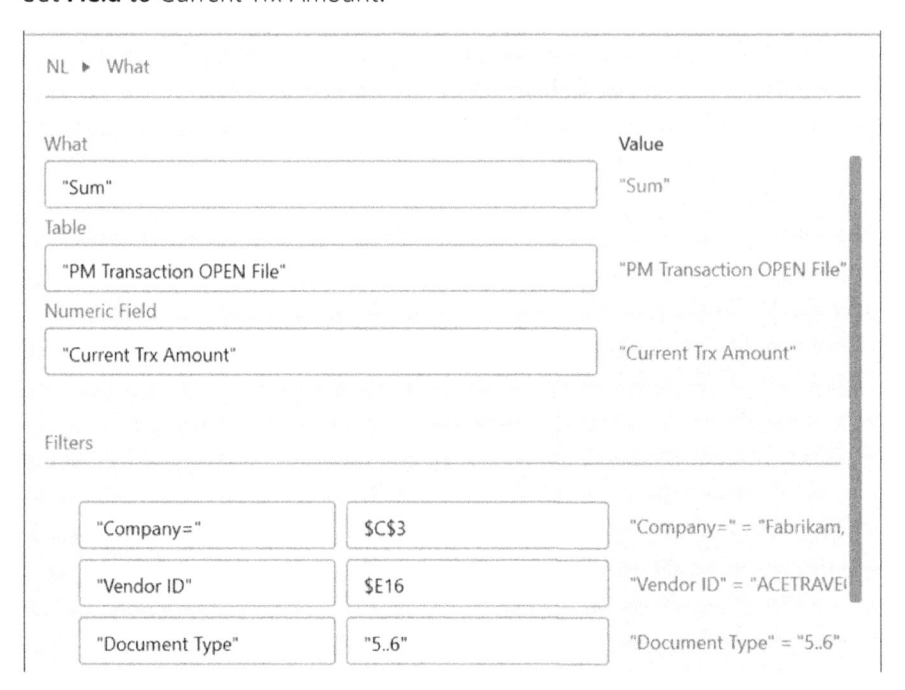

NL ▶ What			
What		Value	
"Sum"		"Sum"	
Table			
"PM Transaction OPEN File"		"PM Transaction OPEN File"	
Numeric Field			
"Current Trx Amount"		"Current Trx Amount"	
Filters			
"Company="	$C$3	"Company=" = "Fabrikam,	
"Vendor ID"	$E16	"Vendor ID" = "ACETRAVE(	
"Document Type"	"5..6"	"Document Type" = "5..6"	

5. Set the first filter field to Company= and the value to a locked cell C3.

Chapter 12: Create a Summary Payables Trial Balance

6. Set the second filter field to Vendor ID and the filter value to E16, with locked column.

7. Set the third filter field to Document Type and the value 5..6 which will return all voucher of types **Credit Menu** and **Payment**.

8. Click **OK** to save the function.

Add Due amount

The **Due** amount is added to cell **I18** by subtracting cell **H18** from **G18**:

| I18 | ▼ | : | × | ✓ | *fx* | =G18-H18 |

Add Current Balance for a vendor

As with the Due balance, the Current balance must be calculated to take into account the unapplied credit transactions.

Add sum of credit transactions

To get a sum of all the credit transactions in **Aging Period 1** can be done using a **NL** function. Do this by following these steps:

1. Place the cursor in cell **J18** and click the **NL** function button.

2. Set **What** to Sum.

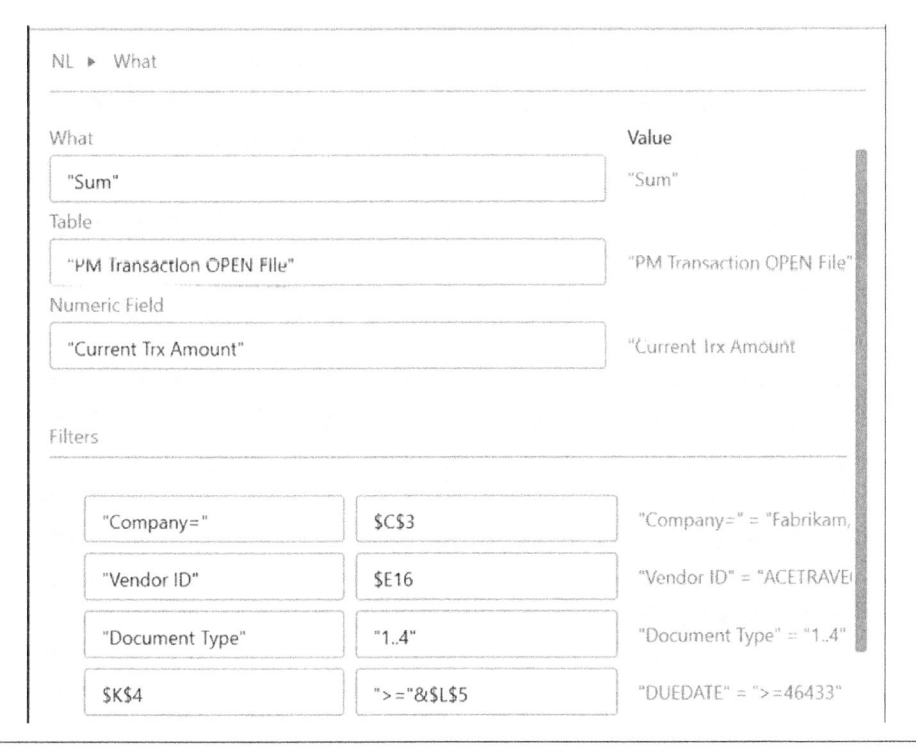

What	Value
"Sum"	"Sum"
Table	
"PM Transaction OPEN File"	"PM Transaction OPEN File"
Numeric Field	
"Current Trx Amount"	"Current Trx Amount"
Filters	
"Company=" $C$3	"Company=" = "Fabrikam,
"Vendor ID" $E16	"Vendor ID" = "ACETRAVE
"Document Type" "1..4"	"Document Type" = "1..4"
$K$4 ">="&$L$5	"DUEDATE" = ">=46433"

113

3. In **Table** select the **PM Transaction Open File** table (**PM20000**).

4. Set **Field** to Current Trx Amount.

5. Set the first filter field to Company= and the value to a locked cell C3.

6. Set the second filter field to Vendor ID and the filter value to E16, with locked column.

7. Set the third filter field to Document Type and the value 1..4 which will return all voucher types except **Credit Menu** and **Payment**.

8. Click **OK** to save the function.

Add sum of debit transactions

To get a sum of all the debit transactions in **Aging Period 1** can be done using a **NL** function. Do this by following these steps:

1. Place the cursor in cell **K18** and click the **NL** function button.

2. Set **What** to Sum.

3. In **Table** select the **PM Transaction Open File** table (**PM20000**).

4. Set **Field** to Current Trx Amount.

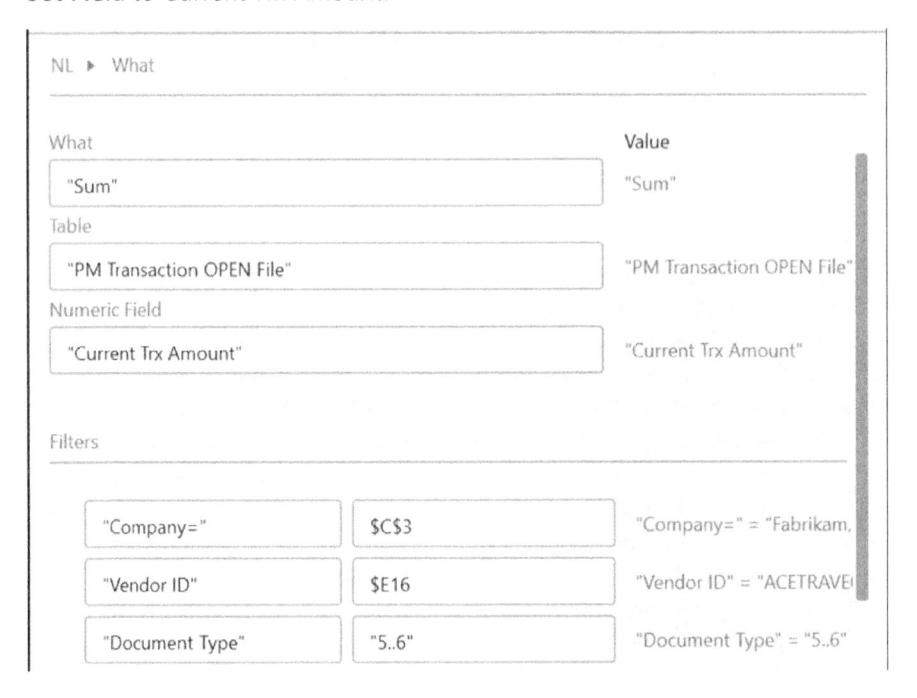

5. Set the first filter field to Company= and the value to a locked cell C3.

6. Set the second filter field to Vendor ID and the filter value to E16, with locked

Chapter 12: Create a Summary Payables Trial Balance

column.

7. Set the third filter field to Document Type and the value 5..6 which will return all voucher of types **Credit Menu** and **Payment**.

8. There is no fourth filter for the credit transactions as we are not aging these.

9. Click **OK** to save the function.

Add Due amount

The **Due** amount is added to cell **L8** by subtracting cell **K18** from **J18**:

L18   fx   =J18-K18

Add aging period 2 balance

The sum of aging period 2 for a vendor can be retrieved using a **NL** function. Do this by following these steps:

1. Place the cursor in cell **M18** and click the **NL** function button.

2. Set **What** to Sum.

3. In **Table** select the **PM Transaction Open File** table (**PM20000**).

4. Set **Field** to Current Trx Amount.

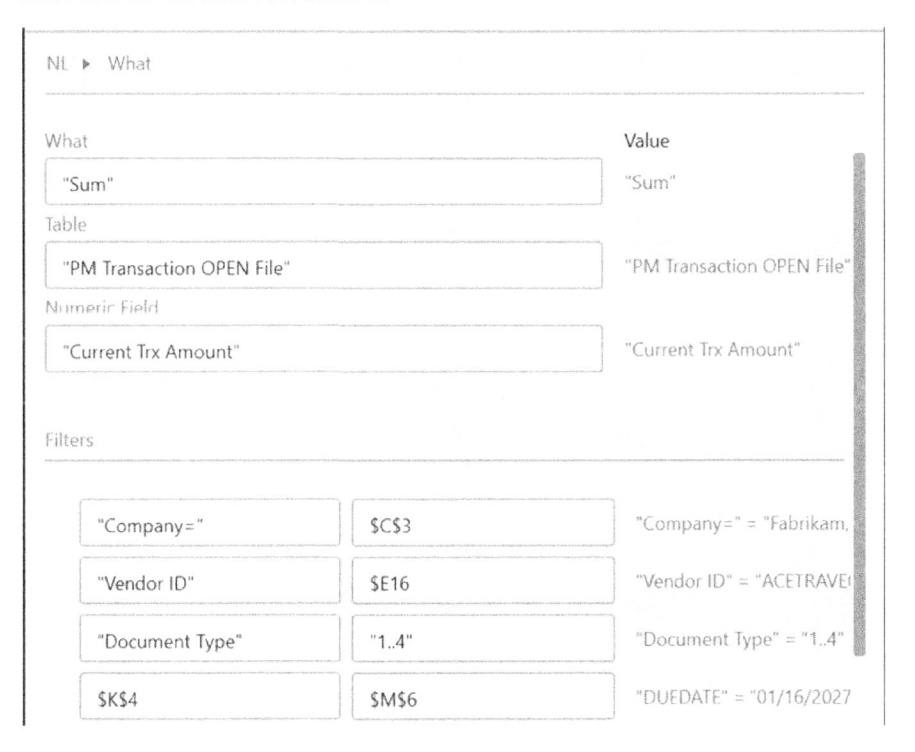

NL ▶ What		
What		Value
"Sum"		"Sum"
Table		
"PM Transaction OPEN File"		"PM Transaction OPEN File"
Numeric Field		
"Current Trx Amount"		"Current Trx Amount"
Filters		
"Company="	$C$3	"Company=" = "Fabrikam,
"Vendor ID"	$E16	"Vendor ID" = "ACETRAVE"
"Document Type"	"1..4"	"Document Type" = "1..4"
$K$4	$M$6	"DUEDATE" = "01/16/2027"

115

5. Set the first filter field to Company= and the value to a locked cell C3.

6. Set the second filter field to Vendor ID and the filter value to E16, with locked column.

7. Set the third filter field to Document Type and the value 1..4 which will return all voucher types except **Credit Menu** and **Payment**.

8. Set the fourth filter field to locked cell **K4** which holds the **Aging By** column and set the value to greater than or equal to the date range in locked cell **M6**.

9. Click **OK** to save the function.

Add aging period 3 balance

The sum of aging period 3 for a vendor can be retrieved using a **NL** function. Do this by following these steps:

1. Place the cursor in cell **N18** and click the **NL** function button.

2. Set **What** to Sum.

3. In **Table** select the **PM Transaction Open File** table (**PM20000**).

4. Set **Field** to Current Trx Amount.

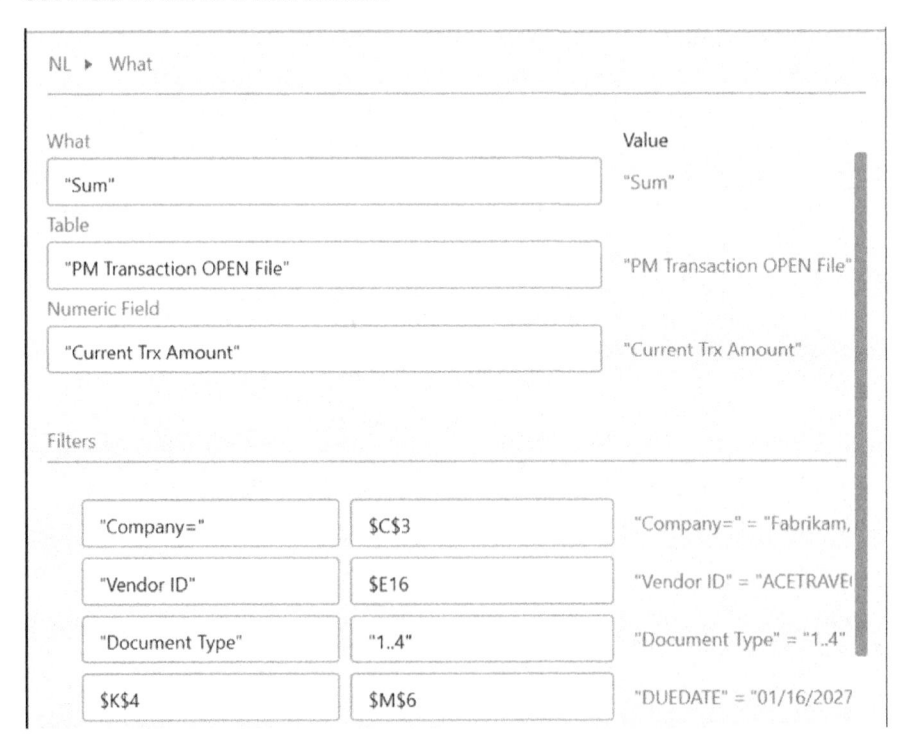

```
NL ▶ What

What                                          Value
"Sum"                                         "Sum"
Table
"PM Transaction OPEN File"                    "PM Transaction OPEN File"
Numeric Field
"Current Trx Amount"                          "Current Trx Amount"

Filters
    "Company="        $C$3                    "Company=" = "Fabrikam,
    "Vendor ID"       $E16                    "Vendor ID" = "ACETRAVE
    "Document Type"   "1..4"                  "Document Type" = "1..4"
    $K$4              $M$6                    "DUEDATE" = "01/16/2027
```

5. Set the first filter field to Company= and the value to a locked cell C3.

Chapter 12: Create a Summary Payables Trial Balance

6. Set the second filter field to Vendor ID and the filter value to E16, with locked column.

7. Set the third filter field to Document Type and the value 1..4 which will return all voucher types except **Credit Menu** and **Payment**.

8. Set the fourth filter field to locked cell **K4** which holds the **Aging By** column and set the value to the date range in locked cell **N6**.

9. Click **OK** to save the function.

Add aging period 4 balance

The sum of aging period 4 for a vendor can be retrieved using a **NL** function. Do this by following these steps:

1. Place the cursor in cell **O18** and click the **NL** function button.

2. Set **What** to Sum.

3. In **Table** select the **PM Transaction Open File** table (**PM20000**).

4. Set **Field** to Current Trx Amount.

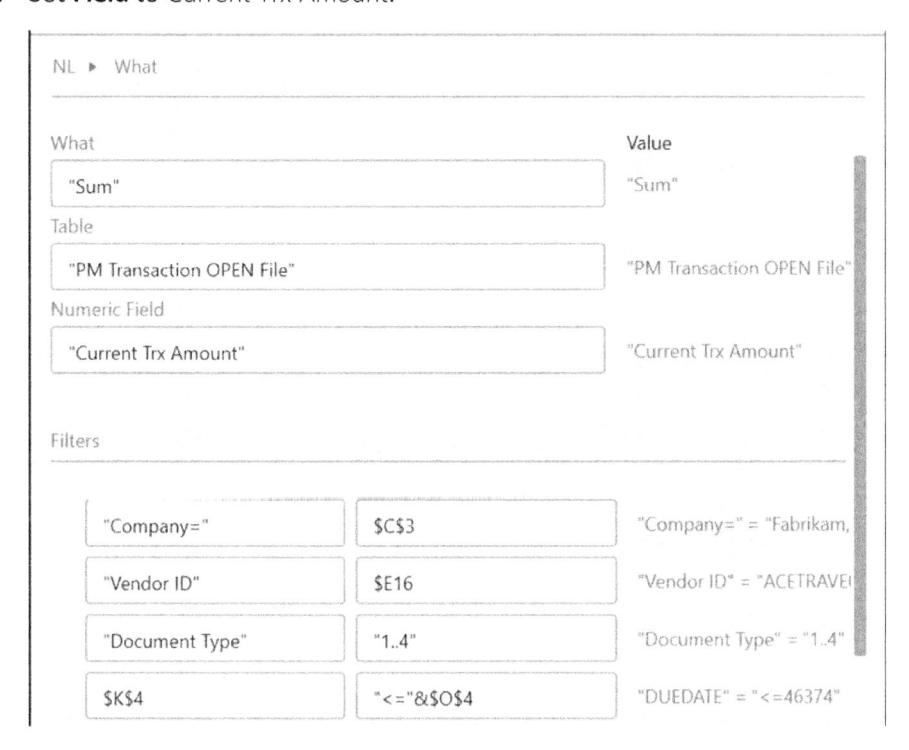

NL ▶ What			
What		Value	
"Sum"		"Sum"	
Table			
"PM Transaction OPEN File"		"PM Transaction OPEN File"	
Numeric Field			
"Current Trx Amount"		"Current Trx Amount"	
Filters			
"Company="	$C$3	"Company=" = "Fabrikam,	
"Vendor ID"	$E16	"Vendor ID" = "ACETRAVE	
"Document Type"	"1..4"	"Document Type" = "1..4"	
$K$4	"<="&$O$4	"DUEDATE" = "<=46374"	

5. Set the first filter field to Company= and the value to a locked cell C3.

6. Set the second filter field to Vendor ID and the filter value to E16, with locked column.

117

7. Set the third filter field to Document Type and the value 1..4 which will return all voucher types except **Credit Menu** and **Payment**.

8. Set the fourth filter field to locked cell **K4** which holds the **Aging By** column and set the value to less than or equal to the date range in locked cell **O6**.

9. Click **OK** to save the function.

Hide vendors with no due balance

Vendors with no due balance are not to be included in this report. To exclude them we can use a formula in column **B** to hide them from view. To do this, I've used an Excel **IF** to check if cell **I18**, locked on column, is equal to zero and, if so, am putting Hide in the cells **D15** to **D19**; if it is not zero, I am putting Show in those cells.

| B15 | ▼ | : | × | ✓ | fx | =IF($I18=0,"Hide","Show") |

Add field for counting creditors

In order to include a count of the included vendors at the bottom of the report we need to include a count for this. There are several approaches that could be taken to get this, but I have opted for a cell containing one which will be included in an Excel SUM function in the report footer.

As the report will be included only vendors with a Due balance, I am checking if cell **I18**, locked on column, is equal to 0 and using 0 in cell **C18** otherwise I am using 1:

| C18 | ▼ | : | × | ✓ | fx | =IF(I18=0,0,1) |

Add total count of vendors

The total count of vendors is added to cell **E21** by using the Excel SUM of cells **C18:C20**:

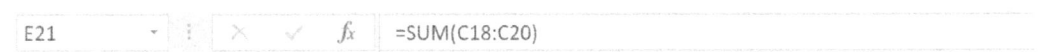

| E21 | ▼ | : | × | ✓ | fx | =SUM(C18:C20) |

Add total count of vouchers

The total count of vouchers is added to cell **F21** by using the Excel SUM of cells **D18:D20**:

| F21 | ▼ | : | × | ✓ | fx | =SUM(D18:D20) |

Add Due total

The total **Due** is added to cell **I21** by using the Excel SUM of cells **I18:I20**:

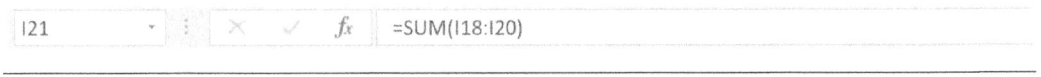

| I21 | ▼ | : | × | ✓ | fx | =SUM(I18:I20) |

Chapter 12: Create a Summary Payables Trial Balance

Add Aging Period totals

The **Aging Period 1** total is added by using the Excel SUM of cells **L18:L20**:

| L21 | ▼ | : | × | ✓ | *fx* | =SUM(L18:L20) |

Repeat this moving across through columns **M**, **N** and **O** for **Aging Periods 2**, **3**, and **4**.

Report ready for testing

If you have followed the instructions the report should look like the example below, and is now ready for testing.

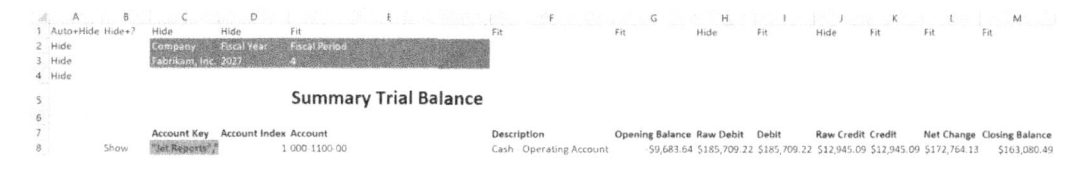

Run report

Run the report by following these steps:

1. Click the **Run** button on the action pane.

2. This will take the Jet Reports out of **Design Mode** and prompt with the **Report Options**:

3. Enter your criteria and click **Run**.

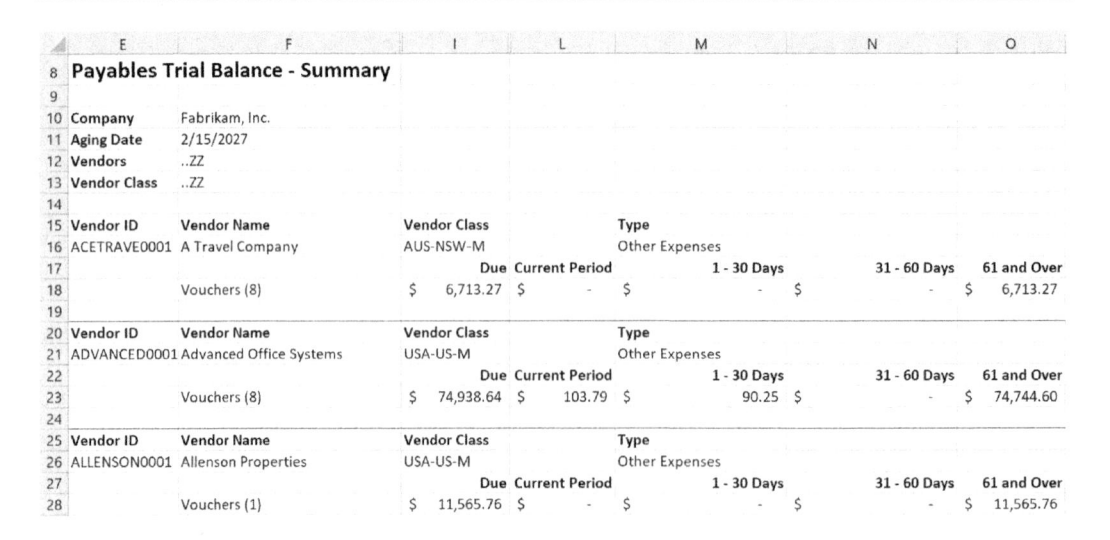

	E	F	I	L	M	N	O
8	**Payables Trial Balance - Summary**						
9							
10	Company	Fabrikam, Inc.					
11	Aging Date	2/15/2027					
12	Vendors	..ZZ					
13	Vendor Class	..ZZ					
14							
15	Vendor ID	Vendor Name	Vendor Class		Type		
16	ACETRAVE0001	A Travel Company	AUS-NSW-M		Other Expenses		
17			Due	Current Period	1 - 30 Days	31 - 60 Days	61 and Over
18		Vouchers (8)	$ 6,713.27	$ -	$ -	$ -	$ 6,713.27
19							
20	Vendor ID	Vendor Name	Vendor Class		Type		
21	ADVANCED0001	Advanced Office Systems	USA-US-M		Other Expenses		
22			Due	Current Period	1 - 30 Days	31 - 60 Days	61 and Over
23		Vouchers (8)	$ 74,938.64	$ 103.79	$ 90.25	$ -	$ 74,744.60
24							
25	Vendor ID	Vendor Name	Vendor Class		Type		
26	ALLENSON0001	Allenson Properties	USA-US-M		Other Expenses		
27			Due	Current Period	1 - 30 Days	31 - 60 Days	61 and Over
28		Vouchers (1)	$ 11,565.76	$ -	$ -	$ -	$ 11,565.76

Summary

In this chapter we have taken a look at creating a **Summary Payables Aged Trial Balance** report. In the next chapter, we'll take a look at creating a **Purchase Order by Vendor** report.

13

Create a Purchase Order by Vendor report

In this chapter, we're going to create a **Purchase Order by Vendor** report which includes both open and historic transactions.

Design the report

The **Purchase Order by Vendor** report we're going to build will:

- Allow the user to specify options for:
    - Company.
    - Vendor ID.
    - Date Range.
- Ordered the output by **Vendor ID** and by **Purchase Order Number**.
- Include only vendors with purchase orders.
- For each vendor include:
    - Vendor Number
    - Vendor Name.
    - Vendor Class.
- Include both work and history purchase orders.
- For each purchase order include:
    - PO Number.

- o Document Date.
- o Required Date.
- o PO Lines including:
  - Item Number.
  - Item Description.
  - Quantity Ordered.
  - Unit Cost.
  - Extended Cost.
  - Inventory/Purchasing Account.
- Include subtotals for each purchase order.
- Include totals at the bottom.

The report will be laid out in this format:

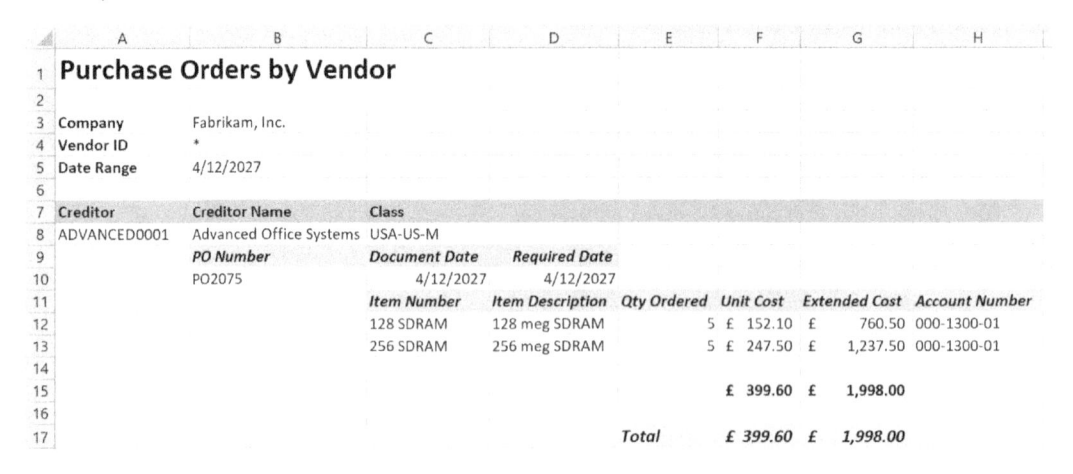

	A	B	C	D	E	F	G	H
1	**Purchase Orders by Vendor**							
2								
3	Company	Fabrikam, Inc.						
4	Vendor ID	*						
5	Date Range	4/12/2027						
6								
7	Creditor	Creditor Name	Class					
8	ADVANCED0001	Advanced Office Systems	USA-US-M					
9		PO Number	Document Date	Required Date				
10		PO2075	4/12/2027	4/12/2027				
11			Item Number	Item Description	Qty Ordered	Unit Cost	Extended Cost	Account Number
12			128 SDRAM	128 meg SDRAM	5	£ 152.10	£ 760.50	000-1300-01
13			256 SDRAM	256 meg SDRAM	5	£ 247.50	£ 1,237.50	000-1300-01
14								
15						£ 399.60	£ 1,998.00	
16								
17					Total	£ 399.60	£ 1,998.00	

Create the Report page

Create a new Excel workbook and change the tab name to **Report**. I have set the layout of the report up with the first five columns and first four rows highlighted in yellow as they will be set to **Hide**.

Column **B** has **Hide+?** added as I will use this column to control visibility of rows depending on if there is data to display or not.

The six fields, **C2** to **E3**, for the options and their headings have had a fill of blue set.

A green fill set for the fields which will hold the **NL** function replicator and the rows they cover:

Chapter 13: Create a Purchase Orders by Vendor report

- **C11** to **C30** for the vendor replicator.
- **D13** to **D19** for the word purchase order replicator.
- **D21** to **D27** for the history purchase order replicator.
- **E16** for the work purchase order line replicator.
- **E24** for the history purchase order line replicator.

The report header and column headings have all been placed and formatting applied with a **Fit** applied for the column widths in the first row. Column **M** is set to hide as it will hold the account index for the inventory/purchasing account which will be used to get the account number string.

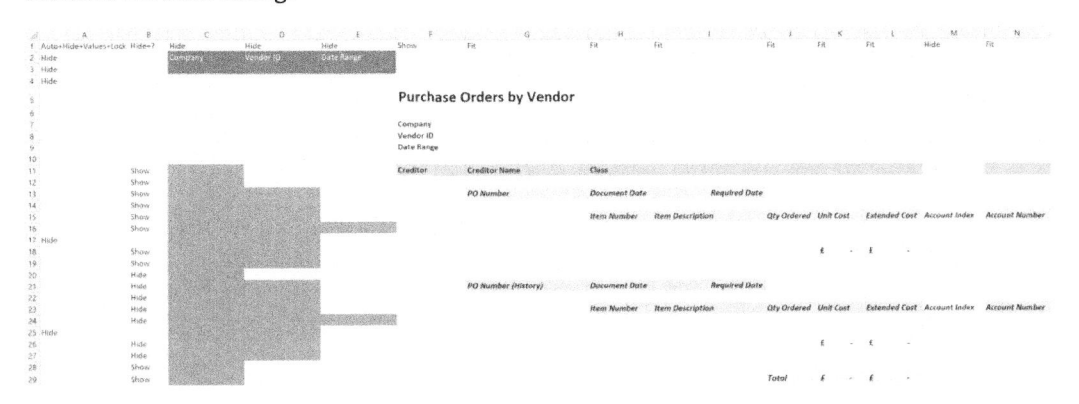

Create the Options page

For the report we will be providing three options for the user to set. To create the options, follow these steps:

1. Click the **Report Options** button on the **Tools** tab of the **Jet** action pane.

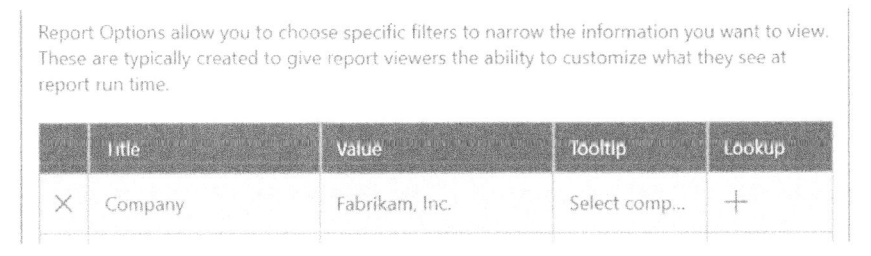

2. Enter a **Title** of Company.
3. Enter a **Value** of Fabrikam, Inc..
4. Enter a **Tooltip** of Select company.
5. Click the plus icon in the **Lookup** column.
6. The **What** will default to Lookup; click the **Nested Jet Function** button on the

action pane and click **Insert NP**.

7. Set the **What** to Companies.

```
NL ▶ Table ▶ NP ▶ What

What                                    Value
"Companies"                             "Companies"
Company Filter

Data Source

```

8. Click **Back** to save the function.

9. Enter Name in **Field** (this must be done manually as the lookup is blank).

```
NL ▶ Field

What                                    Value
"Lookup"                                "Lookup"
Table
NP("Companies")                         "||""Companies"","""",""""
Field
"Name"                                  "Name"
```

10. Click **OK** to save the **Company** lookup.

11. On the second row, enter a **Title** of Vendor ID.

12. Enter a **Value of** * which will give us a range of all vendors.

13. Enter a **Tooltip** of Select vendor.

14. Click the plus icon in the **Lookup** column.

15. The **What** will default to Lookup; select the PM Vendor Master File table (PM00200).

16. Select the **Fields** of Vendor ID and Vendor Name.

17. In the first filter select Vendor Name and in the filter add *.

18. Click the arrows to the left until an up arrow is shown so that the returned vendors are in alphabetic order.

19. Click **OK** to save the **Vendor** lookup.

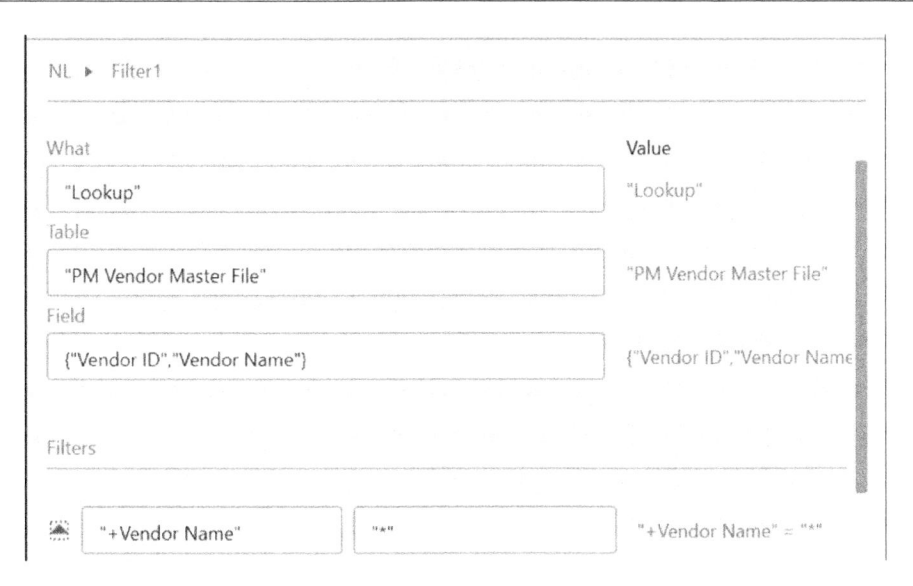

Chapter 13: Create a Purchase Orders by Vendor report

NL ▶ Filter1	
What	**Value**
"Lookup"	"Lookup"
Table	
"PM Vendor Master File"	"PM Vendor Master File"
Field	
{"Vendor ID","Vendor Name"}	{"Vendor ID","Vendor Name"}
Filters	
"+Vendor Name" "*"	"+Vendor Name" = "*"

20. On the third row, enter a **Title** of Aging Date.

21. Enter date in the **Value**.

22. Enter a **Tooltip** of Enter dates.

23. Review the added lookups and ensure they are correct.

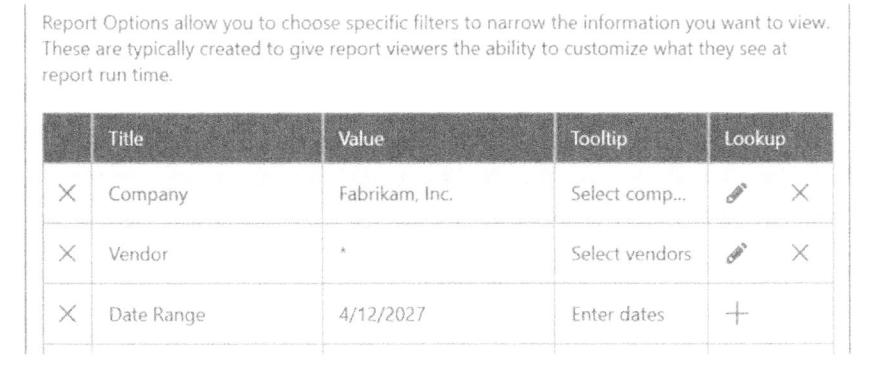

    Report Options allow you to choose specific filters to narrow the information you want to view. These are typically created to give report viewers the ability to customize what they see at report run time.

	Title	Value	Tooltip	Lookup
✕	Company	Fabrikam, Inc.	Select comp...	✏ ✕
✕	Vendor	*	Select vendors	✏ ✕
✕	Date Range	4/12/2027	Enter dates	+

24. Click **Close** to close the **Report Options** window and generate the **Options** page.

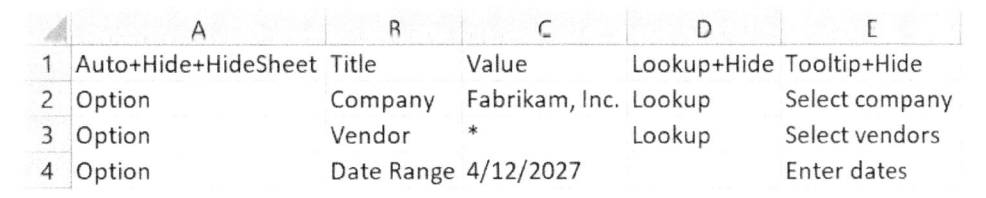

	A	B	C	D	E
1	Auto+Hide+HideSheet	Title	Value	Lookup+Hide	Tooltip+Hide
2	Option	Company	Fabrikam, Inc.	Lookup	Select company
3	Option	Vendor	*	Lookup	Select vendors
4	Option	Date Range	4/12/2027		Enter dates

The options can be edited by clicking the **Report Options** button again or by editing directly through the **Options** page; the **Lookup** can be amended by selecting an entry in column **D** and clicking the **Jet Function** button.

Set Options on Report page

With the **Options** page created, we need to use an **NP** function to bring them to the **Report** page to use:

Do that by following these steps:

1. Place the cursor in cell **C3** and click the **NP** function button.

2. Set the **What** to Eval.

3. Place the cursor in the **Formula** field and select the cell on the **Options** page containing the company value (which is cell **C**), lock the rows and columns.

4. Click **OK** to save the function.

NP ▶ What	
What	Value
"Eval"	"Eval"
Formula	
"='Options'!$C$2"	"='Options'!$C$2"

5. Repeat steps 1 through 4 for the **Vendor ID** and **Date Range**.

The **Report** page should now be showing the values of the **Options** in the blue filled cells.

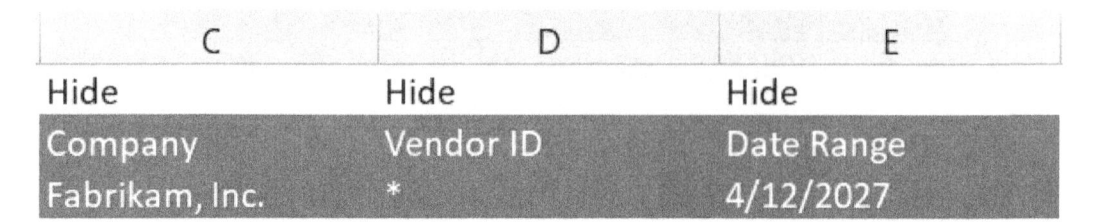

C	D	E
Hide	Hide	Hide
Company	Vendor ID	Date Range
Fabrikam, Inc.	*	4/12/2027

Add parameters to report

On this report I am going to include the report options to the output so people looking at the report will know the options used to generate it. These will be in cells F10 to F13:

As we already have the report options brought through to the blue fill cells, we can use a simple Excel formula to make them visible:

1. To add the **Company**, place the cursor in cell **G7** and enter =C3.

2. To add the **Vendor ID**, place the cursor in cell **G8** and enter =D3.

3. To add the **Date Range**, place the cursor in cell **G9** and enter =E3.

Add Record Key for PM Vendor Master File

The first field to add is the record key replicator from the **PM Vendor Master File** table (**PM00200**). Do this by performing these steps:

1. Place the cursor in cell **C11** and click the **NL** function button.
2. Set **What** to Rows=20.
3. In **Table** select the **PM Vendor Master File** table (**PM00200**).
4. Leave **Field** blank as this is to be a record key replicator.
5. Add a first filter for Company= and the value to a locked cell C3.
6. Set the second filter field to Vendor ID and the filter value to F3, with locked column and row.

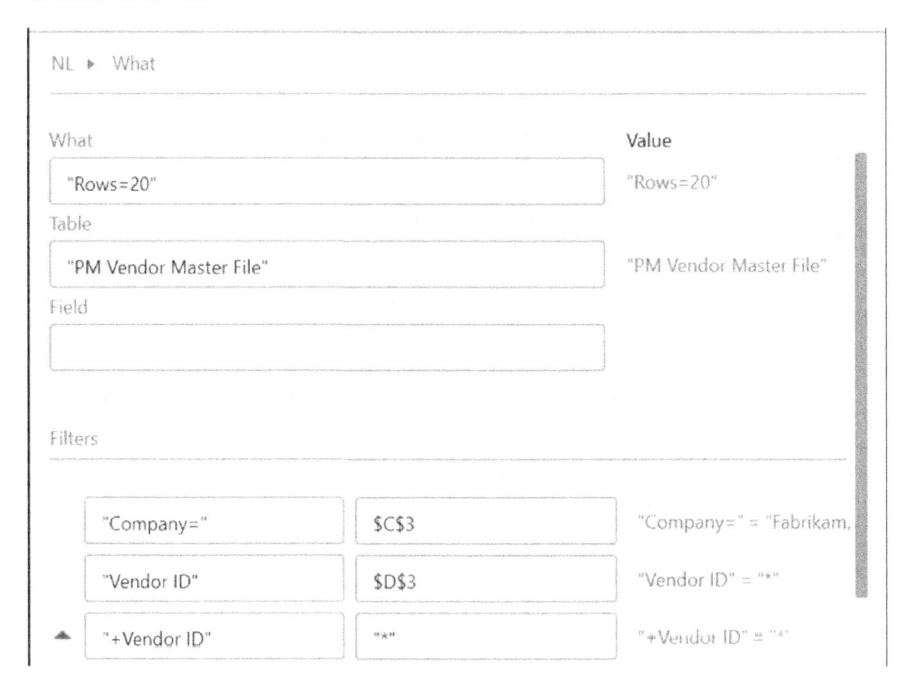

7. To order the accounts in ascending order, set the third filter to Vendor ID and the value to * and click the arrow button till it shows an arrow pointing up.
8. Click **OK** to save the function.

Add Vendor Master fields

There are four fields, **Vendor ID**, **Vendor Name**, **Vendor Class** and **User Defined 1,** which we can extract using the record key. Do this by performing these steps:

1. To add the **Vendor ID**, place the cursor in cell **F12** and click the **NF** function button.

NF ▶ Key	
Key	**Value**
$C11	"""Jet Reports""",""Fabrikam,
Field	
"Vendor ID"	"Vendor ID"

2. In the **Key** select the record key replicator which is in cell **C11** and switch it to lock by the column.

3. In the **Field** select Vendor ID.

4. Click **OK** to save the function.

5. Repeat steps 1 through 4 in cell **G12** and select **Vendor Name**.

6. Repeat steps 1 through 4 in cell **H16** and select **Vendor Class ID**.

Add Record Key for Purchase Order Work

The first field to add is the record key replicator from the **Purchase Order Work** table (**POP10100**). Do this by performing these steps:

1. Place the cursor in cell **D13** and click the **NL** function button.

2. Set **What** to Rows=7.

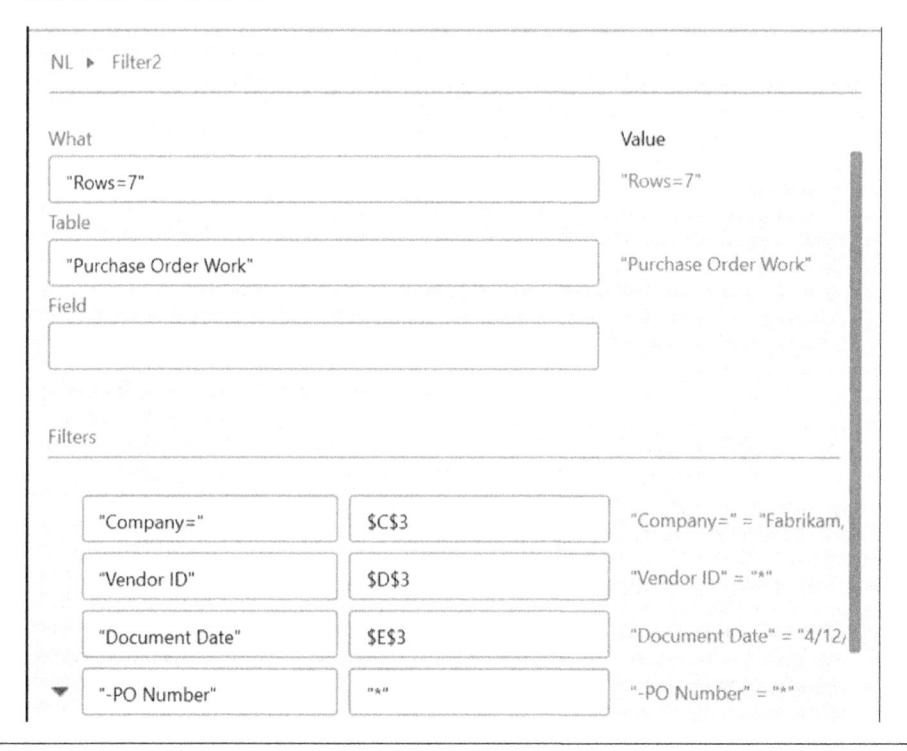

NL ▶ Filter2		
What		**Value**
"Rows=7"		"Rows=7"
Table		
"Purchase Order Work"		"Purchase Order Work"
Field		
Filters		
"Company="	$C$3	"Company=" = "Fabrikam,
"Vendor ID"	$D$3	"Vendor ID" = "*"
"Document Date"	$E$3	"Document Date" = "4/12/
"-PO Number"	"*"	"-PO Number" = "*"

Chapter 13: Create a Purchase Orders by Vendor report

3. In **Table** select the **Purchase Order Work** table (**POP10100**).
4. Leave **Field** blank as this is to be a record key replicator.
5. Add a first filter for Company= and the value to a locked cell C3.
6. Set the second filter field to Vendor ID and the filter value to D3, with locked column and row.
7. Set the third filter field to Document Date and the filter value to E3, with locked column and row.
8. To order the accounts in ascending order, set the fourth filter to PO Number and the value to * and click the arrow button till it shows an arrow pointing up.
9. Click **OK** to save the function.

Add Purchase Order Work fields

There are three fields, **PO Number**, **Document Date** and **Required Date,** which we can extract using the record key. Do this by performing these steps:

1. To add the **Vendor ID**, place the cursor in cell **G14** and click the **NF** function button.

```
NF ▶ Key

Key                                    Value
$D13                                   """Jet Reports""",""""Fabrikam,
Field
"PO Number"                            "PO Number"
```

2. In the **Key** select the record key replicator which is in cell **C11** and switch it to lock by the column.
3. In the **Field** select Vendor ID.
4. Click **OK** to save the function.
5. Repeat steps 1 through 4 in cell **G14** and select **Document Date**.
6. Repeat steps 1 through 4 in cell **H14** and select **Required Date**.

Add Record Key for Purchase Order Line

The first field to add is the record key replicator from the **Purchase Order Line** table (**POP10110**). Do this by performing these steps:

1. Place the cursor in cell **E16** and click the **NL** function button.
2. Set **What** to Rows.
3. In **Table** select the **Purchase Order Line** table (**POP10110**).
4. Leave **Field** blank as this is to be a record key replicator.
5. Add a first filter for Company= and the value to a locked cell C3.
6. Set the second filter field to PO Number and the filter value to G3, with locked column. To ensure there are no errors add "@@" & before the cell reference.
7. To sort the purchase orders by PO number descending, click the arrow button until it changes to an arrow pointing down
8. To make sure blanket purchase orders don't result in extra lines being including, set the third filter field to LineNumber and the filter value to "<>" & 0.

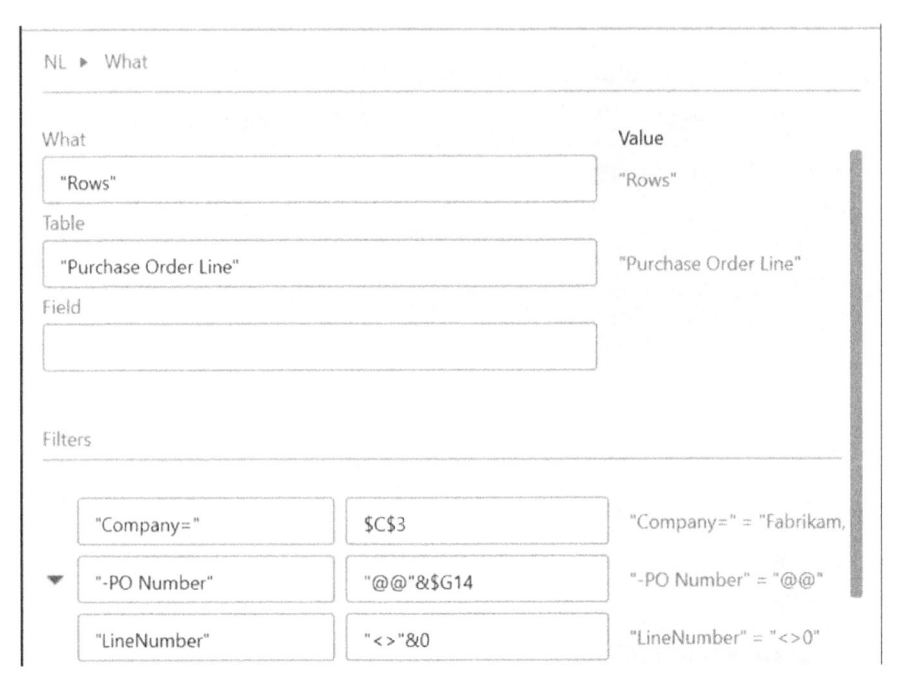

NL ▶ What		
What		Value
"Rows"		"Rows"
Table		
"Purchase Order Line"		"Purchase Order Line"
Field		
Filters		
"Company="	$C$3	"Company=" = "Fabrikam,
"-PO Number"	"@@"&$G14	"-PO Number" = "@@"
"LineNumber"	"<>"&0	"LineNumber" = "<>0"

9. Click **OK** to save the function.

Add Purchase Order Line fields

There are six fields, **Item Number**, **Item Description**, **Quantity Ordered**, **Unit Cost**, **Extended Cost** and **Inventory Index,** which we can extract using the record key. Do this by performing these steps:

1. To add the **Item Number**, place the cursor in cell **H16** and click the **NF** function button.

```
NF ▶ Key

Key                                      Value
┌─────────────────────────────────┐
│ $E16                            │      ""
└─────────────────────────────────┘
Field
┌─────────────────────────────────┐
│ "Item Number"                   │      "Item Number"
└─────────────────────────────────┘
```

2. In the **Key** select the record key replicator which is in cell **E15** and switch it to lock by the column.

3. In the **Field** select Item Number.

4. Click **OK** to save the function.

5. Repeat steps 1 through 4 in cell **I16** and select Item Description.

6. Repeat steps 1 through 4 in cell **J16** and select QTY Ordered.

7. Repeat steps 1 through 4 in cell **K16** and select Unit Cost.

8. Repeat steps 1 through 4 in cell **L16** and select Extended Cost.

9. Repeat steps 1 through 4 in cell **M16** and select Inventory Index.

Add Account Number to Purchase Order Lines

The report is to include the account number which is not directly accessible in the Purchase Order Line table, but the Inventory Index can be used to get this field. To add the account number, follow these steps:

1. Place the cursor in field **N16** and click the **NL** function button.

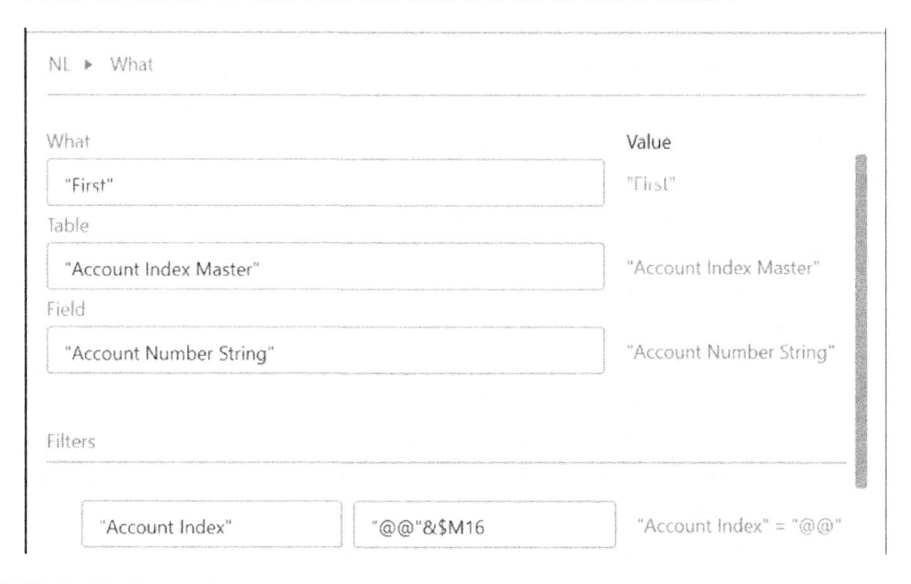

```
NL ▶ What

What                                     Value
┌─────────────────────────────────┐
│ "First"                         │      "First"
└─────────────────────────────────┘
Table
┌─────────────────────────────────┐
│ "Account Index Master"          │      "Account Index Master"
└─────────────────────────────────┘
Field
┌─────────────────────────────────┐
│ "Account Number String"         │      "Account Number String"
└─────────────────────────────────┘

Filters
┌──────────────────┐  ┌──────────────────┐
│ "Account Index"  │  │ "@@"&$M16        │    "Account Index" = "@@"
└──────────────────┘  └──────────────────┘
```

Jet Reports with Microsoft Dynamics GP

2. Set the **What** to **First**.

3. In **Table** select the **Account Index Master** table (**GL00105**).

4. In **Field** select **Account Number String**.

5. Set the filter to **Account Index** and the value to "@@" & $M16, including the **@@** to avoid errors if there are no purchase order lines.

Add subtotals for Purchase Order Lines

Subtotals can be added for the **Unit Cost** and **Extended Cost** columns using standard Excel functionality:

1. To add the **Unit Cost** subtotal in cell **K18**, enter the following formula (the sum spans two rows to ensure it will sum all rows as the replicator expands):

   `K18    fx    =SUM(K16:K17)`

2. Repeat in cell **L18** for the **Extended Cost** subtotal.

Add Record Key for Purchase Order History

The first field to add is the record key replicator from the **Purchase Order History** table (**POP30100**). Do this by performing these steps:

1. Place the cursor in cell **D21** and click the **NL** function button.

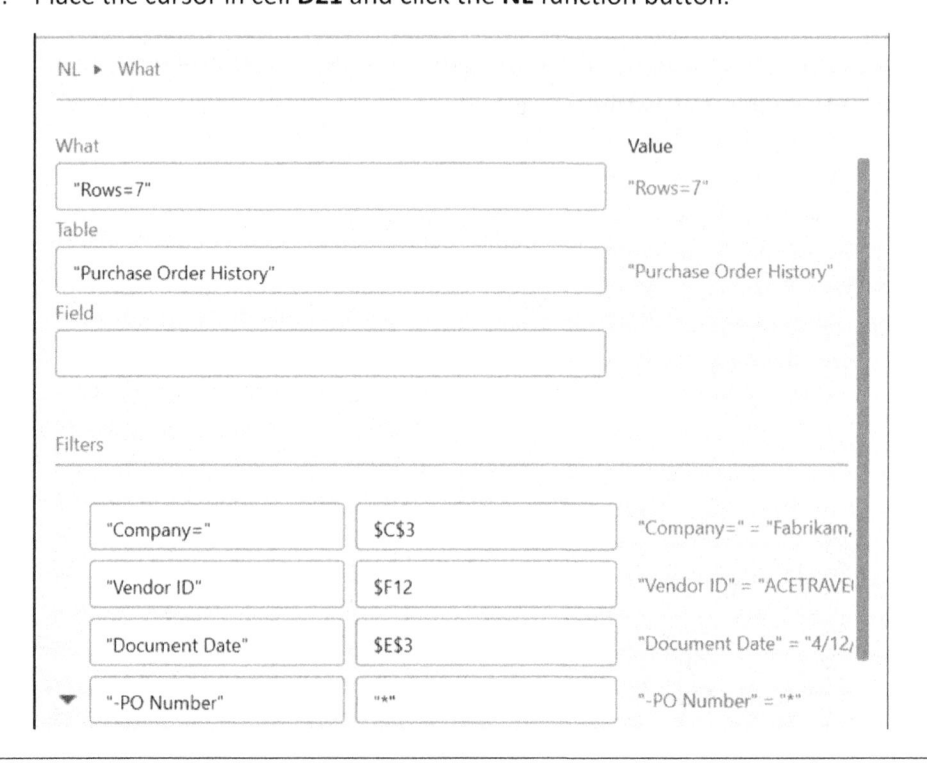

NL ▶ What		
What		**Value**
"Rows=7"		"Rows=7"
Table		
"Purchase Order History"		"Purchase Order History"
Field		
Filters		
"Company="	$C$3	"Company=" = "Fabrikam,
"Vendor ID"	$F12	"Vendor ID" = "ACETRAVE
"Document Date"	$E$3	"Document Date" = "4/12/
"-PO Number"	"*"	"-PO Number" = "*"

132

Chapter 13: Create a Purchase Orders by Vendor report

2. Set **What** to Rows=7.

3. In **Table** select the **Purchase Order History** table (**POP30100**).

4. Leave **Field** blank as this is to be a record key replicator.

5. Add a first filter for Company= and the value to a locked cell C3.

6. Set the second filter field to Vendor ID and the filter value to D3, with locked column and row.

7. Set the third filter field to Document Date and the filter value to E3, with locked column and row.

8. To order the accounts in ascending order, set the fourth filter to PO Number and the value to * and click the arrow button till it shows an arrow pointing up.

9. Click **OK** to save the function.

Add Purchase Order History fields

There are three fields, **PO Number**, **Document Date** and **Required Date,** which we can extract using the record key. Do this by performing these steps:

1. To add the **PO Number**, place the cursor in cell **G22** and click the **NF** function button.

```
NF ▶ Key

Key                                          Value
$D21                                         ""
Field
"PO Number"                                  "PO Number"
```

2. In the **Key** select the record key replicator which is in cell **D21** and switch it to lock by the column.

3. In the **Field** select PO Number.

4. Click **OK** to save the function.

5. Repeat steps 1 through 4 in cell **H22** and select **Document Date**.

6. Repeat steps 1 through 4 in cell **I22** and select **Required Date**.

Add Record Key for Purchase Order Line History

The first field to add is the record key replicator from the **Purchase Order Line History** table (**POP30110**). Do this by performing these steps:

1. Place the cursor in cell **E24** and click the **NL** function button.
2. Set **What** to Rows.
3. In **Table** select the **Purchase Order Line** table (**POP30110**).
4. Leave **Field** blank as this is to be a record key replicator.

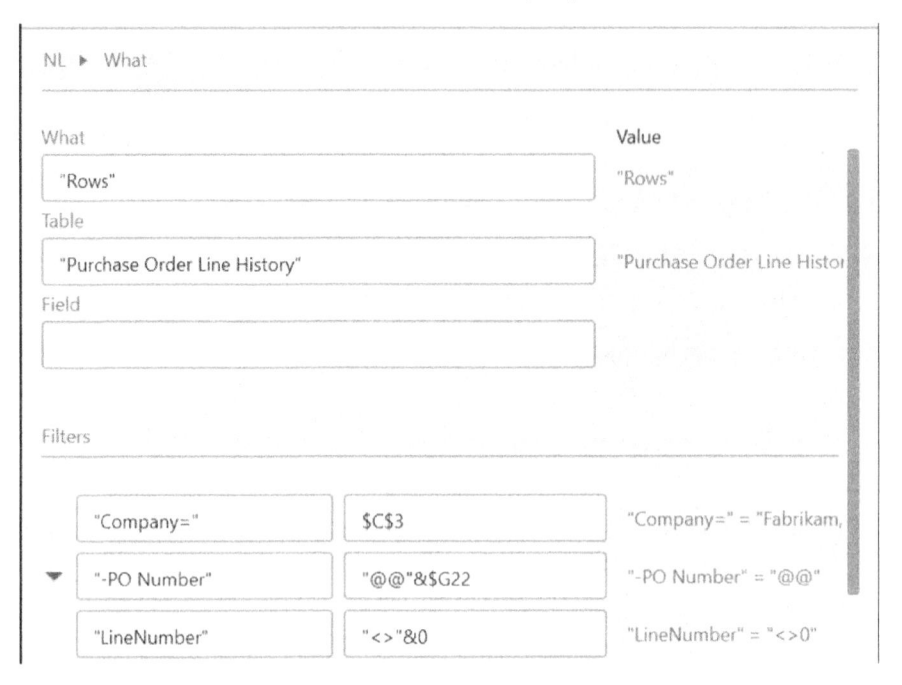

NL ▶ What		
What		Value
"Rows"		"Rows"
Table		
"Purchase Order Line History"		"Purchase Order Line Histor"
Field		
Filters		
"Company="	$C$3	"Company=" = "Fabrikam,
"-PO Number"	"@@"&$G22	"-PO Number" = "@@"
"LineNumber"	"<>"&0	"LineNumber" = "<>0"

5. Add a first filter for Company= and the value to a locked cell C3.
6. Set the second filter field to PO Number and the filter value to G3, with locked column. To ensure there are no errors add "@@" & before the cell reference.
7. To sort the purchase orders by PO number descending, click the arrow button until it changes to an arrow pointing down
8. To make sure blanket purchase orders don't result in extra lines being including, set the third filter field to LineNumber and the filter value to "<>" & 0.
9. Click **OK** to save the function.

Add Purchase Order Line History fields

There are six fields, **Item Number**, **Item Description**, **Quantity Ordered**, **Unit Cost**, **Extended Cost** and **Inventory Index,** which we can extract using the record key. Do this by performing these steps:

1. To add the **Item Number**, place the cursor in cell **H24** and click the **NF** function button.

2. In the **Key** select the record key replicator which is in cell **E24** and switch it to lock by the column.

3. In the **Field** select Item Number.

```
NF ▸ Key

Key                                    Value
$E24                                   ...
Field
"Item Number"                          "Item Number"
```

4. Click **OK** to save the function.

5. Repeat steps 1 through 4 in cell **I24** and select Item Description.

6. Repeat steps 1 through 4 in cell **J24** and select QTY Ordered.

7. Repeat steps 1 through 4 in cell **K24** and select Unit Cost.

8. Repeat steps 1 through 4 in cell **L24** and select Extended Cost.

9. Repeat steps 1 through 4 in cell **M24** and select Inventory Index.

Add Account Number to Purchase Order Line History

The report is to include the account number which is not directly accessible in the Purchase Order Line History table, but the Inventory Index can be used to get this field. To add the account number, follow these steps:

1. Place the cursor in field **N24** and click the **NL** function button.

2. Set the What to **First**.

3. In **Table** select the **Account Index Master** table (**GL00105**).

4. In **Field** select **Account Number String**.

Jet Reports with Microsoft Dynamics GP

NL ► What	
What	Value
"First"	"First"
Table	
"Account Index Master"	"Account Index Master"
Field	
"Account Number String"	"Account Number String"
Filters	
"Account Index" "@@"&$M24	"Account Index" = "@@"

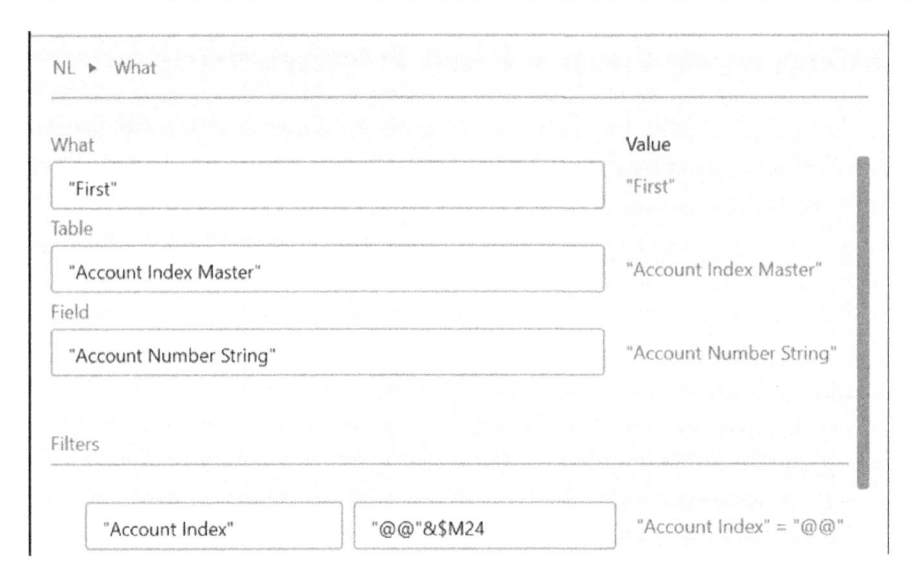

5. Set the filter to **Account Index** and the value to "@@" & $M24, including the **@@** to avoid errors if there are no purchase order lines.

Add subtotals for Purchase Order Line History

Subtotals can be added for the **Unit Cost** and **Extended Cost** columns using standard Excel functionality:

3. To add the **Unit Cost** subtotal in cell **K26**, enter the following formula (the sum spans two rows to ensure it will sum all rows as the replicator expands):

    K26   fx   =SUM(K24:K25)

4. Repeat in cell **L26** for the **Extended Cost** subtotal.

Add vendor total for purchase orders

Totals can be added for the **Unit Cost** and **Extended Cost** columns using standard Excel functionality:

5. To add the **Unit Cost** total in cell **K29**, enter the following formula to sum the subtotals:

    K29   fx   =K18+K26

6. Repeat in cell **L29** for the **Extended Cost** total.

Hide rows when no data to display

Rows can be hidden using a standard Excel formula in column **B**. As this report has several sections, there are several calculations required.

Chapter 13: Create a Purchase Orders by Vendor report

Calculation for Vendor Master rows

Rows **11** and **12** are the **Vendor Master** rows, which can be hidden using a formula checking if the purchase order **Unit Cost** total is equal to 0:

B11   fx   =IF(K29=0,"Hide","Show")

Calculation for Purchase Order Work rows

Rows **13**, **14** and **15** are the **Purchase Order Work** rows, which can be hidden using a formula checking if the **PO Number** is blank:

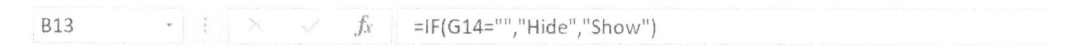

B13   fx   =IF(G14="","Hide","Show")

Calculation for Purchase Order Line rows

Rows **16** is the **Purchase Order Line** row, which can be hidden using a formula checking the **Item Number** is blank:

B16   fx   =IF(H16="","Hide","Show")

Calculation for Purchase Order Work subtotal row

Rows **18** and **19** are the PO subtotal rows, which can be hidden using a formula checking the purchase order **Unit Cost** total is equal to 0:

B18   fx   =IF(K18=0,"Hide","Show")

Calculation for Purchase Order History rows

Rows **20**, **21** and **22** are the **Purchase Order History** rows, which can be hidden using a formula checking if the **PO Number** is blank:

B20   fx   =IF(G22="","Hide","Show")

Calculation for Purchase Order Line rows

Rows **24** is the **Purchase Order Line** row, which can be hidden using a formula checking the **Item Number** is blank:

B24   fx   =IF(H24="","Hide","Show")

Calculation for Purchase Order Work subtotal row

Rows **26** and **27** are the PO subtotal rows, which can be hidden using a formula checking the purchase order **Unit Cost** total is equal to 0:

B26   fx   =IF(K26=0,"Hide","Show")

Calculation for purchase order total row

Rows **28**, **29** and **30** are the vendor total rows, which can be hidden using a formula checking if the total **Unit Cost** is equal to 0 :

| B29 | ▼ | : | × | ✓ | *fx* | =IF(K29=0,"Hide","Show") |

Report ready for testing

If you have followed the instructions the report should look like the example below, and is now ready for testing.

Run report

Run the report by following these steps:

1. Click the **Run** button on the action pane.

2. This will take the Jet Reports out of **Design Mode** and prompt with the **Report Options**:

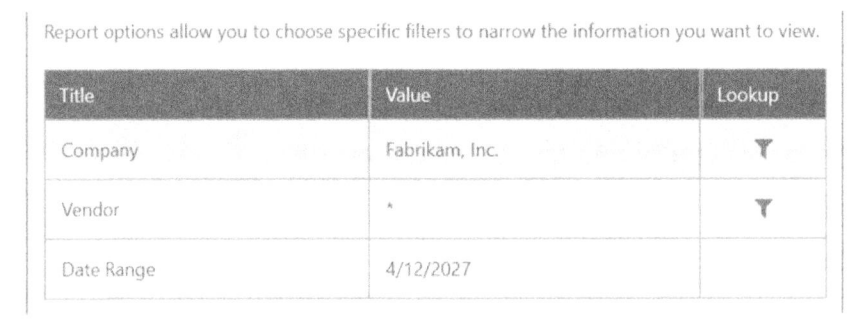

3. Enter your criteria and click **Run**.

Chapter 13: Create a Purchase Orders by Vendor report

	F	G	H	I	J	K	L	N
5	**Purchase Orders by Vendor**							
6								
7	Company	Fabrikam, Inc.						
8	Vendor ID	*						
9	Date Range	4/12/2027						
10								
31	Vendor	Vendor Name	Class					
32	ADVANCED0001	Advanced Office Systems	USA-US-M					
33		PO Number	Document Date	Required Date				
34		PO2075	4/12/2027	4/12/2027				
35			Item Number	Item Description	Qty Ordered	Unit Cost	Extended Cost	Account Number
36			128 SDRAM	128 meg SDRAM	5	£ 152.10	£ 760.50	000-1300-01
37			256 SDRAM	256 meg SDRAM	5	£ 247.50	£ 1,237.50	000-1300-01
39						£ 399.60	£ 1,998.00	
40								
49								
50					Total	£ 399.60	£ 1,998.00	
51								
92	Vendor	Vendor Name	Class					
93	ASSOCIAT0001	Associated Insurance Inc.	USA-US-M					
94		PO Number	Document Date	Required Date				
95		PO2074	4/12/2027	4/12/2027				
96			Item Number	Item Description	Qty Ordered	Unit Cost	Extended Cost	Account Number
97			100XLG	Green Phone	1	£ 28.46	£ 28.46	000-1300-02
99						£ 28.46	£ 28.46	
100								
109								
110					Total	£ 28.46	£ 28.46	

Summary

In this chapter we have taken a look at creating a **Purchase Orders by Vendor** report. So far, the four reports we have created, have been created manually; in the next chapter, we're going to take a look at some of the tools available in Jet Reports which can assist in the creation of reports.

14

Report creation tools

There is a number of tools included in Jet Reports which can assist in the creation of reports. In this chapter I'm going take a look at these tools.

Report Wizard

You can easily create an entire report from a single table, or view, in your database using the **Report Wizard**, which is accessible from the **Jet** ribbon. As this type of report is limited to only a single table, the reports possible from it are much more basic than the ones you can create manually. However, the reports created can then be manually amended to link them to other tables or views.

To use the **Report Wizard** to create a **GL transaction** report, follow these steps:

1. Click the **Report Wizard** button on the toolbar to start the wizard.
2. The **Company** will be set to the default, but can be changed.
3. Select the **AccountTransactions** view (it is better to use this view as it contains fields such as the **Account Number** and not just the **Account Index**.

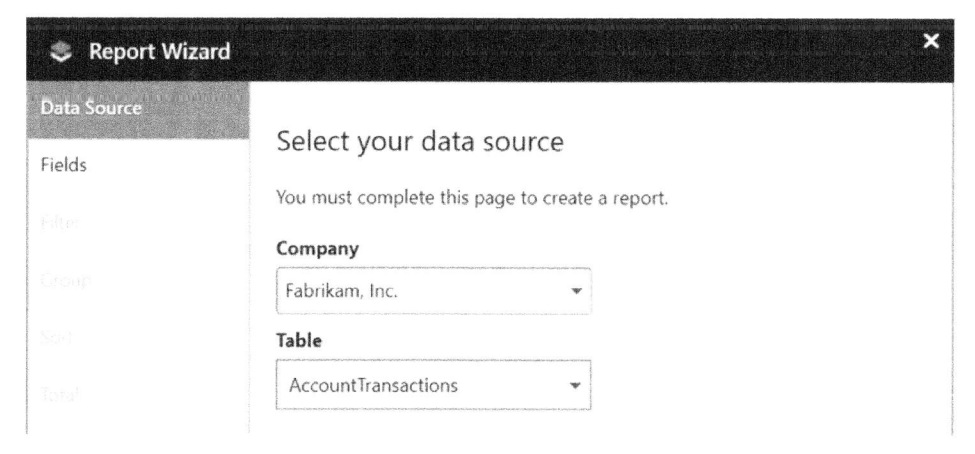

4. Click **Next** to continue.

5. Multiple fields can be selected in the **Add Fields (AccountTransactions)** list. Select the following fields:

    a. Open year.

    b. Period ID.

    c. Account Number.

    d. Account Description.

    e. Batch Number.

    f. Reference.

    g. Debit Amount.

    h. Credit Amount.

    i. Currency ID.

    j. Originating Debit Amount.

    k. Originating Credit Amount.

    l. Description.

    m. TRX Date.

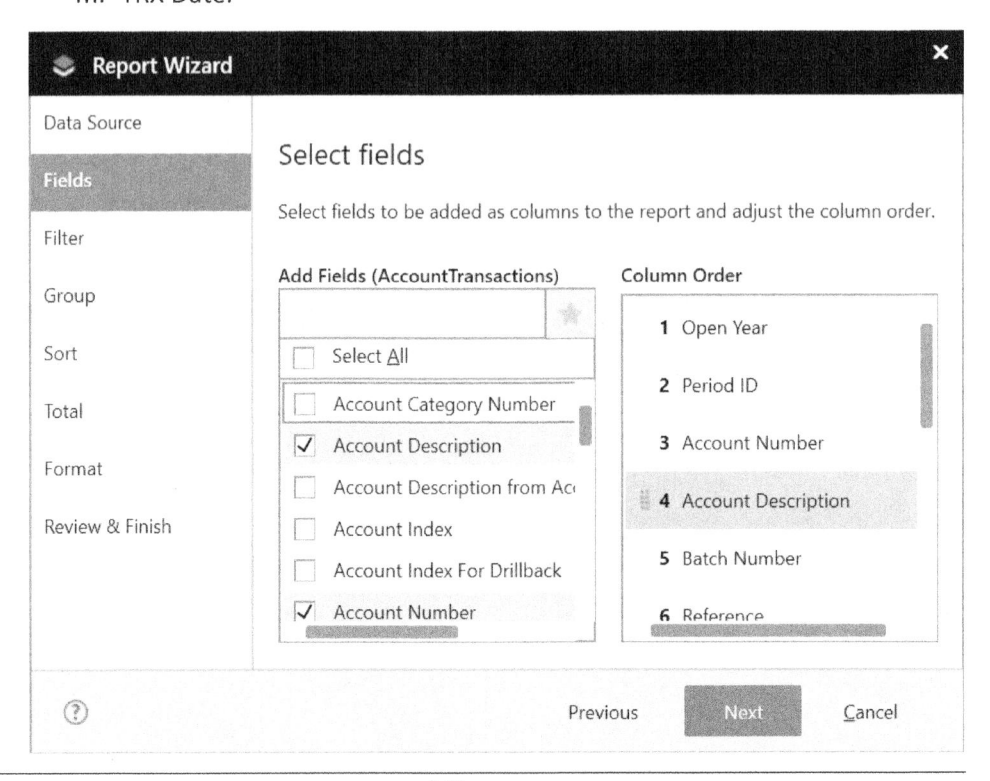

Chapter 14: Report Creation Tools

Fields can be reordered, by dragging and dropping; do this by hovering over a field in the **Column Order** list until the icon appears at the left and then click, drag and drop.

6. Multiple filters can be added; these can form the **Options** page of the report. Filters can be created for any field in the table or view, not just the ones included in the report output. To add a filter for **Open Year**, click the **Add Filter** button.

7. Select **Open Year** and set a **Filter value**.

8. Mark the checkbox **Add as report option (user sets at report run time)** to add as an option to the **Options** page; if this is left unmarked, the filter will be added to the **Report** page which can only be amended in **Design Mode**.

9. To add a second filter for **Period ID**, click the **Add filter** button.

10. Set the **Filter field** to **Period ID** and enter a **Filter value**.

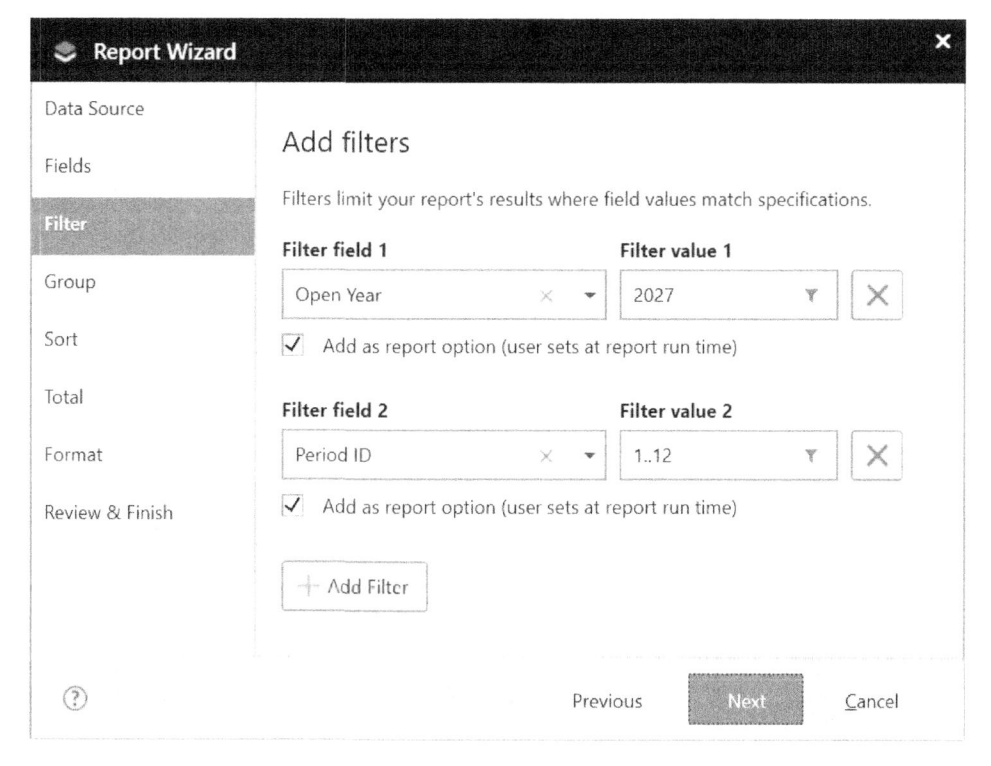

11. Click **Next** to continue.

12. Groups can be used to organize data in the report and to add subtotals for numeric fields. To add a filter for **Period ID**, click the **Add group** button and set the **Group by** to **Period ID**.

13. To add a second grouping on **Account Number**, click **Add group** and set the **Then by** to **Account Number**.

143

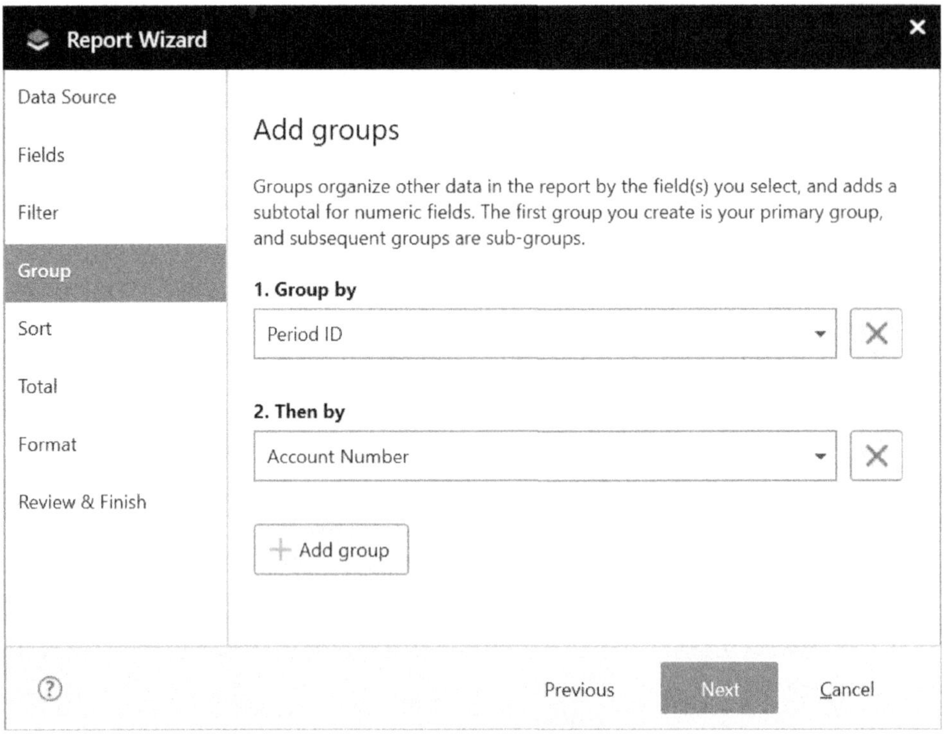

14. The report can be sorted by multiple fields; when using grouping, I'd recommend sorting by the same fields.

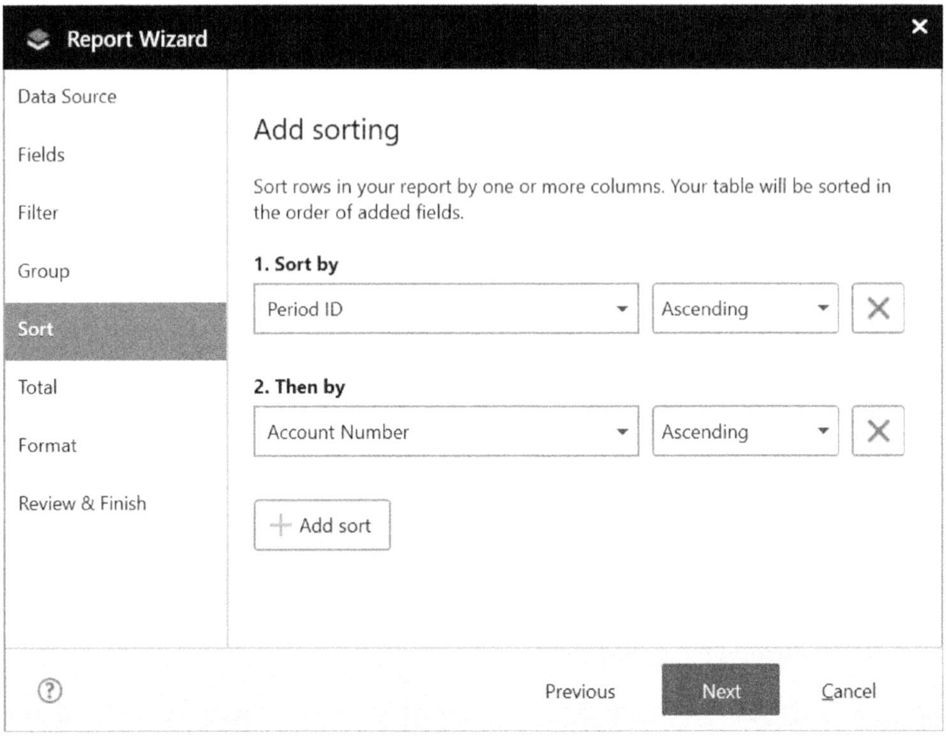

15. Click the **Add sort** button and set the **Sort by** to **Period ID Ascending**.

16. Click the **Add sort** button and set the **Then by** to **Account Number Ascending**.

17. The Report Wizard allows the fields which should have **Grand Totals** and **Subtotals** for the groups added. Mark the following fields and then click **Next**:

    a. Debit Amount.

    b. Originating Debit Amount.

    c. Credit Amount.

    d. Originating Credit Amount.

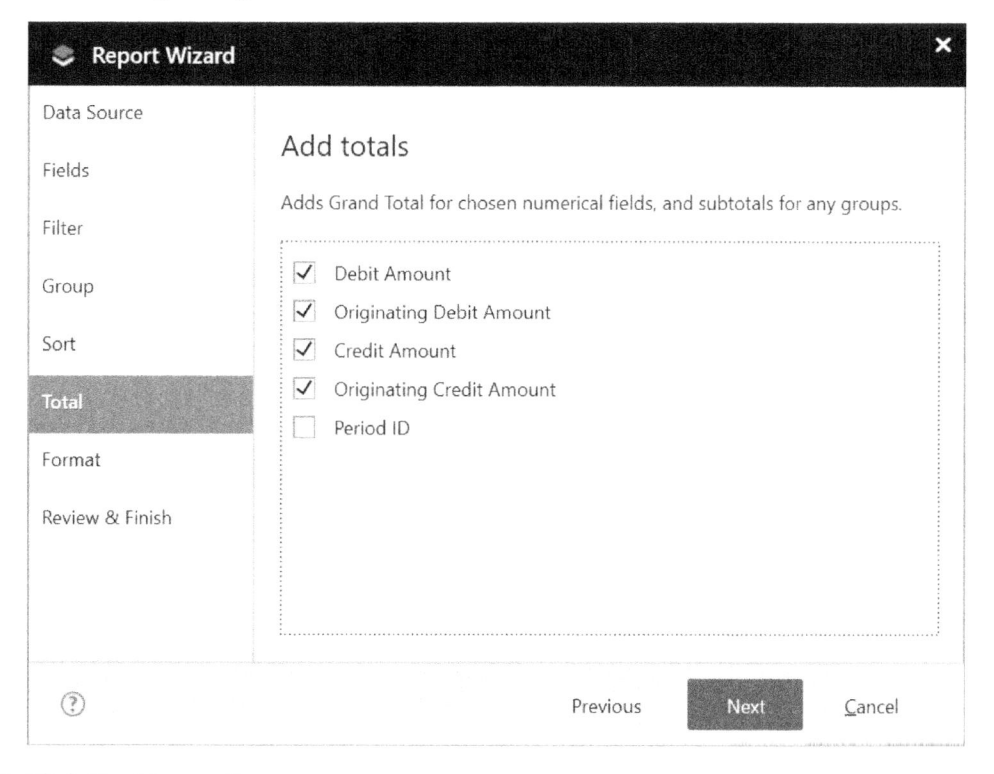

18. Click **Next** to continue.

19. There are two format options available which take advantage of standard Excel formatting.

    The first, will add basic Excel formatting such as bold column headings, adds freeze panes, and bolds and adds borders to subtotal and total lines.

    The second will outline groups using the Data Grouping feature; groups will be collapsed by default when the report runs.

20. Mark the **Add basic Excel formatting to the report** and click **Next**.

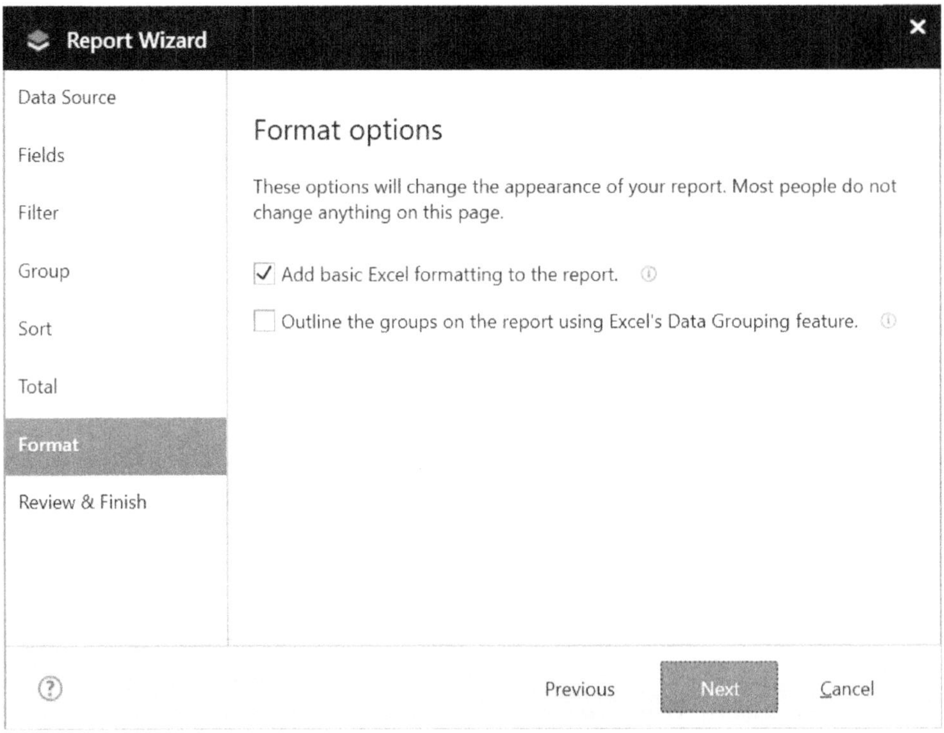
Report Wizard
Data Source
Fields
Filter
Group
Sort
Total
Format
Review & Finish
Format options
These options will change the appearance of your report. Most people do not change anything on this page.
Add basic Excel formatting to the report.
Outline the groups on the report using Excel's Data Grouping feature.
Previous
Next
Cancel

21. Review your selections; click **Previous** to make any necessary changes or click **Finish** to generate the report.

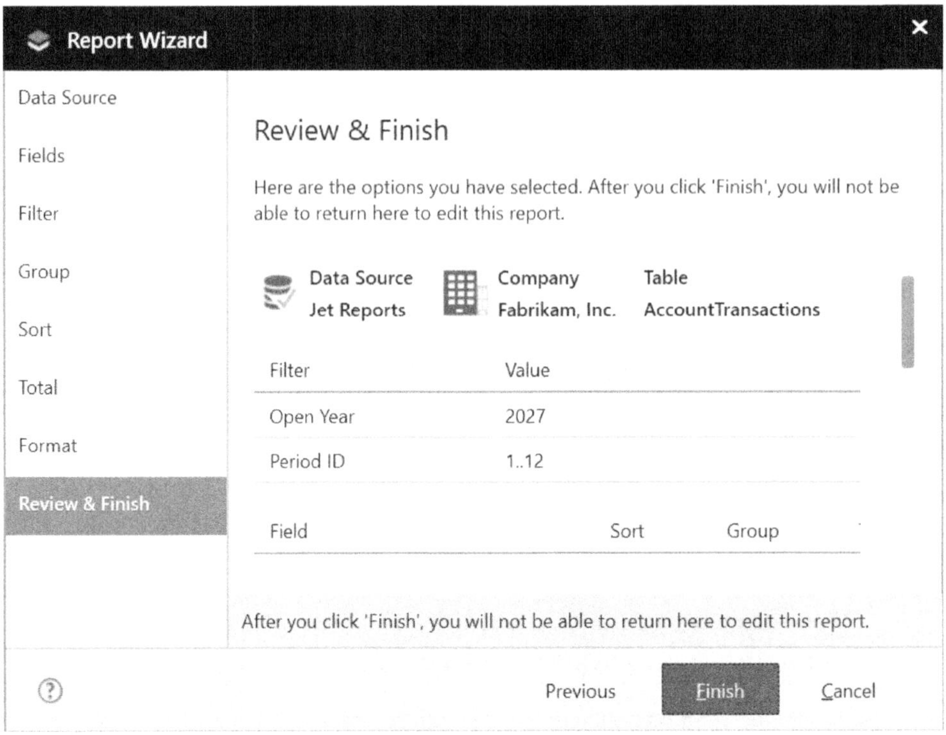
Report Wizard
Data Source
Fields
Filter
Group
Sort
Total
Format
Review & Finish
Review & Finish
Here are the options you have selected. After you click 'Finish', you will not be able to return here to edit this report.
Data Source
Jet Reports
Company
Fabrikam, Inc.
Table
AccountTransactions
Filter
Value
Open Year
2027
Period ID
1..12
Field
Sort
Group
After you click 'Finish', you will not be able to return here to edit this report.
Previous
Finish
Cancel

The report will be returned to a sheet in a new workbook. The report is created by adding the Jet functions in the same way we did in earlier chapters. This means the report can now be amended further if required.

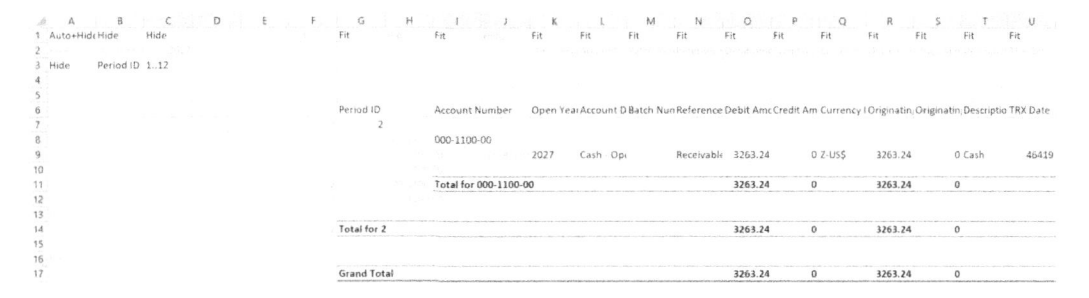

Table Builder

The **Table Builder** function helps you to create and insert an **NL("Table")** function in your workbook which creates an Excel table (from one or more database tables) which can be used as the basis for pivot tables or charts.

Create Table Builder report

To create a vendor addresses report with email addresses, launch **Table Builder** by clicking on the button in the **Tools** section of the **Jet** tab:

1. Add the first table by clicking the **Add Table** button.

2. Select the **Jet Vendor Master** view by finding it in the list, you can use the search at the top or scroll down to find it manually, and double-click.

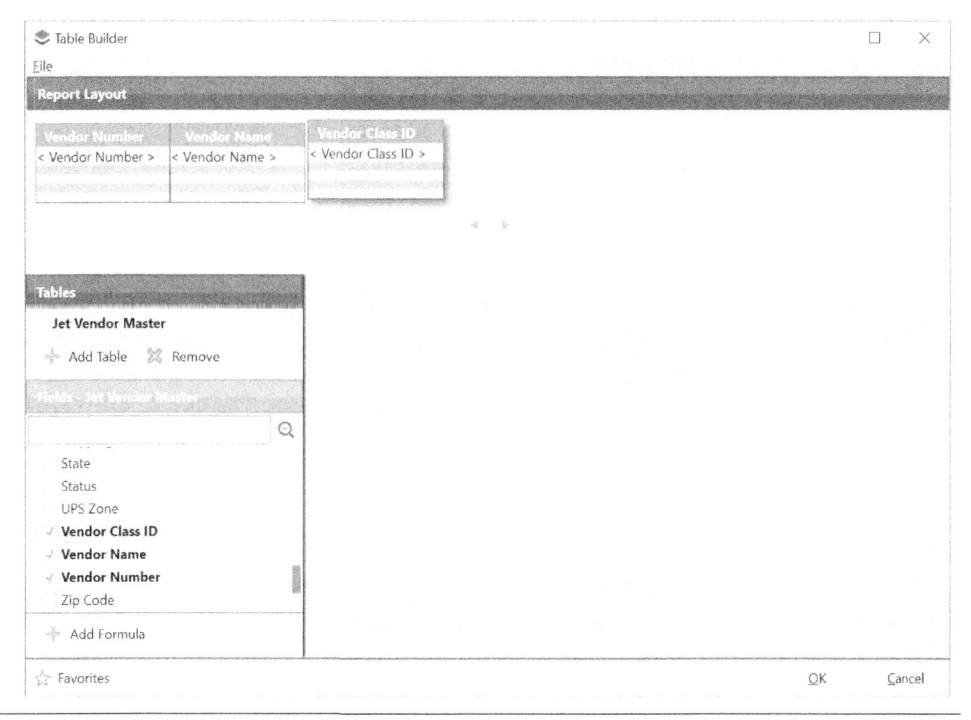

147

Jet Reports with Microsoft Dynamics GP

3. Mark the **Vendor Number**, **Vendor Name** and **Vendor Class ID** fields.

4. Click the **Add Table** button and select the **VendorAddress** view.

5. On the right hand **Links** pane, click the **Add Link** button.

6. The join will default to the first fields on each table; change them to **Vendor ID** and **Vendor Number**.

7. From the **VendorAddress** view, select the **Address 1**, **Address 2**, **Address 3**, **City**, **State**, **Zip Code** and **Country** fields.

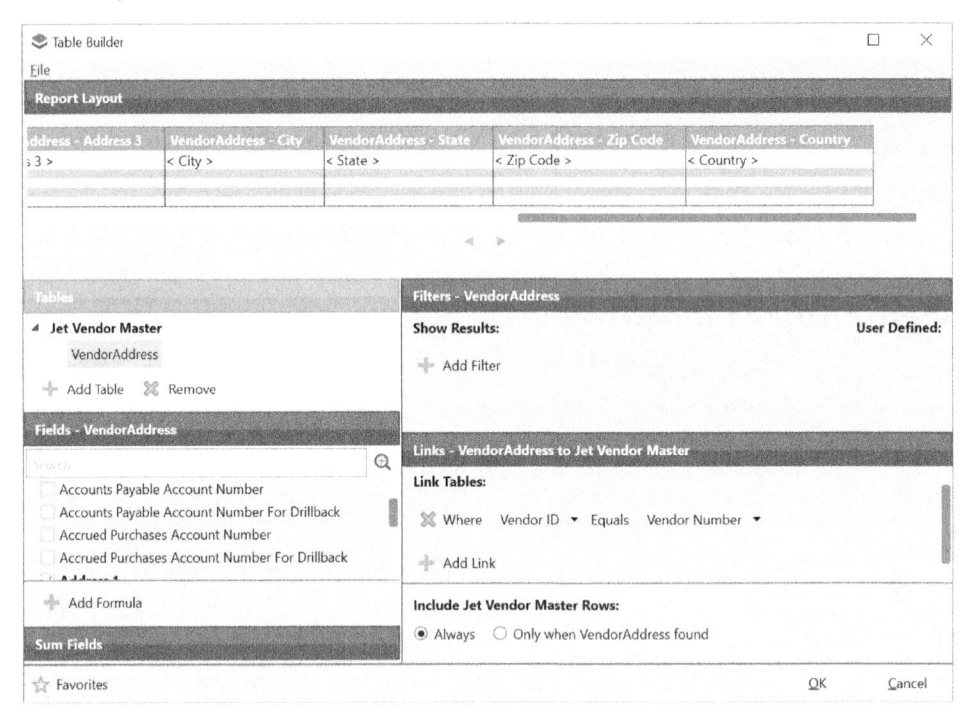

8. To add the **Internet Addresses (SY01200)** table, click the **Add Table** button and change the dropdown at the bottom from **View** to **Table**.

9. Select **Internet Addresses** by double-clicking.

10. On the right hand **Links** pane, click the **Add Link** button.

11. The join will default to the first fields on each table; leave the first as **Address Code (ADRSCODE)** and change the second to **Address Code**.

12. Click **Add Link**.

13. Change the first field to **Master ID** and set the second to **Vendor ID**.

14. As the **Internet Addresses** table holds information for vendors, customers, items and the company, we need to add a filter to make sure only vendors are returned. Do this by clicking **Add Filter** in the **Filters** pane.

Chapter 14: Report Creation Tools

15. Set the field to **Master Type (Master_Type)**.

16. Leave the filter type set to **equals** and enter VEN in the value.

17. Select the **Email To Address**, **Email Cc Address** and **Email Bcc Address** fields.

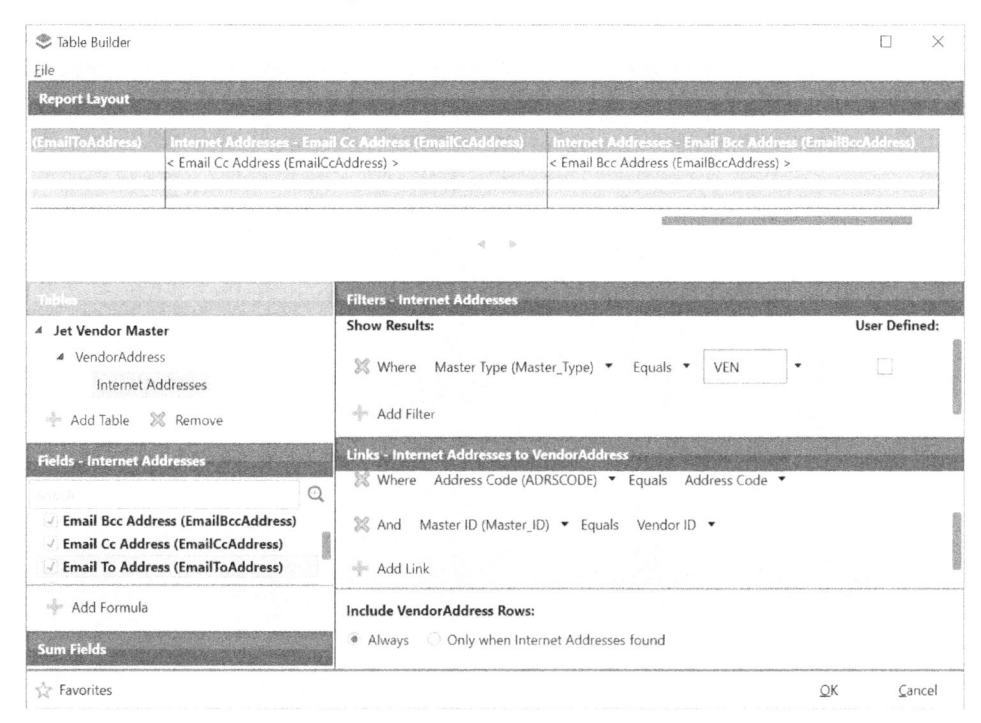

18. Review your configuration and click **OK**.

19. You will be prompted to save your work as a **Table Builder template**; doing this will allow you to open the template and amend it in future, rather than starting from scratch. Click **Yes**.

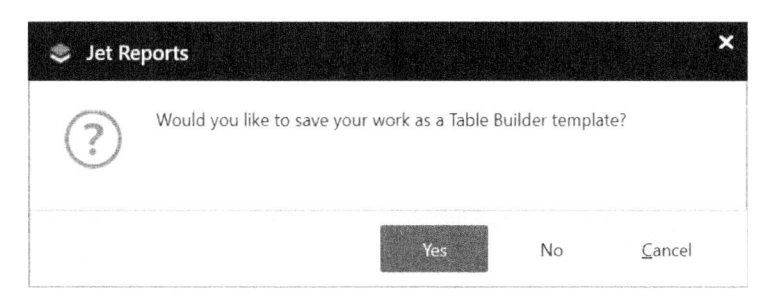

20. Select a save location, make this a shared drive or network location to share the template with other people; give the file a name and click **Save**.

A new workbook will be created with the **Report** page containing the output of the **Table Builder**. The report can be run or amended in design mode if required.

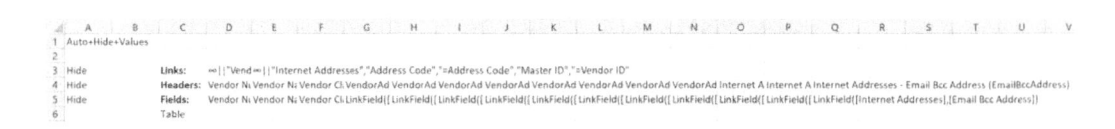

Amend Table Builder template

In the last section, we created a report using Table Builder and saved the work as a template. This means we can reload the template and make changes through **Table Builder** rather than amending directly.

To open a template, launch **Table Builder** and, on the **File** menu, click **Open**. Select the required template and click the **Open** button. The **Table Builder** window will be loaded with the settings from the template, where it can be amended.

Browser

The **Browser** provides an easy-to-use interface for report designers to utilize advanced searching and drag-and-drop functionality to create reports. The drag-and-drop fields are placed as standard Jet functions which can be amended as we did in earlier chapters.

In addition, the **Browser** allows you to flag tables and fields as favorites, making them easier to find in future.

To create a report from the **Jet Vendor Master** view, launch the **Browser** from the **Tools** section of the **Jet** action pane.

1. Select the **Jet Vendor Master** view from the tables list (which despite the name includes both tables and views.

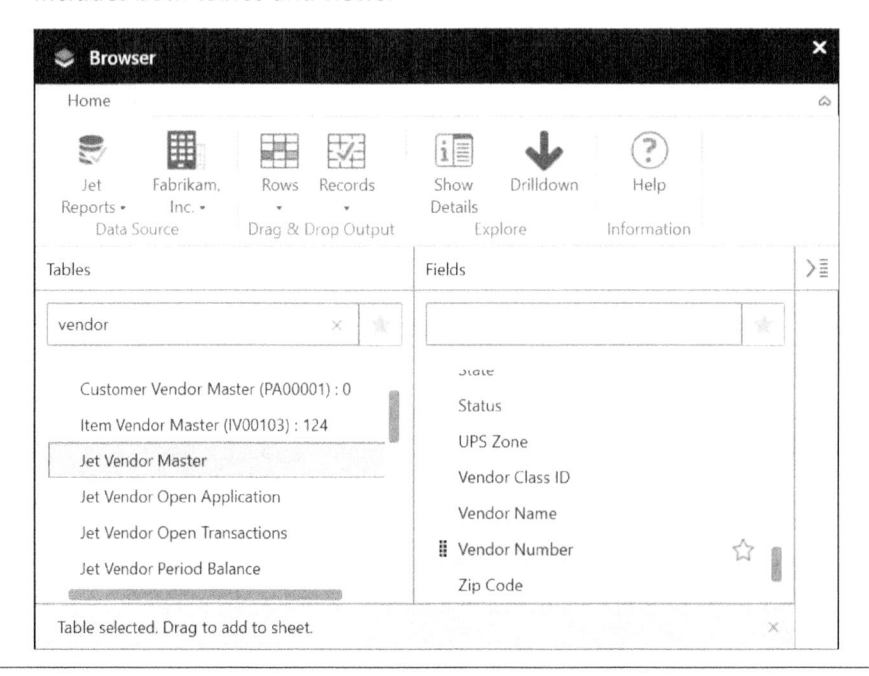

2. The fields from the view will be displayed on the left.

3. Drag-and-drop the **Vendor Number** field onto the worksheet in cell **E5**; the **NL** replicator function on the view will be added to cell **D5** with the **Vendor Number** as an **NF** function in cell **E5**.

4. Drag-and-drop the **Vendor Name** field into cell **F5**.

5. Repeat with any other fields to be added.

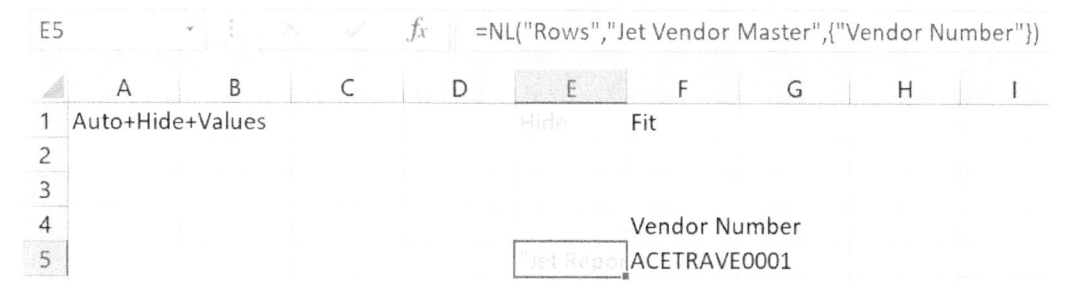

	A	B	C	D	E	F	G	H	I
	\multicolumn{9}{l	}{E5 fx =NL("Rows","Jet Vendor Master",{"Vendor Number"})}
1	Auto+Hide+Values				Hide	Fit			
2									
3									
4						Vendor Number			
5					Jet Repo	ACETRAVE0001			

Fields from multiple tables will be added to the report; if you select a field from another table or view, a new replicator will be added. This can then be configured using the **NL** function as we did when creating the reports manually earlier.

Adding fields using the **Browser**, can make creating reports manually easier, but the point to remember, is that reports created using the browser are not complete reports. There is still effort required to create options and amend the fields dropped from the browser to limit using the options.

Snippets

Jet Reports **Snippets** are small, reusable report parts which can be easily reused to speed report creation. They can also be shared between Jet Reports users by copying them using **Windows Explorer**.

Add snippet

To add a snippet for a financial report **Options** page, perform these steps:

1. Launch Snippets from the Tools section of the **Jet** action pane.

2. Highlight the section to use in the snippet.

	A	B	C	D	E
1	Auto+Hide+HideSheet	Title	Value	Lookup+Hide	Tooltip+Hide
2	Option	Fiscal Year	2027	Lookup	Select fiscal year
3	Option	Fiscal Period	4	Lookup	Select fiscal period
4	Option	Company	Fabrikam, Inc.	Lookup	Select company

151

3. Click the **New Snippet** button.

4. Select the **New Snippet 1** text and overtype with name of the snippet.

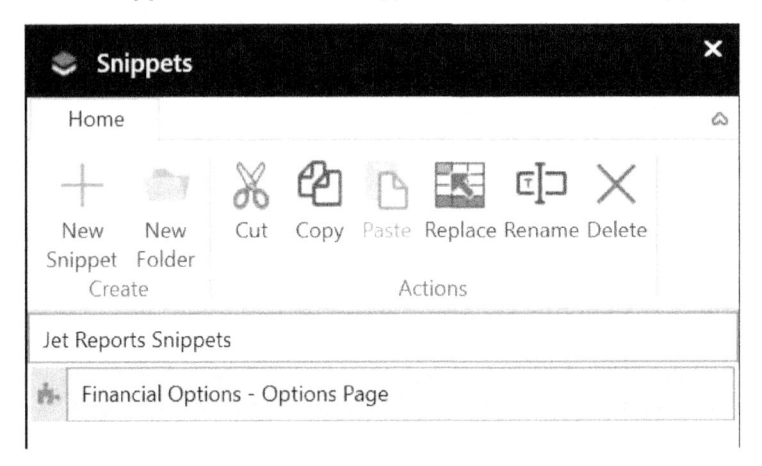

Edit snippet

Unfortunately, snippets cannot be edited; they can only be replaced.

Replace snippet

To replace a snippet, follow these steps:

1. Launch **Snippets** from the **Tools** section of the **Jet** action pane.

2. Select the section of the report to use as the snippet replacement.

3. Select the snippet to replace and click the **Replace** button.

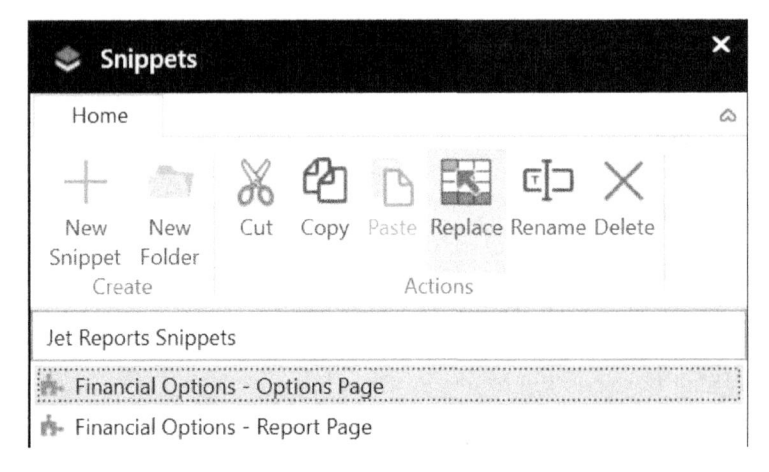

4. When prompted, click, **Yes** to replace the snippet.

Rename snippet

Snippets can be easily renamed, by launching the Snippets window, selecting the snippet and clicking the **Rename** button on the action pane and entering the new name.

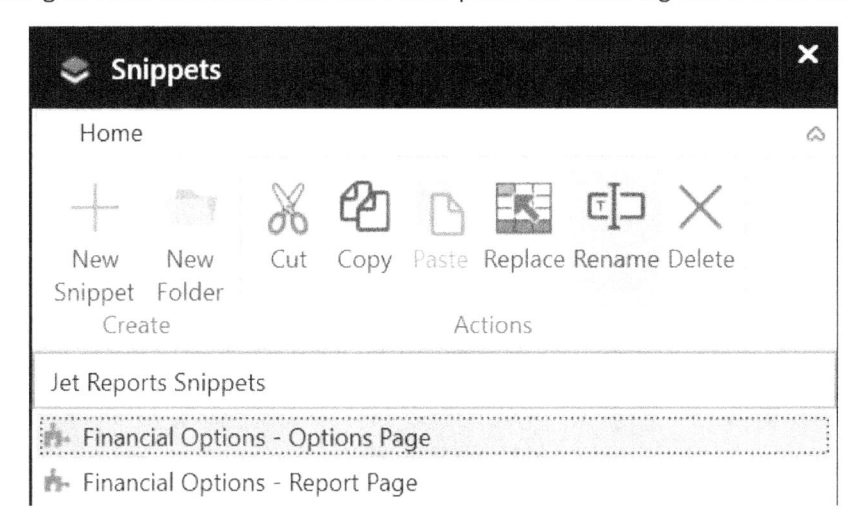

Delete snippet

If a snippet is no longer required, it can be deleted by launching the **Snippets** window, selecting it in the list and clicking the **Delete** button on the action pane:

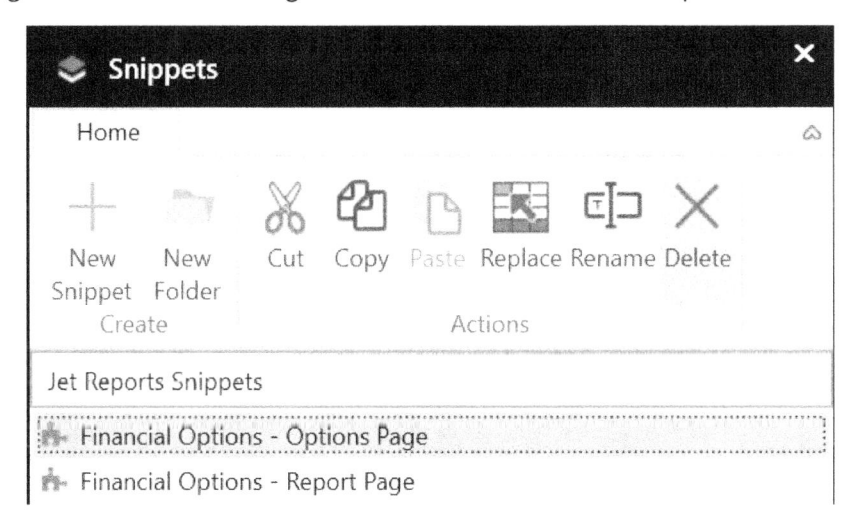

When prompted, click, **Yes** to replace the snippet.

Organize snippets

Snippets can be organized into folders to make finding them easier. To create a new folder, click the **New Folder** button on the action pane and giving it a name. Then you can drag-and-drop, or cut and paste, snippets into the folder.

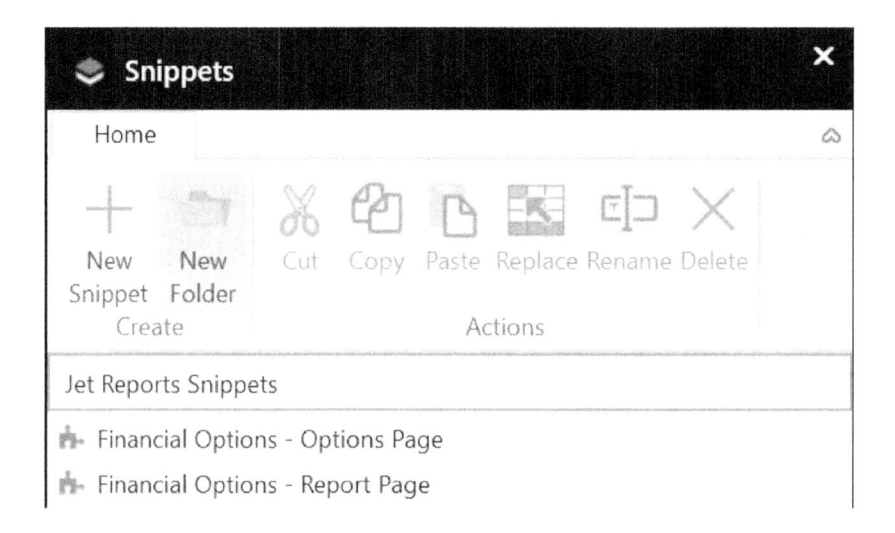

Share snippet

Snippets can be shared by copying and pasting them between users **Documents** folders. The snippet library is stored in a subfolder called Jet Reports **Snippets**. Each snippet is stored individually as a file with a .snippet extension.

Any organization structure to the snippets, is reflected in the same folder structure in Windows Explorer.

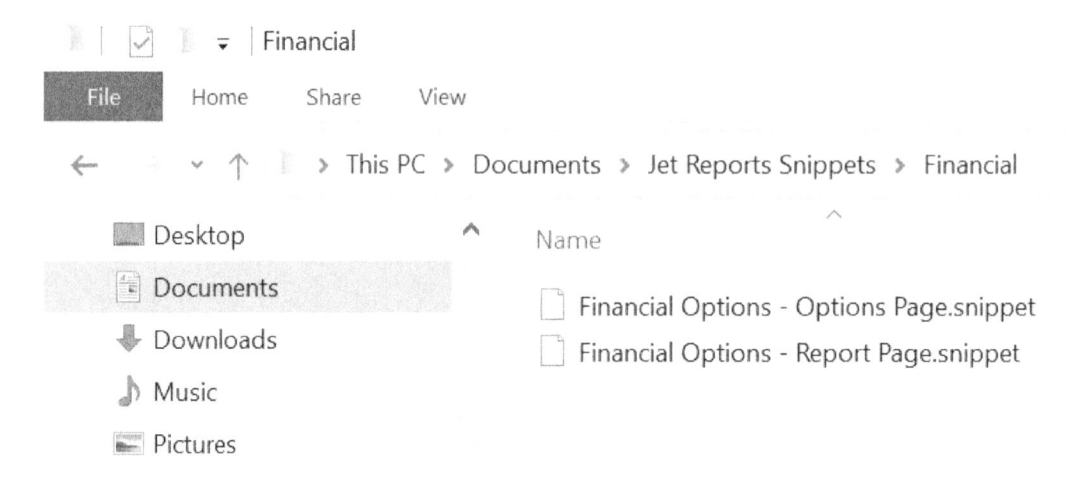

Sample snippets

There are a number of **Snippets** available for Microsoft Dynamics GP users to download; these can be downloaded from https://azrcrv.co.uk/jetsnippets.

The download file is a zip file which you can then extract into the **Jet Reports Snippets** folder in your **Documents** folder. When the **Snippets** window is opened the snippets will be available.

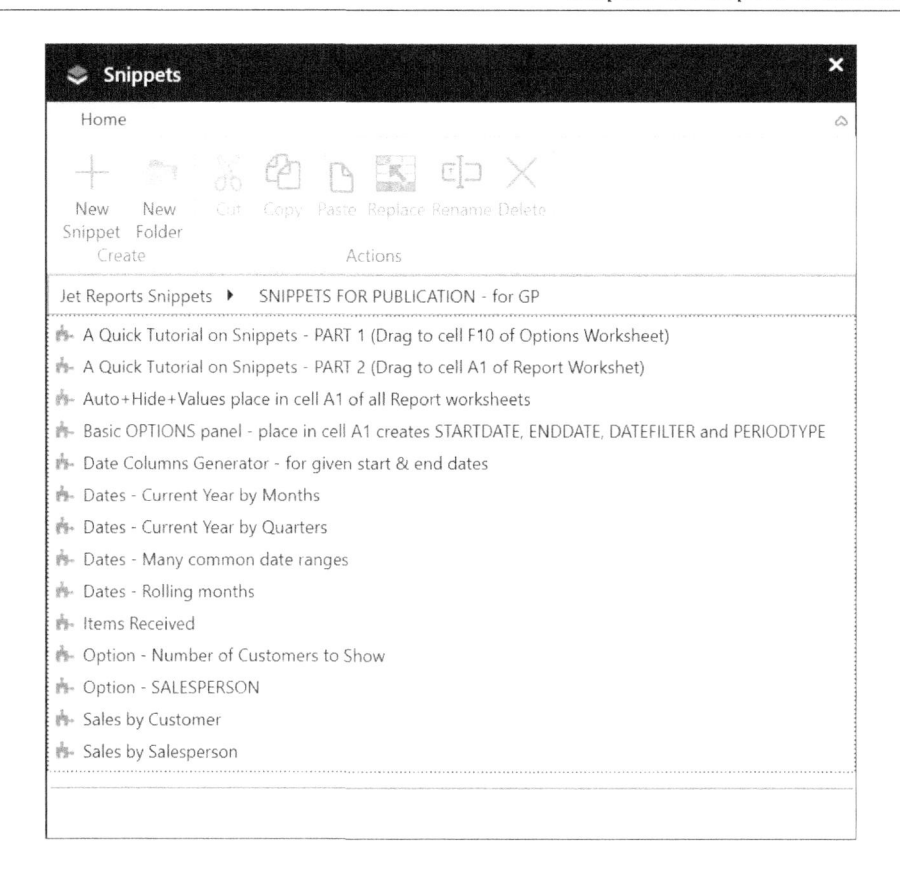

Summary

In this chapter, we've taken a look at the tools available in **Jet Reports** which can make creating reports quicker and easier. In the next chapter, we're going to take a look at the **Jet Hub**.

15

Using Jet Hub

In this chapter, we're going to take a look at **Jet Hub** and the functionality it offers to users to access Jet Reports from wherever they are and on any device.

Introducing Jet Hub

Jet Hub allows users to access reports using almost any device through a simple web interface. Through this web portal, they can manage, run and view reports without needing to install any software (an **Office365** logon is required to view reports).

Jet Hub allows you to easily find the desired report and to specify report parameters when running the report, allow you to get up-to-the-minute data and view it in **Excel Online**. It also includes report history and version control of changes.

Accessing Jet Hub

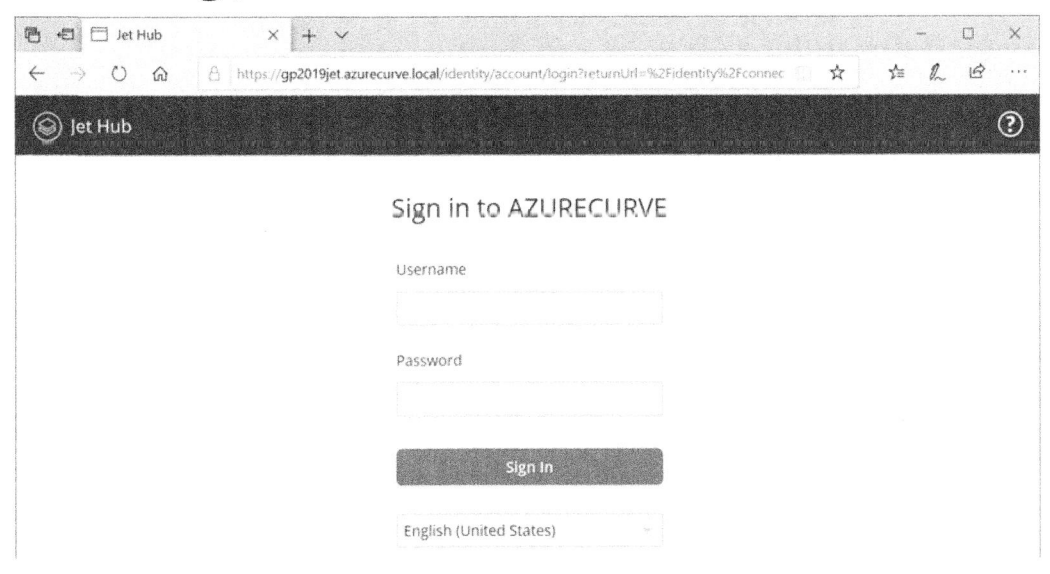

Only users with a license for Jet Reports are able to log into the **Jet Hub**; access is by logging in with their Windows domain user and password.

Once logged in, you will be taken to the **Reports** view, which until a report is uploaded will not find any reports to display.

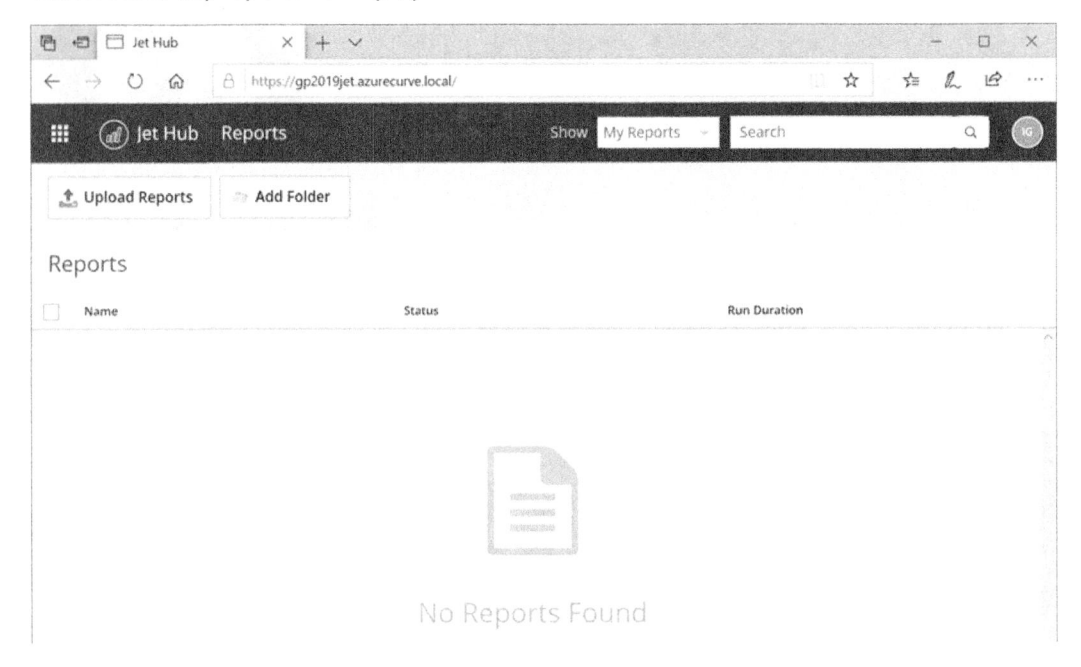

Uploading reports

When first installed, there will be no reports available in the **Jet Hub** until they are uploaded. Reports can be uploaded through **Jet Hub** itself or from the **Jet Excel add-in**.

Upload through Jet Hub

To upload a report to **Jet Hub**, follow these steps:

1. Log into **Jet Hub** and navigate to the **Reports** page.
2. Click the **Upload Reports** button.
3. In the **Data Source** box, select the data source to be used by the report.

Chapter 15: Using Jet Hub

Upload Reports	×

Data Source ⓘ

Jet Reports

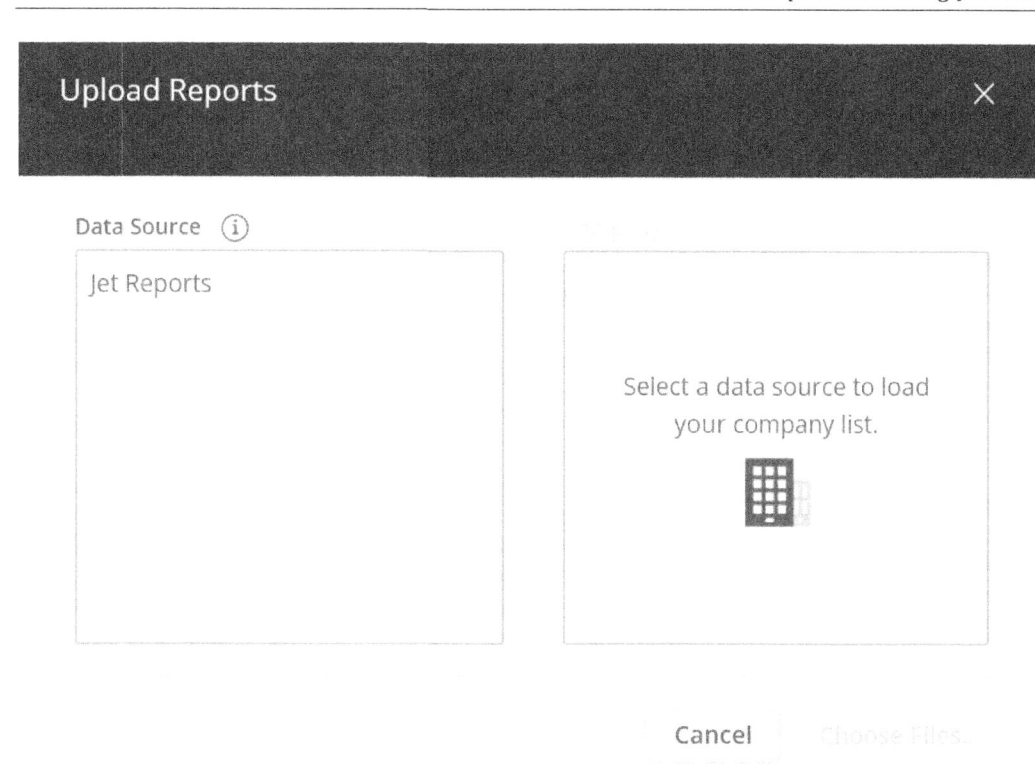

Select a data source to load your company list.

Cancel   Choose Files

4. Enter your password to authenticate that you have access to the selected data source (this is required as a user may have a data source not available in **Jet Hub**).

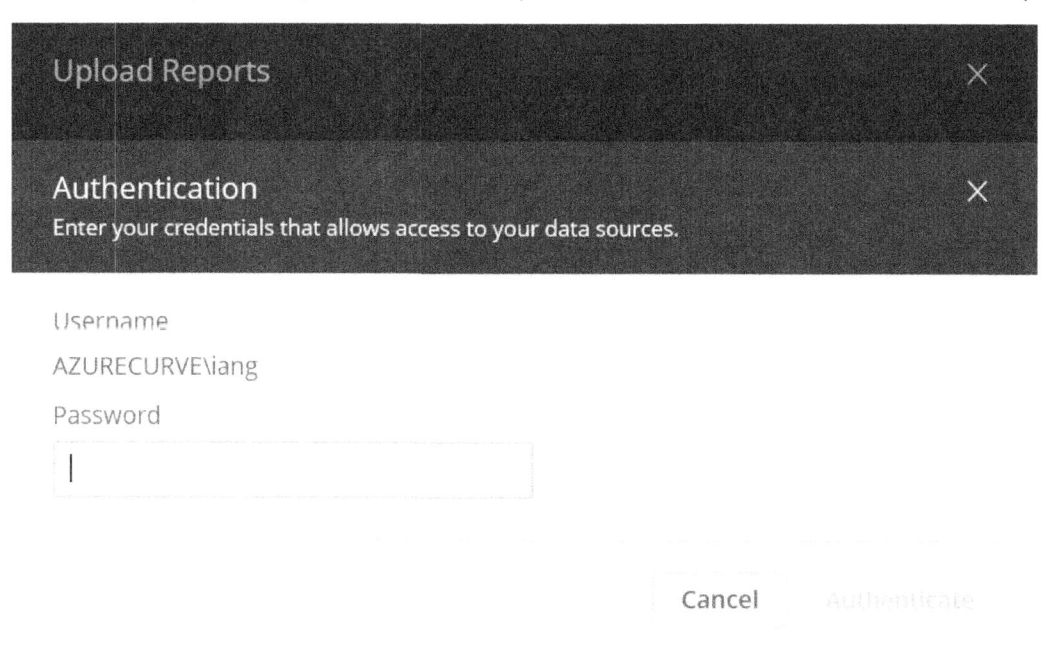

Upload Reports	×

Authentication ×
Enter your credentials that allows access to your data sources.

Username
AZURECURVE\iang

Password

Cancel   Authenticate

5. Click **Authenticate**.
6. Select the default **Company** for the uploaded report.

159

Jet Reports with Microsoft Dynamics GP

Upload Reports

Data Source ⓘ

Jet Reports

Company

ISC Software Solutions Ltd.

Fabrikam, Inc.

Cancel   Choose Files...

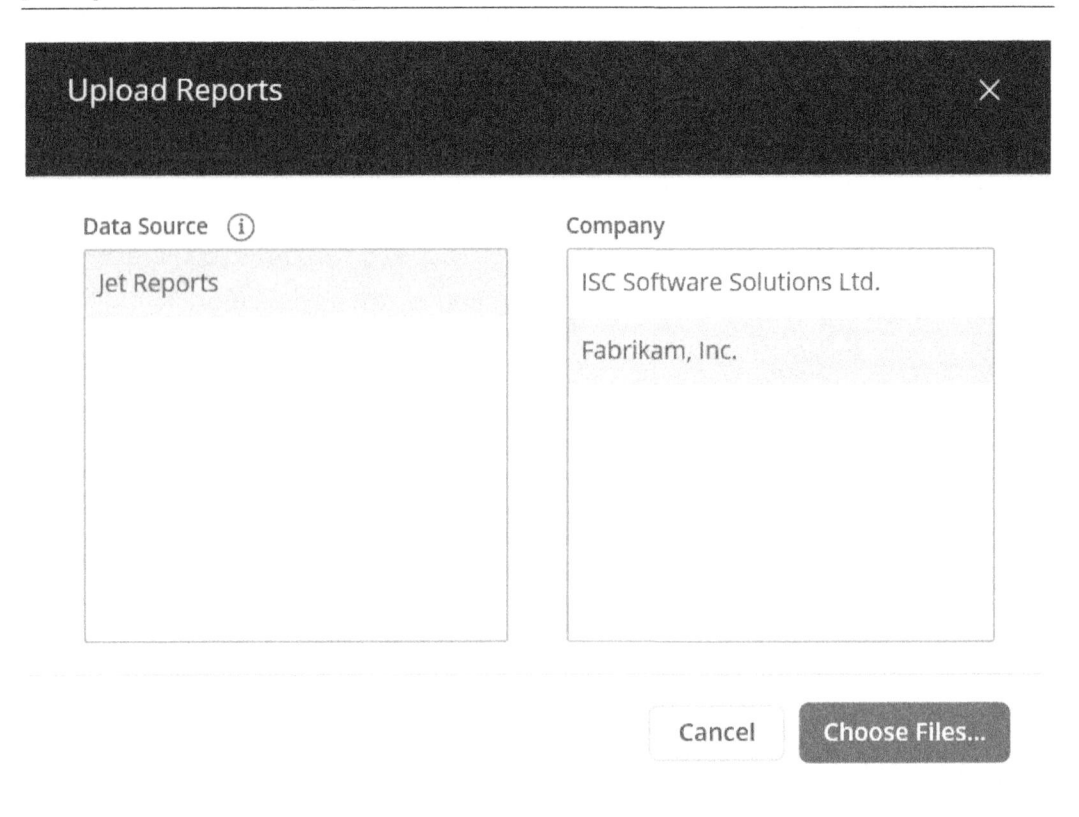

7. Click **Choose Files**.

8. Select the report(s) to upload in the dialog and click **Open**.

Upload through the Excel add-in

To upload a report using the **Jet Excel add-in**, perform these steps:

1. Open the report to upload in **Excel**.

2. On the **Jet** action pane, in the **Jet Hub** section, click **Upload**.

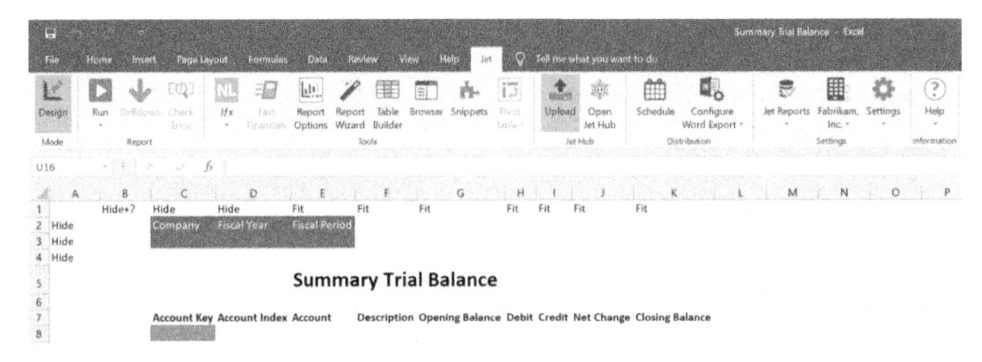

3. Check the settings on the **Upload Report** page and click **Upload**.

160

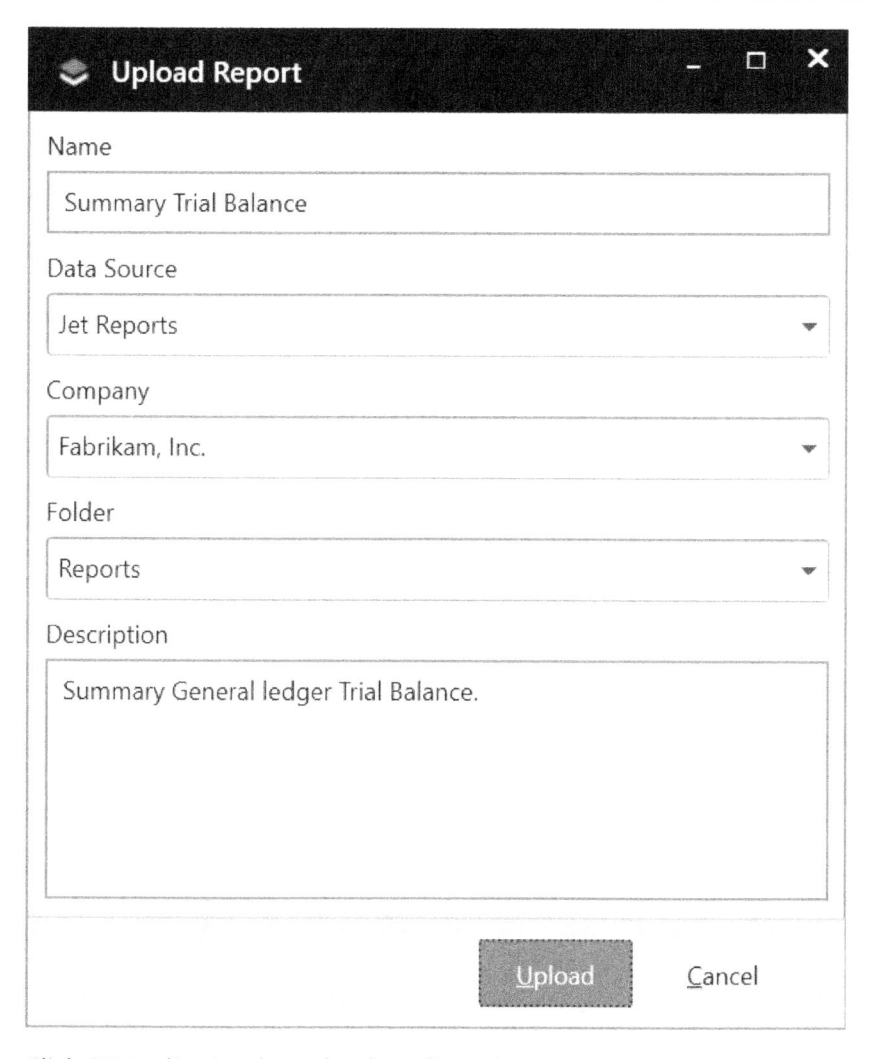

4. Click **OK** to dismiss the upload confirmation message.

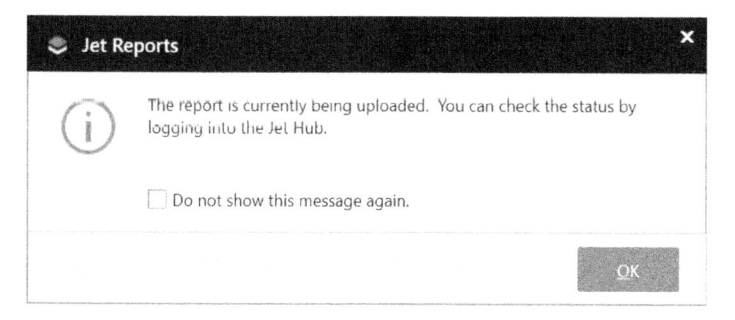

Running a report

Once reports have been uploaded to **Jet Hub** they are immediately available. To run a report:

1. Log into Jet Hub and access the **Reports** page.

2. Hover the mouse the report to run and click the **Play** button.

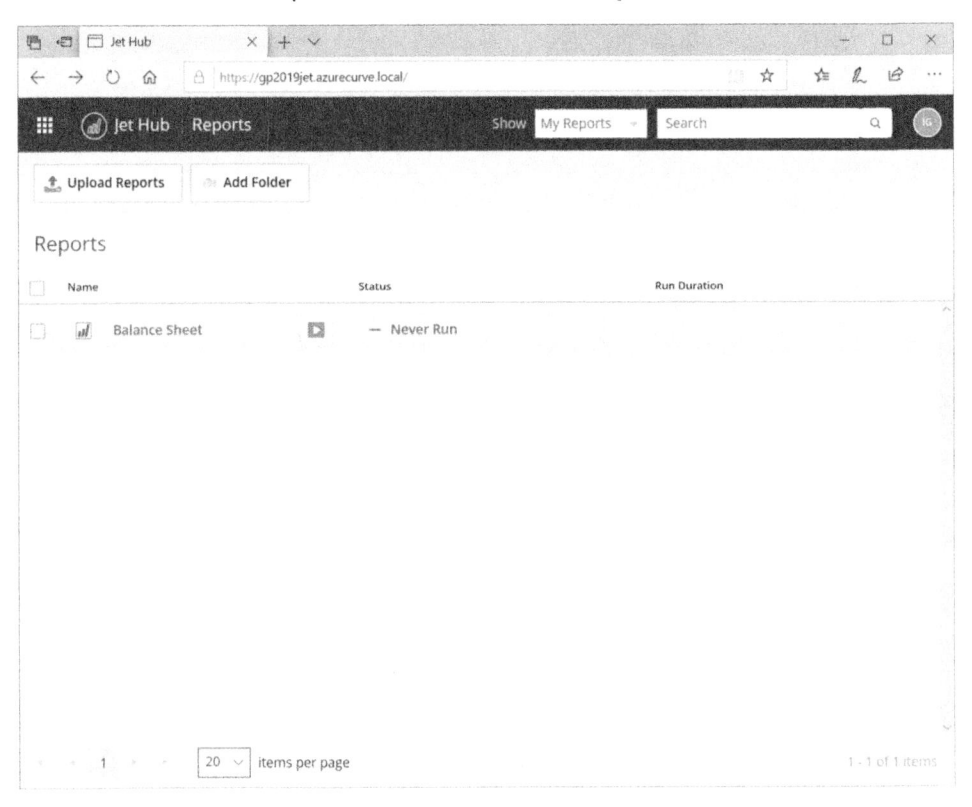

3. Set the report options as required and click **Run Report**.

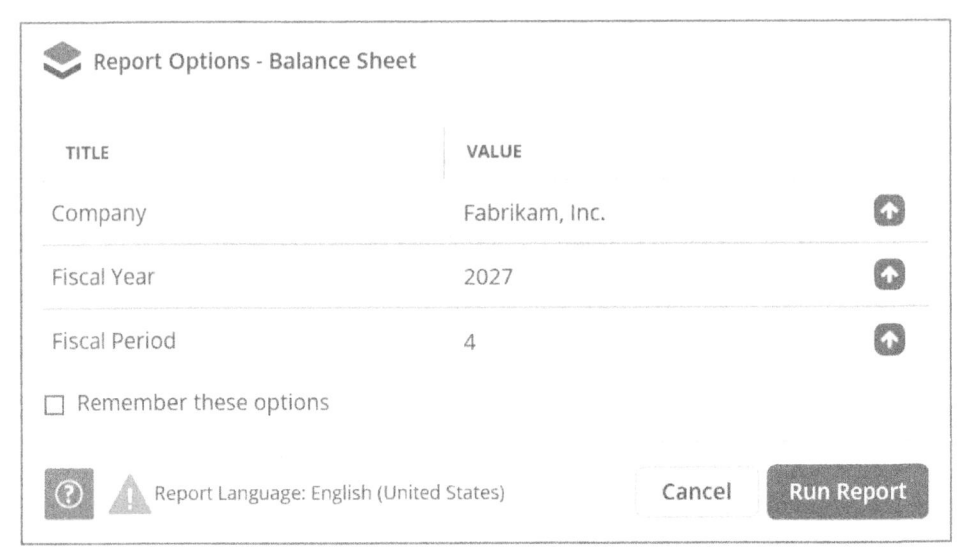

4. The report will generate and show the **Status** of **Complete** when finished.

Chapter 15: Using Jet Hub

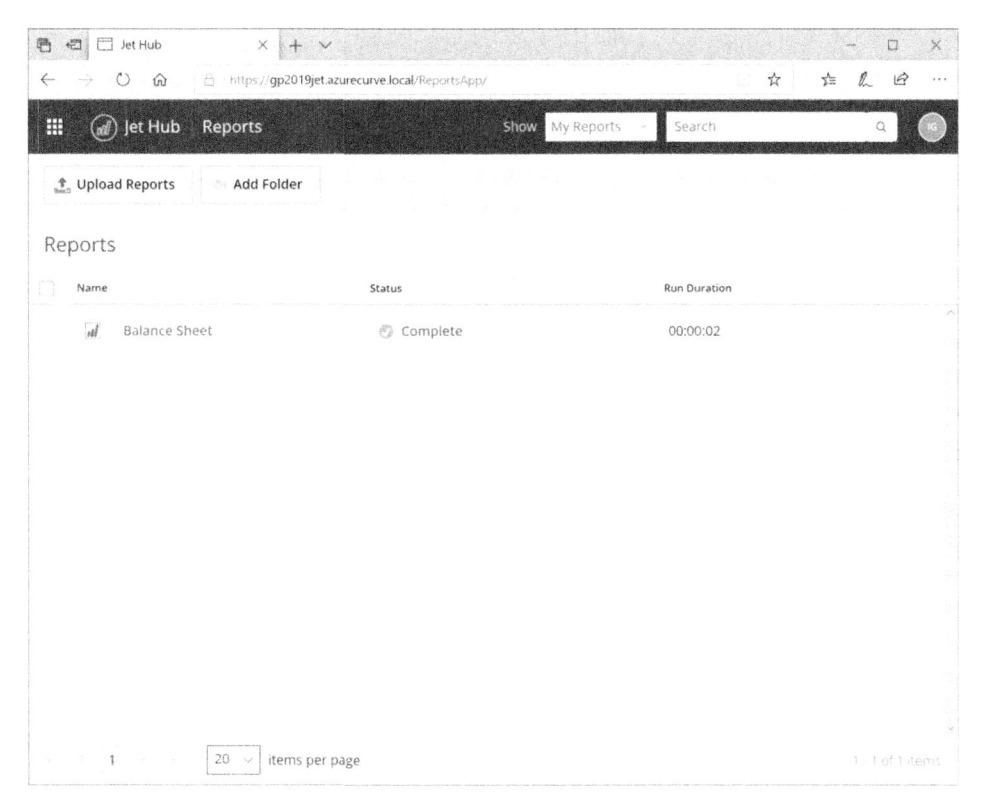

Reports which are run in the Jet Hub, do not automatically open. This allows a user to run a report once and have that version of the report available to all users.

Opening a report

Once a report has been run, it is available for users to view:

1. Log into **Jet Hub** and access the **Reports** page.

2. Click the report name to view.

3. Click the **Open** button at the top left.

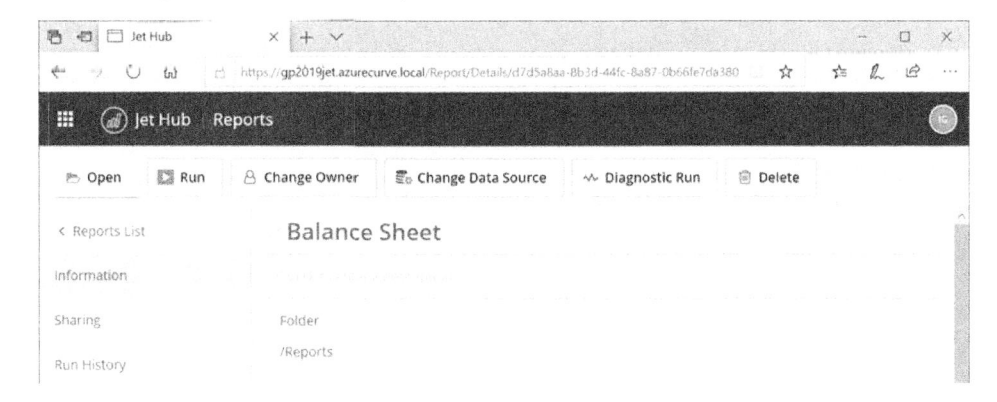

4. If you have an **Office365** account, you can click **Open in Excel Online**, otherwise

you will have to click **Download**; the latter options requires you to have **Microsoft Excel** installed, but you do not need the **Jet Excel Add-in** (this is only required to run the report).

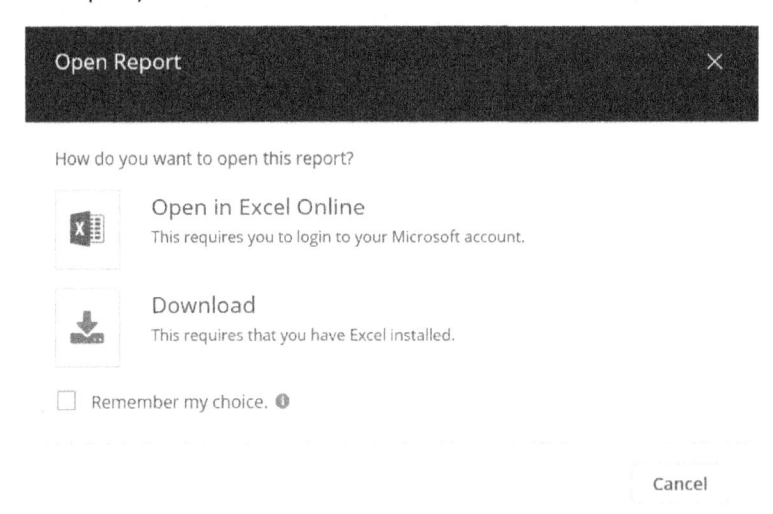

Run History

When a report has been opened in **Jet Hub**, there is the facility to view a historic version of the report:

1. Log into **Jet Hub** and access the **Reports** page.

2. Click the report name to view.

3. Click the **Run History** button on the left-side navigation pane.

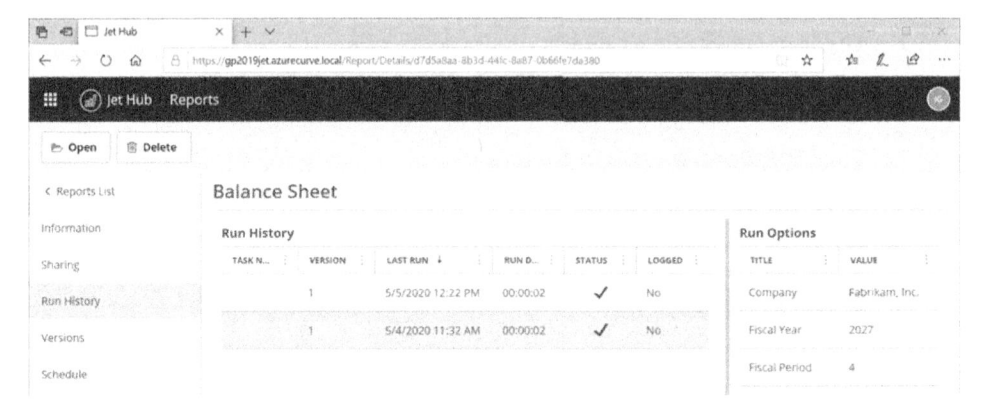

4. Select the report to view and click the **Open** button in the top left.

5. Choose whether to open the report in **Excel Online** or download and view in **Microsoft Excel**.

Chapter 15: Using Jet Hub

Versions

When a version of a report is uploaded to **Jet Hub**, it is version controlled, which means you can go back and either run an old version to download the file; this means you could then upload again as the new current version if the existing current version wasn't working correctly.

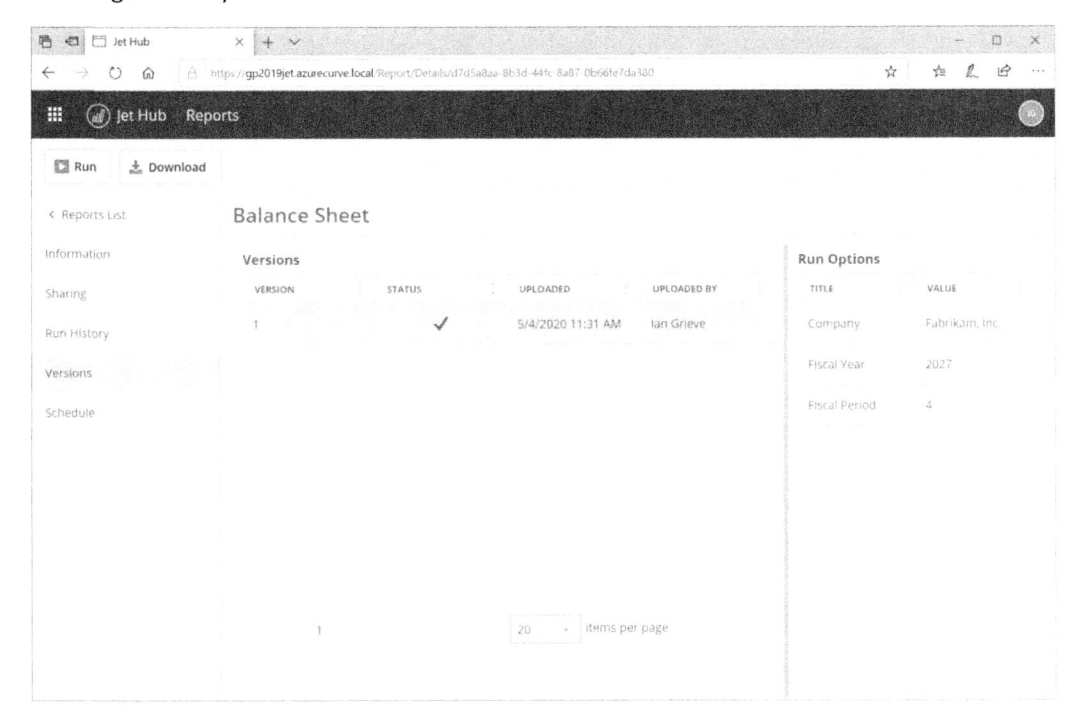

Scheduling a report

If you have reports which need to be run at regular times, a schedule can be created. To create a schedule to run the **Balance Sheet** on the second Tuesday of every month, follow these steps:

1. Log into Jet Hub and access the **Reports** page.
2. Click the **Balance Sheet** report to open it.
3. In the left-side navigation pane, click **Schedule**.
4. **Click the** New Task **button.**
5. Set **Repeat** to **Monthly**.
6. Set the **Start Time** to the required date and time.
7. Leave **Every** set to **1**.
8. Change **Repeat On** to **Other**.

165

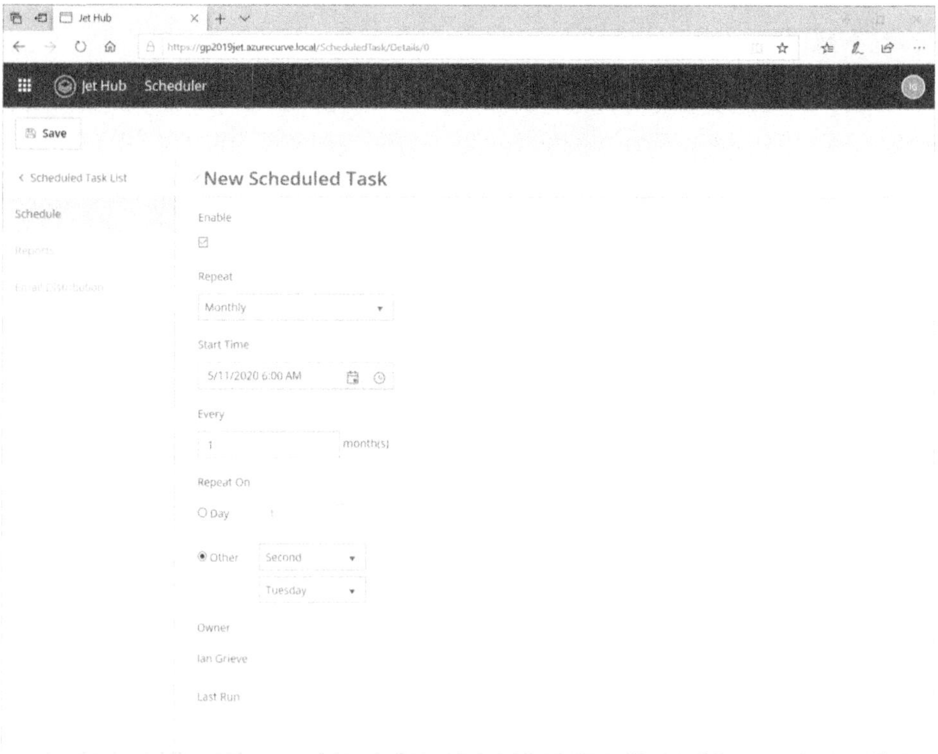
Jet Hub
Jet Hub Scheduler
Save
Scheduled Task List
Schedule
New Scheduled Task
Enable
Repeat
Monthly
Start Time
5/11/2020 6:00 AM
Every
1
month(s)
Repeat On
Day
Other
Second
Tuesday
Owner
Ian Grieve
Last Run

9. Set the dropdown lists to **Second** and **Tuesday**.
10. Click the **Save** button.
11. Clicking on the **Reports** item on the navigation pane will show the report options and allow you to amend them.

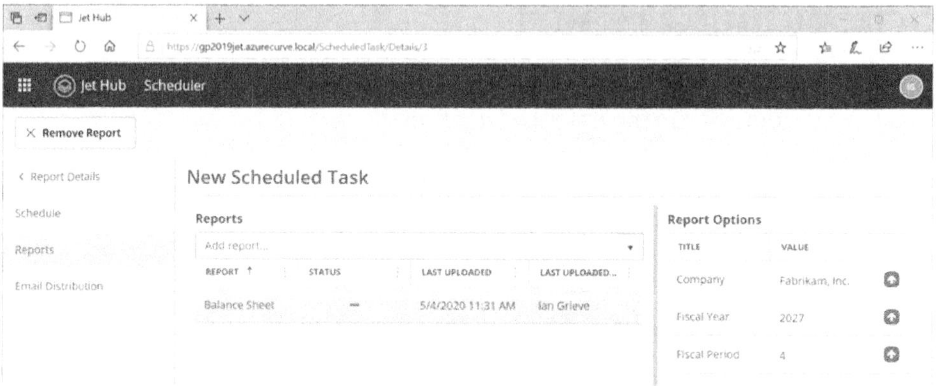
Jet Hub
Jet Hub Scheduler
Remove Report
Report Details
Schedule
Reports
Email Distribution
New Scheduled Task
Reports
Add report...
REPORT
STATUS
LAST UPLOADED
LAST UPLOADED...
Balance Sheet
5/4/2020 11:31 AM
Ian Grieve
Report Options
TITLE
VALUE
Company
Fabrikam, Inc.
Fiscal Year
2027
Fiscal Period
4

Summary

In this chapter, we've taken a look at **Jet Hub** and the functionality it offers for accessing reports via the browser, including creating schedules.

Index

Aged Trial Balance, xv, 98, 99, 120
Balance, xiii, xiv, xvi, 53, 60, 61, 62, 70, 71, 74, 78, 80, 81, 83, 85, 87, 92, 93, 94, 95, 99, 113, 165
Balance Sheet, xiv, 70, 71, 74, 78, 83, 85, 87, 165
Excel Add-in
    Jet Excel Add-in, x, xi, xii, 7, 9, 10, 11, 17, 18, 28, 29, 32, 37, 164
Formula, 51, 57, 77, 90, 104, 126
Friendly Names, 26
    Caption, 26
    Name, xii, 24, 26, 38, 43, 50, 55, 56, 74, 76, 89, 99, 101, 102, 109, 110, 121, 124, 127, 128, 148, 151
IIS, 11, 12, 15, 17
Income Statement, xiv, 83, 85, 91, 98
Jet Administration Console, xi, 17, 18, 23, 24, 26
Jet Analytics, 5, 6
Jet Basics, 5, 6, 7
Jet Express, 5
Jet Function, 7, 36, 37, 49, 56, 57, 74, 101, 104, 123, 125
    GL, xii, 6, 7, 37, 42, 43, 44, 59, 60, 61, 62, 79, 80, 85, 91, 92, 93, 94, 95, 97, 141
    NF, xii, 30, 37, 40, 41, 66, 67, 68, 69, 110, 127, 129, 130, 133, 135, 151
    NL, xii, 7, 30, 34, 35, 36, 37, 38, 39, 40, 41, 42, 54, 58, 60, 61, 66, 67, 71, 100, 104, 105, 106, 107, 109, 110, 111, 112, 113, 114, 115, 116, 117, 122, 127, 128, 130, 131, 132, 134, 135, 147, 151
NP, xii, 34, 37, 39, 41, 42, 49, 51, 56, 57, 59, 74, 77, 90, 101, 104, 124, 126
Jet GP Updater, 19
Jet Hub, x, xi, xviii, 6, 9, 11, 12, 13, 14, 15, 16, 17, 31, 111, 155, 157, 158, 159, 160, 161, 163, 164, 165, 166
Jet Reports, iii, ix, x, xi, 1, 2, 5, 6, 7, 9, 10, 11, 12, 13, 17, 19, 21, 23, 24, 28, 32, 37, 63, 70, 82, 96, 119, 138, 139, 141, 151, 154, 155, 157, 158, 168
Jet Service Tier, x, xi, 2, 9, 11, 13, 14, 15, 16, 17, 23
Lookup, xiii, 35, 48, 49, 54, 55, 56, 57, 74, 75, 76, 88, 89, 101, 102, 103, 104, 123, 124, 125
Microsoft Dynamics GP, iii, vii, viii, ix, 1, 2, 5, 6, 7, 10, 19, 25, 28, 29, 32, 37, 45, 78, 91, 111, 154, 168
Office 365, 10, 11, 12
Options, xii, xiii, xiv, xv, xvi, 30, 34, 35, 41, 47, 49, 50, 51, 54, 57, 58, 63, 70, 74, 77, 78, 82, 87, 90, 96, 101, 103, 104, 119, 123, 125, 126, 138, 143, 151
Report Wizard, xvii, 30, 141, 145
Schedule, 6, 31, 165
    Scheduling, xviii, 165
Snippets, xvii, 6, 30, 151, 152, 153, 154
SQL Server, 2, 9, 10, 11, 12, 13, 15, 19, 25
Table Builder, xvii, 30, 147, 149, 150
Trial Balance, 7, 64, 71, 85
    Detailed Trial Balance, xiii, 64, 65, 70, 71
    Summary Trial Balance, xiii, 52, 53, 64, 65, 70

Thank you for buying

Jet Reports with Microsoft Dynamics GP

For information on other titles from azurecurve Publishing, please visit
https://publishing.azurecurve.co.uk/

Printed in Great Britain
by Amazon